Working Mothers

An Evaluative Review
of the Consequences
for Wife, Husband, and Child

Lois Wladis Hoffman
F. Ivan Nye

with

Stephen J. Bahr, Arthur C. Emlen,
Joseph B. Perry, Jr., Marion Gross Sobol

WORKING
MOTHERS

 Jossey-Bass Publishers
San Francisco • Washington • London • 1975

WORKING MOTHERS
An Evaluative Review of the Consequences for Wife, Husband, and Child
by Lois Wladis Hoffman and F. Ivan Nye

Copyright © 1974 by: Jossey-Bass, Inc., Publishers
615 Montgomery Street
San Francisco, California 94111
&
Jossey-Bass Limited
3 Henrietta Street
London WC2E 8LU

Library of Congress Catalogue Card Number LC 74-6744

International Standard Book Number ISBN 0-87589-243-4

Manufactured in the United States of America

JACKET DESIGN BY WILLI BAUM

FIRST EDITION
First printing: December 1974
Second printing: August 1975

Code 7434

The Jossey-Bass
Behavioral Science Series

Preface

The aim of *Working Mothers* is to pull together research findings
on the effects of maternal employment on the family from the
fields of psychology and sociology, to organize these diverse findings by substantive topics, and to summarize them in nontechnical
language. A major goal is to retain the scientific quality of the research and to avoid premature generalizations to practical issues,
yet to make the data useful by organizing the findings and emphasiz-
ing the conditions that affect their meaning and applicability. One
goal will be achieved if the reader at least learns to avoid the question "Is maternal employment good or bad?" and to ask instead
"What is the effect on specific attitudes, behavior, or health under
specified conditions?" The view that guides the present volume is
that the research findings have value but must be qualified. For
example, the effects of maternal employment differ under alternative
socioeconomic conditions, at different stages in the family cycle, and
in various social and familial settings. Data that appear to be inconsistent are usually answering different questions.

The topics reflect the research that has been accomplished. It
would have been desirable, for example, to include a chapter on the
effects of maternal employment in the fatherless home, but an extended search indicated too few studies to warrant a separate
chapter. Instead, the existing data on such families have been reported under the appropriate substantive topics. Similarly, it would
have been desirable to report additional findings on the effects of

ix

maternal employment among black Americans, the effects with different child-care arrangements, and the effects under the newly emerging social conditions, in which maternal employment has become the normative pattern for many groups. All these are topics currently in need of additional empirical investigation.

While historical background materials and cross-cultural studies are considered where these provide a perspective for the topic under discussion, the focus of the book is on maternal employment in America since 1940. This focus, like the topics, covers most available data. More recent research was emphasized to avoid overlap with previous volumes on this topic (Michael, 1971; Nye and Hoffman, 1963; Yudkin and Holme, 1963). All the chapters are interpretive summaries of the literature written for this volume. (Chapters Four and Six were written for this volume, although they were published previously.) The first three chapters provide a socio-psychological description of maternal employment. The first chapter gives the statistical picture, tracing changes in rates for different segments of the population and interpreting these trends in the light of other sociocultural events. The second chapter deals with personal motivations for employment. The third chapter considers studies of women's commitment to work, the extent to which they remain in the labor force once they decide to join it. The fourth and fifth chapters deal with special aspects of maternal employment. The fourth chapter addresses the relationship between female employment and fertility patterns, viewing the changing rates of each in sociocultural perspective and exploring their significance for personal motivation. In the fifth chapter, the child-care arrangements of working mothers are discussed in terms of their historical development, current prevalence, and future prospects. The remaining chapters, Chapters Six through Nine, deal with the effects of maternal employment on family relationships and family members. Chapter Six is an integrative summary of research findings on the effects on the child. Chapter Seven analyzes the concept of conjugal power relations, summarizing the literature on the effects on the influence patterns and division of labor between the husband and wife. In Chapter Eight, the affective relationship between the spouses is explored. Several criteria for evaluating the relationship are considered: divorce, conflict, satisfaction, and a combination of rewards and tensions. Chapter Nine focuses on the mother herself. The research reviewed deals with the mother's physical and mental health, her general self-concept, and her evaluation of herself in each of her roles. A final chapter provides an overview of the present state of knowledge, pointing out the limitations of the current empirical picture and providing suggestions for further research.

Ann Arbor, Michigan   Lois Wladis Hoffman
Pullman, Washington   F. Ivan Nye
September 1974

Contents

Working Mothers

An Evaluative Review
of the Consequences
for Wife, Husband, and Child

1

Sociocultural Context

F. IVAN NYE

Whether millions of mothers look for and find paid employment depends on whether a society can offer such employment and whether the household roles women usually enact allow them to take a major set of additional responsibilities. In this chapter we review (a) the principal changes which have resulted in the need of employers for the labor of women with children still in the home; (b) the traditional household roles, to determine what changes in them allow women simultaneously to be mothers and full-time paid employees; and (c) what has happened to the nature of work traditionally considered unsuitable to women which now renders almost all types of employment equally appropriate for men and women.

Historical Perspective

Women have always worked to produce goods and services for themselves and their families. In almost every society this work has included the processing and preparation of food and of clothing, household care and repair, and similar housekeeping tasks. In most societies it also has included agricultural and collecting tasks, in which some of the goods to be consumed in the family were pro-

Work on this chapter was supported in part by Project #2008 of the Agricultural Research Center, Washington State University.

1

duced directly by women. In many other societies, it included production of items either in the household or in factories and offices which were sold or exchanged for salary or wages. The issues, then, are hardly whether women shall work, but rather at what tasks, for how many hours a week, in or away from their homes, for salaries paid to them or for an undifferentiated share of total family income, and how shall the responsibilities of full-time employment away from the home intersect with responsibilities for child care, family recreation, and housekeeper tasks?

Looking back to colonial times, we find that, in America in contrast to Europe, employment of women in the fields was not common, although it occurred. However, women were busy inside the home in the manufacture of items for family use and for sale or barter; after development of the factory system, an increasing number were employed outside the home. In 1789, a petition on behalf of the first cotton factory in Massachusetts stated that it would "afford employment to a great number of women and children, many of whom will be otherwise useless, if not burdensome to society" (Abbott, 1910, p. 43). Early American society was thus not adverse to women being employed productively and contributing to family income; such work not only was desirable economically, but was also considered conducive to good morals, as the following suggests: During the tariff controversy of the 1830s, free traders and protectionists alike agreed in commending the manufacturing industries which had furnished employment for women. "It was no new thing for 'Friends of Industry' to argue that the decline of our manufacturing interests would mean that women employees would become 'the tenants of charitable institutions or be consigned to prisons and penitentiaries by the vices contracted during idleness' " (Abbott, 1910, p. 53). Later (1910), the New York Times was "earnestly advocating the employment of females as clerks in stores—particularly all retail dry goods stores. It is an employment for which they are well fitted and would properly enlarge their sphere of action and occupations, and it is a business that they can handle better than men" (quoted in Abbott, 1910, p. 3). While not everyone supported the idea of women in paid work, it had extensive and influential support.

While systematic statistics are not available for the first half of the nineteenth century, thirty-nine thousand females were employed in cotton factories alone in 1831. The economic contribution made by these women was impressive to a contemporary observer: "[The] immense sum paid for the wages of females may be considered so much clear gain for the country" (quoted in Abbott, 1910, p. 55). In 1846, it was estimated that 13,311 women were working in Massachusetts alone in making hats and bonnets.

The first census of manufacturing, in 1850, showed 731,137 men and 225,922 women employed; thus, 24 percent of the total were women. The 1905 census showed a slightly lower proportion, 19 percent. The two censuses are not exactly comparable, however (Abbott, 1910, p. 81). In 1910, women were 21 percent of the labor force, 22 percent in 1930, 25 percent in 1940, and 37 percent in 1970 (U.S. Bureau of the Census, 1930, 1941, 1971).

Thus, economically productive women are a phenomena as ancient as humanity itself, and their employment for wages and salaries was a familiar part of the Industrial Revolution. By 1940, with one worker in four a woman, the gainful employment of women was a well established and accepted aspect of the American economic structure. However, prior to World War II, most employed women were single; in 1890, only 14 percent of employed women were married and, in 1900, 15 percent. Therefore, although approximately one paid worker in five was a woman in 1900, only a seventh of these—or about 3 percent of the total working force—were married. We have no data on what proportion of those married women had minor children, but the proportion of all workers who were mothers with dependent children at home must have been less than 1 percent of all workers in gainful employment.

From another perspective, only 5 percent of all married women were gainfully employed in 1890, increasing to 12 percent in 1930 (LaFollette, 1934, p. 2). Census data prior to 1940 provided no information as to whether married women in employment had dependent children; but, from what we have learned since concerning the inhibiting effects of children on the acceptance of employment by mothers, the proportion of mothers employed must have been substantially less than the proportions for all married women.

Although the gainful employment of women has a long and economically significant place in the development of American society, a change has occurred in the incorporation of a large number of married women into the labor force. By 1930 this number had reached one in eight, more than double that of 1890. By 1940, one worker in four was a woman, and 30 percent of all employed women were married and living with husbands. Newer still is the incorporation of increasing proportions of married women with dependent children into gainful employment; in 1940 this figure had reached only one mother in twelve (see Table 1).

Besides the increase in maternal employment which accompanied and followed World War II, two events highlighted the impression of an abrupt change. First, in the Great Depression, because of high rates of unemployment of men, including many with families, a conscious effort was made to keep married women out of employment. Frequently women were discharged when it became known that they were married. Second, census analyses did not, until after World War II, distinguish between married, employed, childless women and those with children. Thus, systematic data on the number or proportion of mothers in the labor force were lacking, and awareness of the phenomenon seemed to parallel the lack of such organized data. It was known and accepted that a large proportion of single women were employed and, to a lesser extent, married childless women, but it was still assumed that, barring exceptional circumstances, "a mother's place is in the home." Therefore, it came as a surprise following World War II that a large and increasing proportion of married women with dependent children were employed. It happened, too, that the post-World War II period was one of increased divorce, juvenile delinquency, and mental health problems. Many journalists and some amateur social scientists were not slow to assert a causal relationship and to voice concerns about working mothers.

Following World War II. Just prior to World War II, a large surplus of labor existed, male as well as female. This surplus offered little opportunity for the participation of married women in employment. But the situation changed during World War II and with the end of that war, the American economy entered a period of unprecedented expansion, resulting in a shortage of labor. This expansion presented a most favorable milieu—economic, political, and

Table 1.

WOMEN IN THE LABOR FORCE, 1940–1972

Employed Women

Marital Status	1940	1944	1948	1955	1960	1965	1971	1972
					Number (Millions)			
Single	6.7	7.5	5.9	5.1	5.4	5.9	7.2	7.5
Married, living with husband	4.2ᵃ	6.2	7.6	10.4	12.3	14.7	18.5	19.2
No children under 18 years	2.7	ᵇ	4.4	5.2	5.7	6.8	8.4	ᵇ
Children 6–17 only	1.5ᵃ	ᵇ	1.9	3.2	4.1	4.8	6.4	ᵇ
Children 0–5			1.2	2.0	2.5	3.1	5.5	ᵇ
Widowed, divorced, living apart	2.9	4.7	3.7	4.6	4.9	5.4	6.0	6.2
All women	13.9	18.5	17.2	20.1	22.6	26.0	31.7	32.9
					Percent			
Single	48.1	58.6	51.1	46.6	44.1	40.5	52.7	54.9
Married, living with husband	14.7	21.7	22.0	27.7	30.5	38.3	40.8	41.5
No children under 18 years		ᵇ	28.4	32.7	34.7	34.7	42.1	42.7
Children 6–17 only	8.6ᵃ	ᵇ	26.0	34.7	39.0	42.7	49.4	50.2
Children 0–5			10.7	16.0	18.6	22.8	29.2	30.1ᶜ
Widowed, divorced, living apart	35.4	42.0	38.3	38.5	40.0	35.7	38.1	40.0ᵈ
All women	25.7	35.0	31.0	33.4	34.8	36.7	42.5	43.6

ᵃ Estimated. Source: U.S. Department of Labor, Women's Bureau (n.d.). Data for 0–5 and 6–17 are combined for 1940.
ᵇ No information available.
ᶜ With no children under three, 36 percent were employed; with children under three, 27 percent.
ᵈ For 1972, the proportions employed were: widowed, 27 percent; living apart, 42 percent; divorcees, 70 percent (with preschool children, 62 percent).
Sources: U.S. Bureau of the Census (1971, 1972); U.S. Bureau of Labor Statistics (1971); and Hayghe (1973).

ideological—for the entry of millions of married women, most of them mothers, into paid employment.

Oppenheimer (1973) analyzes the needs of industry for the services of married women, including those with children: "My argument is that continued economic development in our society has increased the demand for female labor, which, combined with demographically induced shifts in the supply of women, has resulted in the considerable post-World War II rise in women's labor force participation" (p. 948).

Decline in Single Female Population. Part of the demographic pressure to move married women into the labor force originated in the decrease in the number of single women available for employment (Oppenheimer, 1973). The absolute number of single women employed declined from 6.7 million in 1940 to a low of 5.1 million in 1955 (Table 1). The proportion of single women who were in employment also declined slightly from 48 to 47 percent as a larger proportion of the young females married, resulting in a larger proportion of women past retirement age in the single population. In order to maintain their 1940 proportion in the population, the number of single women would have had to increase by about 1.5 million from 1940 to 1955. Instead, it declined 1.6 million, to a "deficit" of 3.1 million, or about 46 percent of the 1940 figure.

Several changes contributed to the decline in numbers and proportion of single females. The birth rate, which had been 30.1 in 1910 declined to 21.3 in 1930 and to 18.7 in 1935 (a reduction of more than a third), where it remained almost unchanged until 1945, when it stood at 20.5 per thousand (U.S. Bureau of the Census, 1972). As a consequence, beginning as early as 1945, there was a scarcity of young workers, proportionate to the older population, entering the labor force, a scarcity which continued into the 1960s.

Another reason for the scarcity of young, single, employable women was the increase in the proportion who married and the earlier age at marriage. Between 1930 and 1950 the proportion of women over fourteen years who were single declined from 28 to 20 percent, concentrated in the age group from sixteen to twenty-five, in which high proportions of single women are employed. During these decades, age at marriage also declined. In 1940, only 35 percent of women married by age twenty, but in 1950 the proportion had increased to 49 percent. Since many became pregnant within a year, many young women were removed from the labor force earlier.

Increase in Birth Rate. Not only did young women marry younger, but they began having larger families. The birth rate jumped from 20.5 in 1945 to 25.0 in 1955 and did not fall below 20.0 again until 1965. Thus, many of the young married women who would have been available to the work force between 1945 and 1965 were involved in bearing and caring for small children. This lack of young women opened many opportunities for employment for older mothers with no preschool children. Oppenheimer (1970) also observes that a major expansion occurred in the proportion of young women eighteen to nineteen years old who after 1945 were enrolled in college rather than working.

The shortage of unmarried women and childless married women could not be relieved by employing men for several reasons. The overall supply of young male workers was inadequate even to fill positions traditionally occupied by men. The low birth rate from 1930 to 1945 reduced the number of young men entering employment from 1945 to 1965. As with women, a much larger proportion of men eighteen to twenty-one were, after 1945, enrolled in advanced education. Finally, the age group from twenty to thirty experienced major casualties during World War II.

Besides the unavailability of young men to fill positions traditionally occupied by women, there were other reasons a switch did not occur. Employer preferences had been developed for women in secretarial, nursing, primary teaching, waitressing, and other occupational categories. Also, the comparatively low pay in most of these rendered them relatively unattractive to men.

Increase in Demand for Women Workers. The enormous expansion of the economy after World War II multiplied the demand for female labor. Overall, the labor force expanded from 52.0 million in 1940 to 59.6 million in 1950, 66.7 million in 1960, and to 80.6 million in 1972 (U.S. Bureau of the Census, 1940, 1972). As seen, not much of this increase could come from the male sector. The increase for men was only from 39.4 million in 1940 to 49.8 million in 1972. The combination of low birth rates from 1930 to 1945, the increased enrollment in advanced education, and casualties in World War II held the increase in male employment to a modest 25 percent. Since children were in school or prohibited from most employment, the largest part of the expansion of the economy had to come from the addition of women workers. Since there was a decline in single women and married women increased their birth rate, a major part of the increase had to come from women with children.

The needs for increased labor supply developed primarily in white-collar occupations, where physical strength was irrelevant. Thus, of the total increase in the labor force of 30.6 million, 22.6 million (about 70 percent of the gain) was in the white-collar occupations. For example, professional, technical, and kindred workers increased from 3.9 to 11.6 million, a gain of 400 percent, and clerical employment from 5.3 to 14.2 million, an increase approaching 300 percent. Many of the occupations in these categories were staffed primarily with women employees.

We have seen the convergence of several changes conducive to the expansion of employment among mothers: (1) a tremendous expansion in the economy; (2) the concentration of the expansion in the white-collar and service areas which had long been staffed largely by women; (3) a shortage of men and single females available for such expansion. This convergence provided extremely favorable opportunities for the employment of women and for major increases in pay in areas of chronic shortages, such as teaching, nursing, and secretarial positions. Probably because of the shortage of available labor, employers developed an increased willingness to employ married women, with less regard for their familial status or responsibilities. Thus, after 1945, there was a chronic need for the services of women with children, a group traditionally defined as being outside the labor force.

Social Changes

In most of the world in most periods of history, women have made an important, direct contribution to the economic support of the family. This contribution has almost always included the processing of food and fiber, and the cleaning and ordering of utensils, clothing, and the dwelling. These clusters of economic activities have been characteristic of the American family as well as those of other societies. However, slowly at first, but with increasing momentum, these economic activities within the home moved outside of it and this change, with a long-term downward trend in the birth rate, has basically altered the role structure of the American family.

Earliest among these changes was the shift of clothing manufacture from the home to the factory. Manufacturing soap, tending gardens, and keeping chickens were other tasks early transferred to production and manufacture outside the home (Oppenheimer, 1973). Later, canning fruits and vegetables, making jams and jellies, baking bread and pastries, and dry cleaning clothing became the task of specialized factories and establishments. Still more recently, the TV dinner, precooked meats, and vegetables cleaned and prepared for the pot have become commonplace. At the same time new fabrics requiring no ironing have been developed. Finally, the preparation and serving of food outside the home has become an increasingly important item.

Concurrent with this transfer of economic activities out of the home has been the mechanization of tasks within it. The old wood range and fireplace as sources of heat for cooking have been replaced with electric, gas, and now electronic ovens. The refrigerator and deep freeze replace the old storage pits. The dishwasher replaces several pans of dish and rinse water. As a consequence, those housekeeper tasks still performed in the home can be done in a fraction of the time once required.

Reduced Role of Child and Elderly Care. Perhaps as important as the reductions in household tasks is the control of fertility and planning for small families. The birth rate, which stood at 52 per thousand population in 1820, gradually declined until it was 18.9 in 1935. An upturn in 1945 took it to 25 in 1955, but after that the downturn resumed until in 1973 it was 14, hardly more than one-fourth of the 1820 rate (*U.S. Monthly Vital Statistics Report,* 1974). It was also less than one-half of the 1910 rate of 30.1.

As important as the reduction in size has been the concentration of child-bearing in a few years following marriage. The majority of mothers see their youngest child off to school before their thirty-second birthday (Leslie, 1973, p. 263), which leaves them with some thirty-five years of healthy, active adulthood and considerable time and energy to devote to activities beyond the home. The husband is likely to be away from home from before 8:00 until after 5:00; school-age children are gone from about 8:30 until 3:30. Much time, although probably not enough to add a full-time job, has become available to the mother with children of school age.

The care of the aged has also been transferred from the young family, primarily to the aged themselves, as governmental and business retirement plans have become more adequate and retirement annuities purchased from insurance companies have added substantially to retirement income. The majority of retired people prefer to live by themselves rather than with their grown children, and adequate economic provisions for retirement have made this possible. Medicare has provided some of the nursing care needed by the elderly and may have resulted in a reduction in chronic illness in old age. The development of retirement communities with extensive recreational facilities and of social clubs for the elderly has decreased the dependence of many of the elderly on their children for social interaction and recreation. As a result of these and related developments, many young women who would in previous years have devoted much of their time to the care of elderly parents have that time available for other activities, including employment.

New Pressures on Family Incomes. The transfers of economic productivity and the mechanization of homes do not occur without economic costs. Although precise data are not at hand, the cost of served meals in restaurants may be double the cost of the food and fuel required to produce it in the home. A suit or dress purchased is likely to increase even more in cost. Similarly, the preprocessing of vegetables and the marketing of these in small portions multiply their costs.

The increase in costs has also been dramatic in the mechanization of the home. The modern refrigerator and deep freeze replace the air cooler or the storage pit, the cost of which was nil. The expensive dishwasher replaces the dishpan; the vacuum cleaner replaces a minimum-cost broom and dust pan. Expensive central heating (and sometimes a cooling system) replaces fireplaces and heating stoves. Finally, the separation of most homes spatially from the husband's place of employment and also from shopping districts and schools has created a perceived need for two automobiles.

The transfer of economic activities from the home, the elaborate mechanization of household equipment, and the separation of the residence from the place of employment and from service centers have placed pressure on the earning power of the husband. Especially in the early years of family formation, during which men's earnings are low, and during the time that major household equipment is purchased, the strain on many one-income families is severe.

Changing Normative Structure

Historically, the care of the home and of small children has been allocated to the mother. The inference was that either she should personally care for the home and such children as were there or she should personally supervise servants in their duties. The employment of women away from the home for any considerable time was believed to be incompatible with good care of the home and children. Therefore, it was believed wrong for mothers to be employed outside of the home.

The assumed neglect of home and children was not the only basis for objecting to the employment of mothers. Many scholars earlier believed that the behavior required in the marketplace—aggressiveness, rationality, and competitiveness—were incompatible with the role requirements of mothers to be accepting, nurturant, and accommodative (Lundberg and Farnham, 1947). The same scholars believed that having wives share the provider role would be a threat to the self-confidence and security of the husband.

As a consequence of the assumption that paid employment was incompatible with the efficient enactment of the housekeeping, child care, and other feminine roles, and the fear of resulting personality damage to both men and women, the initial reception of the movement of mothers into the labor force was hostile. Employed mothers were accused of being responsible for juvenile delinquency, divorce, mental illness among both mothers and children, frigidity, and other behavior considered problematic. At least one social agency supported research on employed mothers with the expectation that the results could be utilized as a basis for legislation to discourage their participation in the labor force. In Nye and Hoffman (1963a), however, the reports of more than twenty social scientists were generally reassuring with respect to the effects of maternal employment.

As more mothers have taken paid employment outside the home (Table 1) and the predicted catastrophies have not resulted, the proscriptions against mothers in employment have relaxed. Over half of the women sixteen to sixty-four are now in the labor force (U.S. Department of Labor, Women's Bureau, 1972), as are half of the mothers who have children six to seventeen years of age and none under six. These figures are for women employed or looking for work during a given week and greatly understate the proportion employed sometime during the year.

Since the behavior of most women now contradicts the traditional proscriptions against mothers taking paid employment, feelings against it cannot be generally strong or sanctions effectively applied. Yet, the negative feelings have not entirely disappeared. A sampling of opinion in the state of Washington by Nye and coworkers (1973) showed the following sentiment concerning the employment of married women (Table 2). The question to the respondents was: "There has also been a trend toward more women being employed outside the home than in the past. Do you think this trend toward more women working is desirable or undesirable?" In the total population of adults, sentiments were about equally divided, but a decisive majority of younger adults is now supportive of the em-

Table 2.

ATTITUDES TOWARD THE GAINFUL EMPLOYMENT
OF MARRIED WOMEN, PERCENT

	Favorable	Unfavorable	Undecided
Males, all ages	49	42	9
Females, all ages	43	44	13
Males, under 35	61	31	8
Females, under 35	63	28	8

ployment of married women. This finding suggests that the norms against paid employment for women are disintegrating and that women, unless they are members of groups holding beliefs different from the society as a whole, need not anticipate generalized disapproval and opposition to their employment.

Trends in Maternal Employment. Census data show a steadily increasing proportion of women in paid employment since 1910, but, unfortunately, early reports do not distinguish between women who were mothers and those who were not. Estimates are available starting with the 1940 census, and after 1948 adequate data indicate the presence and age of children in the family.

There has been a moderate increase in the proportion of all women gainfully employed, from 25.7 percent in 1940 to 44 percent in 1972. In contrast, the proportion of employed married women living with their husbands increased from 14.7 to 42 percent in the same period, and the proportion of mothers with children under eighteen increased even more dramatically (Table 1). About three-fourths of these are full-time workers—that is, employed an average of thirty-five hours weekly or more. This proportion varies, however, by age of child, race, and other variables. The average work week for mothers of preschool children is about thirty-two hours compared with thirty-seven for women with no children under eighteen (Bowen and Finegan, 1969, p. 101).

Women with children of school age have entered the labor force in greater numbers than have mothers of preschool children, but the rate of increase until 1965 was about equal. The increase from 1948 to 1965 was 152 percent for the mothers of school-age children and 158 percent for the mothers of preschool children. Since 1965, the numbers of women with children of school age entering the labor force has been greater than the number of those with preschool children, but the proportionate increase has been larger among those with preschool children. Since 1965, the increase for those with school-age children was from 42.7 to 50.2 percent; with the earlier percentage as a base, this is a gain of 18 percent. The increase for those with preschool children was from 22.8 to 30.1 percent; again, based on the earlier percentage, the increase is 32 percent (Table 1).

Three societal changes occurred in these seven years that

appear relevant to the larger increase in employment among mothers of preschool children. The birthrate fell from 19 to 14 per thousand and the divorce rate increased from 2.5 to 3.9 per thousand (U.S. Bureau of the Census, 1973).[1] During the same period, substantial subsidies for day care of preschool children were initiated both through federal funding (U.S. Department of Labor, 1972) and by voluntary organizations. Thus women were having fewer children of preschool age for whom care was required, more financial support of day care became available, and a much larger proportion of young mothers, because of divorce or separation, needed to supplement their income by taking employment. Since half of all divorces and more than half of all terminal separations occur in the first seven years of marriage, younger mothers were affected disproportionately.

About two-fifths of employed women in 1972 were mothers with children under eighteen. Divorced, widowed, and separated women in the labor force increased by about 100 percent and the increase in the number of single women employed was slight, while that group married and living with husbands expanded some 800 percent from 1940 to 1971. Within this period, the employment of mothers changed from a negligible social and economic phenomenon to one that affected more than two in five families with children under eighteen and one in two with children six to seventeen years and none under six years of age. The proportion who worked for pay sometime during the year was even greater, 58 percent of those

[1] These changes are rendered complex, possibly confusing, by the fact that only the *numbers* of women with school children continue to grow much faster than did the numbers of those with preschool children. This growth is due partly to the fact that the total number of mothers with school children is larger, but also to the fact that the "pool" of women with preschool children declined in numbers during this seven-year period. The number of children born in the United States was less for every year during this period than it was in 1964; therefore the number of mothers with preschool children declined during the period, while the number with school children continued to grow because of the high birth rates from 1950 to 1965. The fact that the number of employed women with preschool children continued to grow substantially during this period of seven years while the total pool from which they were drawn became smaller resulted in a relatively rapid gain in the *proportion* of women with preschool children in gainful employment.

with school-age but none younger, and 47 percent of those with preschool children (Waldman and Gover, 1972).

The presence of preschool children has reduced the flow of well-educated, energetic young woman into the labor force, and very young children reduce it more than do older preschool children. Sweet (1970) found that the presence of a child under the age of one reduces the proportion of women in the labor force 17 percentage points below the average for all women with children under eighteen. A child one year of age reduces it 9 points; of age two, 7 points; three, 5 points; four or five, 3 points. Mothers are much more likely to be ready to leave an older preschool child than a small baby with a relative or other care-giver.

Occupational Changes. Since the beginning of this century the occupational composition of the United States has changed tremendously. Much of this change is reflected in women's occupations (Table 3). In 1900, almost half of all employed women were working in agriculture or as private household workers, but by 1960 this proportion had declined to about one in ten and is less than that today. A moderate decline has occurred in the proportion of women in factories (operatives). The primary increase has been in clerical work, which has increased eightfold, with moderate increases in sales, managerships and proprietorships and in professional and technical occupations. Thus, not only the mechanization of labor but the occupational trends toward white-collar work have been conducive to the entry of women into paid employment. The changes have been somewhat uneven, with a large proportion of older women still employed in blue-collar jobs. Black women are also more likely than white women to be in blue-collar positions: In 1971, 17 percent of the employed black women were in private household work compared with 3 percent of employed white women, and 27 percent were in service occupations compared with 16 percent of white women. Only 22 percent were clerical and 11 percent professional and technical compared with 36 and 15 percent, respectively, for white women (U.S. Department of Labor, Women's Bureau, 1972).

Compared with men, employed women were as likely to be in professional and technical positions (Table 3) but less likely to be

Table 3.

OCCUPATION COMPOSITION OF U.S. EMPLOYED FEMALE POPULATION, 1900–1973, AND MALES, 1973, PERCENT

Occupation	Women								Men
	1900	1910	1920	1930	1940	1950	1960	1973[a]	1973[a]
Professional, technical, kindred workers	8.1	9.7	11.6	13.4	12.7	12.2	13.3	14.9	13.4
Managers, officials, proprietors, excluding farmers	1.4	2.0	2.2	2.7	3.2	4.3	4.6	4.9	13.4
Clerical, kindred workers	4.0	9.2	18.6	20.8	21.4	27.4	30.0	34.3	6.6
Sales workers	4.3	5.1	6.2	6.8	7.3	8.6	7.2	6.8	6.3
Craftsmen, foremen, kindred workers	1.4	1.4	1.2	1.0	1.1	1.5	0.9	1.5	20.7
Operatives, kindred workers	23.8	22.9	20.2	17.4	19.5	19.9	16.1	13.5	19.2
Private household workers	28.7	24.0	15.7	17.8	18.1	8.8	9.8	} 21.9[b]	8.1[b]
Service workers, excluding private household	6.7	8.4	8.1	9.7	11.3	12.6	15.4		
Farm workers	18.9	15.7	13.5	8.3	3.9	3.6	2.4	1.4	4.8
Laborers, excluding farm and mine workers	2.6	1.4	2.3	1.5	1.1	0.8	0.3	0.8	7.6
Total	99.9	99.9	100.0	100.0	99.9	100.0	100.0	100.0	100.0

[a] April 1973.
[b] Data not separately available for private household and service workers. Data for married women, husband present in 1972, showed 3 percent employed as private household and 16.7 percent as service workers.
Sources: U.S. Bureau of Labor Statistics (1971) and U.S. Bureau of the Census (1958, 1973).

in those requiring graduate degrees. They were outnumbered three to one in managerial and proprietary positions but almost completely dominate the clerical occupations. Women are found occasionally in the craft occupations but have almost left farm work, 60 percent are in occupations usually classified as white collar compared with 40 percent of the men. Therefore, compared with men, they are more heavily concentrated in white collar occupations but in those paying lower salaries.

These changes in the structure of American occupations away from agriculture and factory to white-collar employment have increased the proportion of jobs in which physical strength is irrelevant. As accompanying mechanization of agriculture and factory jobs reduced the amount of physical strength needed to a fraction of what it was before, it may have made employment more attractive to more women. Even so, Duncan, Schuman, and Duncan (1972) found in the Detroit Metropolitan Area that 62 percent of the women and 74 percent of the men interviewed felt that there were some jobs women should not take. However, this finding represented a considerable change from 1956, when 75 percent of the women and 85 percent of the men felt some jobs were unsuitable for women.

Education. Well-educated women have moved into the labor force much faster than those with little education (Figure 1). The proportion employed among those with graduate degrees is more than three times that for those with less than an eighth-grade education. This statistic may seem surprising since the earning power is lower for husbands of women with little education and, therefore, economic need in an absolute sense would be greater for women with less education. A glance at Table 3, however, shows that all the growth in female employment has come in the white-collar occupations, where an average to a higher education is required, or at least preferred, by employers. The occupations with the least educational requirements, such as private household work and farm labor, have declined the most rapidly, leaving few opportunities for women in those occupational categories. In contrast, the white-collar occupations have experienced substantial to exceptional growth, thus providing opportunities for the well-educated.

The increase in labor force participation with increased education has been analyzed by Bowen and Finegan (1969) for the

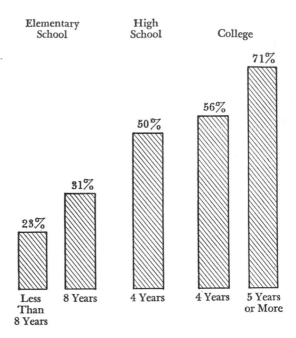

FIGURE 1. Proportion of women in the labor force by highest year of education completed, 1970. Source: U.S. Department of Labor, Women's Bureau (1971).

influence of other related variables, including income earned by the woman, age of children, and race. They report (p. 118) that women with some graduate training earn about two and one-half times as much as do those with less than fourth-grade education. This, they believe, is a major reason for the higher participation of women with more education, but they also list such "psychic rewards" as pleasant work and a preference for "market" work rather than "home" work.

Differences in the proportion of women employed by education level are less for women with children under six, suggesting that the inhibiting effects of the child-care role are greater for highly educated women, and, therefore, the availability of jobs, including comparatively well-paid positions, has less effect on their decision to enter the labor force.

A unique relationship was found for black women. They were (1960 data) about as likely to be employed if they had no education as if they had a high school diploma. However, black women with a four-year degree or graduate training were found in the labor force in the highest proportions of any female group (83 percent). A disproportionately high proportion of black women are in such occupations as private household and service jobs, which require little or no education. Relatively few clerical and sales jobs, for which a high school education is especially relevant, have been available to blacks until recently. As more of these positions become available to black women, more women with high school educations may take employment.

Husband's Earnings and Other Income. The wife's motivation to take employment is affected by the amount her husband earns, but at lower income levels other income such as public assistance, disability pay, and annuities may also become important. One indication of this is supplied by data showing that the average income of families in which neither the husband nor the wife is in the labor force is not zero but about forty-five hundred dollars (Waldman and Gover, 1971, p. 23).

A better measure of economic need than the husband's income is the sum of all other income (than that of the wife). Bowen and Finegan (1969) utilized this figure in relating economic need to the proportion of women employed (Table 4) and showed a continuous decline in employment of women with increases in other income.

Comparable data are not at hand from the 1970 census. More limited data from the U.S. Bureau of Labor Statistics (1971) show a substantial drop in the proportion employed—from 55 percent when the husband's income is $7,000–$9,999 to 42 percent for families in which the husband earns over $10,000 (families with children six to seventeen). In families with children under six years the drop was from 33 to 21 percent. These figures are not directly comparable with the data in Table 4 but indicate that if there are children, the proportion of mothers employed declines substantially as the husband's income rises above the median level. Other 1970 data (Waldman and Young, 1971) showed that the participation of married women with no children under eighteen was as high for women whose husbands earned over $10,000 as for the average of all income levels.

Table 4.

OTHER FAMILY INCOME AND LABOR FORCE PARTICIPATION:
MARRIED WOMEN FOURTEEN TO FIFTY-FOUR YEARS
OF AGE IN URBAN AREAS, CENSUS WEEK OF 1960

Total of other family income	*Percentage of population*			*Proportion of wives in labor force*[a]		
	No children under 6	Children under 6	Black with and without children under 6	No children under 6	Children under 6	Black with and without children under 6
Less than $999	3.2	1.9	7.2	60.0	37.4	61.8
$ 1,000–$ 1,999	4.0	3.3	12.0	55.1	24.8	46.9
2,000– 2,999	6.0	6.3	18.4	57.8	28.8	49.9
3,000– 3,999	8.8	10.2	17.3	57.5	24.9	39.3
4,000– 4,999	12.8	14.7	16.7	56.2	24.4	46.5
5,000– 5,999	15.8	18.9	13.4	52.4	21.0	48.0
6,000– 6,999	12.9	14.1	—	48.1	17.6	—
7,000– 8,999	16.5	15.9	5.8	41.3	12.9	48.2
9,000– 10,999	8.2	6.4	3.3	34.9	12.2	41.3
11,000– 14,999	6.1	4.9	—	31.2	9.7	—
15,000– 24,999	4.1	2.5	—	21.6	8.1	—
25,000+	1.6	0.9	—	3.4	1.2	—
Total	100.0	100.0	100.0	46.8	19.4	47.0

[a] Unadjusted. In the original source the authors also give proportions adjusted for effects of color, presence of children, schooling, age, and, in one set of data, employment status of the husband. These are sample data from the census, totaling about twenty-three thousand families.
Sources: Adapted from Bowen and Finegan (1969).

Sweet (1970) elaborates the strategy for determining need by including the number of persons in the family. Using this number and the total income other than that of the wife, he derived a score to measure "income adequacy": the "less adequate" the family income from other sources, the more likely the woman is to be in the labor force. There are limitations to this generalization, however. Since the expansion of demand for women's labor has come in the white-collar occupations (Table 3), where a high school diploma is likely to be a requirement and college education may be essential or at least deemed desirable, women with such education can find jobs more easily. Furthermore, motherhood operates as a barrier to employment, regardless of economic need.

Number of Children. Early research showed the not-surprising finding that married women with no children and mothers with only one or two children were more likely to be employed than were mothers with more children. Child care not only takes time but usually takes place in the family home, away from offices and factories that provide the greatest proportion of employment opportunities. However, children also require increased income since each additional one adds expenses for food, clothing, and a larger residence.

Sweet's (1970, p. 197) analysis of 1960 census data shows that the proportion of women employed declines with the number of children:

Number of Children	Proportion of Women Employed
None	43%
1	33
2	25
3	20
4	19
5	15
6+	12

Thus, while more children increase the need for income, that need is more than offset by the greater "costs" of work for women with large families. These costs include such things as child care if the children are of preschool age, and the greater amount of housework, child supervision, and other duties characteristic of large families. Women with large families may also encounter more adverse comment about "leaving their families" to take employment than do women with small families. The relationship that mothers with smaller families are more likely to be employed holds for white and black families and at all income levels, but for all husband-wife families, the difference, 0.23 children, is surprisingly slight.

Minority Families. A greater proportion of minority women are employed (Table 5). Fifty-four percent of minority women presently or previously married are employed compared with 41 percent of ever-married white women (U.S. Department of Labor,

Table 5.

MOTHERS IN LABOR FORCE BY RACE, AGE OF CHILDREN,
AND MARITAL STATUS, MARCH 1971, PERCENT

Race and Age of Children (years)	*Married* (Husband Present)	*Widowed or Divorced* (Husband Absent)	*Total Ever Married*
Minority, Total[a]	53.1	55.7	53.9
6–17 only	60.5	62.7	61.3
Under 6	46.9	46.3	46.8
White, Total	38.4	61.5	40.7
6–17 only	48.4	69.4	50.9
Under 6	27.7	48.5	29.3

[a] Composed of 90 percent Negro, 10 percent other races. Spanish-speaking persons included in this category.
Source: Adapted from U.S. Department of Labor, Women's Bureau (1972).

Women's Bureau, 1971). For all minority women, including those never married, the proportions are more similar, 56 percent of minority compared with 50 percent of whites. The income of minority women is less than that of white women, except for those with graduate education; minority women "fully employed" (over thirty-five hours weekly, fifty or more weeks yearly) earned 85 percent of the average for white women, and 71 percent of the average for minority men. Minority wives contributed 31 percent to family income compared with 26 percent contributed by white married women. Forty-four percent of minority women were in private household and service occupations compared with 19 percent of the white women workers. Minority women with college degrees or graduate education earned as much as white women, but the proportion of those who had completed four years of college was smaller—8 compared with 12 percent. Minority women workers are rapidly narrowing the education gap; they averaged 12.1 years of education in 1971, an increase of three years since 1959 and were approaching the 12.5-year level of white women and men (U.S. Department of Labor, Women's Bureau, 1972, p. 8).

Although minority women still are employed disproportionately in unskilled jobs, they have made major gains in the past decade. They have almost doubled in professional and technical positions from 6 to 11 percent and more than doubled in clerical jobs from 9 to 22 percent of their numbers. These gains should not, however, obscure the fact that they are still disproportionately employed in private household and service jobs.

In husband-wife families, minority mothers are much more likely to be in the labor force, but not in families headed by women. In minority families, the mother is as likely to be employed regardless of whether a husband is present, but in white families women are much more likely to be in paid employment if no spouse is present. The difference for white mothers with children six to seventeen years is between 38 percent (spouse present) and 62 percent (spouse absent), an increase of 63 percent of the figure for spouse present; for mothers of preschoolers, the increase from 28 to 49 percent represents an increase of 75 percent over the spouse-present proportion (U.S. Department of Labor, Women's Bureau, 1971).

The presence of a husband does not appear to appreciably affect the participation of black women in employment. The greater instability of the marital bond, the higher level of male unemployment and intermittent employment, and the larger proportion of income contributed by black compared with white wives are probably important in the decision of black women to take or retain employment regardless of the presence of a spouse.

Age. The largest proportion of women in the labor force have completed their education, have not yet had their first child, and are between twenty and twenty-four years of age. There is a major decrease in employment while there are children of preschool age in the family, then a return to a high level while children are of school age and the mothers are thirty-five to fifty-four years of age. Finally, a sizable decline of 11 percent precedes retirement age from fifty-five to sixty-four (U.S. Department of Labor, Women's Bureau, 1971).

A number of reasons have been given for the lower employment rate after age fifty-five; however, it should be noted that a similar drop in participation occurs for men, from 96.2 to 87.5 percent (Bowen and Finegan, 1969, pp. 45, 287). The drop in participation is larger for women than men, but not much (11 compared with 8.7 percent). Some reasons for men leaving the labor force after age fifty-five include early retirement, physical disability, and inability to find employment. All of these may be reasons for the lesser participation of older women. In addition, pressure on the husband's income eases after the mid-fifties, and permits the wife to leave the labor force. Most children have left home and are supporting themselves. Major home furnishings have been purchased, and the home mortgage may be paid. In many families, it may be possible to do without the wife's income without reducing the level of living. Relevant here also is a finding (presented in Chapter Nine) that shows that younger employed mothers are better satisfied with their lives than housewives are, but, in the postparental period, housewives are better satisfied than employed wives. Finally, there is much more movement into and out of the labor force by women than men. After fifty-five it is easy for women to leave employment but more difficult to enter it if they have not worked previously (Conyers, 1963).

Part- and Full-Time Employment. The employment of mothers has involved large numbers of part-time as well as full-time workers. In fact, a minority (41 percent) of women work full time the year around, although the proportion is increasing slightly (U.S. Bureau of the Census, 1973). Three general types of part-time employment may be found: full-time employment for only part of the year, part-time employment for the full year, or part-time employment for part of the year. Among women who work thirty-five or more hours weekly about three-fourths are employed the year around. Thus, although a minority of women work full time the year around, most who work full time on the basis of hours per week also work on a year-around schedule. Of those who work less than thirty-five hours weekly, few work a full year. Half of the part-time workers work less than twenty-six weeks a year, about one-fifth work twenty-six to forty-nine weeks yearly, and only about 30 percent hold jobs on a year-around basis (U.S. Department of Labor, Women's Bureau, 1968, p. 1).

The proportion of full-time and part-time employment differs considerably by marital status, age of children, and race (Table 6). Women with a husband present and children under six

Table 6.

HOURS AND NUMBER OF WEEKS WORKED DURING THE PREVIOUS
YEAR BY EMPLOYED WOMEN ON DAY OF 1970 CENSUS, PERCENT

Married (Husband Present)	Number of weeks worked during 1969			
	1–26	27–49	50–52	Total
With children under 6				
All races	45	29	27	101
Races other than white[a]	34	33	33	100
With children 6–17 (none under 6)				
All races	25	30	45	100
Races other than white	19	34	48	101

	Hours worked during census week				
	1–14	15–34	35–40	41+	Total
With children under 6					
All races	12	26	52	10	100
Black women	6	20	66	8	100
With children 6–17 (none under 6)					
All races	9	28	53	11	101
Black women	7	22	63	8	100

[a] Composed of about 90 percent blacks and including Native Americans and persons of Oriental ancestry.
Source: Data are taken from U.S. Bureau of the Census (1973, Tables 17 and 21). Analytic categories are not identical.

are less likely to work the full year, although if employed, they are almost as likely to work full time during the weeks they work as are the women without preschool children. Taking both types of part-time employment into account, only 16 percent of employed married women (spouse present) with children under three are fully employed, increased to 31 percent for those with children three to five years, and to 39 percent for those with children six to seventeen (U.S. Department of Labor, Women's Bureau, 1968).

For women with spouse absent, preschool children have less effect on whether they take full- or part-time employment. Their participation in employment more closely resembles that of women with children six to seventeen than those with preschool children.

Married women of minority races with husband present work more hours per week and more weeks per year, but if separated, widowed, or divorced, they average fewer weeks per year than white women.

Unemployment. The entry into and continued employment of married women are contingent on their desire for paid employment and the existence of jobs or positions. Frequently a considerable mismatch exists between the supply of women who want employment and its availability. In 1970, the unemployment rate for women aged sixteen and over was 5.3 percent; it was 8.8 percent for black women. The rate for women was considerably higher than for comparable categories of men: all men, 3.8 percent; black men, 6.1 percent (U.S. Bureau of the Census, 1973, p. 98).

However, unemployment among married (and previously married women) varies greatly by age, education, and race. Minority women in most categories have higher unemployment rates than white women, principally in the younger categories and especially at the teenage level. Minority females aged sixteen to nineteen had an unemployment rate of 35.5 in 1971 compared with 15.2 percent for white females (U.S. Department of Labor, Women's Bureau, 1972, p. 2). The racial differences are less for married women sixteen to nineteen, but in this category the unemployment rate for minority women was more than 50 percent higher than for white women. However, for women with four or more years of college, the unemployment rate of 1.9 percent for minority women is less than that for white women (2.5 percent).

Young married (and formerly married women) experience greater problems than older women in finding employment. The rate is 15.6 percent among married women sixteen to nineteen; for those twenty to twenty-one, it is considerably less but still high at 9.0 percent. By age thirty to thirty-four, it declines to 5.1 percent, reaching a low of 3.7 percent for married women fifty-five to fifty-nine years of age. It increases again to 8.3 percent for women over sixty-five. These figures are for married women, spouse present, but the relationship of age to unemployment is similar for separated and formerly married women (U.S. Bureau of the Census, 1973, Table 3).

The relationship of education to unemployment is equally dramatic. For example, in the thirty to thirty-four age category, the rates for those with no more than an eighth-grade education is 9 percent for white and 10 percent for minority women, compared with 3.7 and 5.4, respectively, for high school graduates, and 2.5 for white and 1.9 for minority women with a college degree. A similar relationship between education and employment is found at all ages.

These data may be summarized as follows: There is a large surplus of female labor younger than twenty-one; the size of the surplus declines with increasing years but is still rather high in the thirty to thirty-four age category (5.1 in 1970). Thus, there is a surplus throughout the period in which women have preschool children at home. After age thirty-five, unemployment declines further, even though a much larger supply of labor is available during the years when no minor children are at home. Supply and demand appear reasonably in balance for women aged thirty-five to sixty-five.

Minority women experience more unemployment in their late teens and twenties than do white women, especially the minority women who have dropped out of school. After thirty-five, minority and white unemployment is about equal. Unemployment is also especially severe for minority women with no more than an eighth-grade education, but those with college or graduate degrees have the lowest unemployment rate of any category.

The large oversupply of labor is concentrated among the poorly educated as well as the young women, with rates approximately three times as high for those with no more than eight years of education than for those with college degrees. The labor market is greatly oversupplied with relatively uneducated women and is in reasonable balance for those with high school diplomas; there is an apparent shortage of women with four years or more of college education especially minority women.

Thus, the entry of women into paid employment is not merely a matter of their decisions. Currently, young women who wish to work are having more difficulty in finding employment than are men of the same age. Women over thirty-five have about the same success ratio as men of that age, and women who have a bachelor's or advanced college degree are in an especially advantageous position in the employment picture.

Comparative Income Analysis

Employment of married women moves families from less than average income to higher than average levels. For whites, the average for all families in 1971 was $11,551 (Hayghe, 1973, p. 35). For families in which the wife worked at some time during the year, the figure was $12,932, but since the wife earned an average of $3,870 (U.S. Department of Labor, Women's Bureau, 1972, p. 9), without her income these families would have had an average of only $9,062. Thus, white families with two wage earners averaged about $1,400 more than all white families, but without the wife's income, they would have had almost $2,500 less than the average white family. The situation can be viewed productively utilizing the concept of relative deprivation. Without the wife in the labor force, the family income was about $200 a month less than the average of other families, but with her employment the family moved into a favored position with about $120 more per month gross than the average. Without maternal employment, the family is a relative "have not," looking up at the level of living enjoyed by others. If the wife is in the labor force and the position of the family is reversed, it is able not only to improve its own level of living but to have a bit more than others. If the mother works full time, year around, the advantage becomes over $3,000 more (gross income) than that of the average family.

For minority races, the difference is even greater. The income of minority families averaged $8,157 in 1971. In families in which the wife was employed at some time during the year, it was $10,339, so these families had about $2,200 a year, or almost $200 a month more than average minority family income (Hayghe, 1973; (U.S. Department of Labor, Women's Bureau, 1972). But since the

wife contributed an average of $3,285, these families wo[...]
averaged only $7,054 without her employment, or about $1,10[...]
than the average minority family. Thus, the minority family witho[...]
the mother in the labor force is almost $100 a month behind the
average minority family, but adding her employment brings the
family almost $200 ahead. Adding full-time employment of minority
women brings family income to $13,259 (gross), more than $5,000
ahead of average minority family income and nearly double the
figure the family would have without her employment. It also brings
it well ahead of the average income for white families.

To sum up, families without a working wife lag appreciably
behind the income and level of living of all families. Part-time employment brings them to the average salary for their race, and full-
time employment brings them well ahead of the average. For
minority families, those without an employed wife are moderately
deprived with respect to other minority families and extremely deprived compared with whites, but full-time employment of the
wife moves them ahead of the average for both groups. The impact
of maternal income on the family's relative position in the society,
as well as the absolute gain, provides important rewards to the employed mother and her family.

While money provides some of the added rewards for
maternal employment, it should not obscure some noneconomic rewards such as a better self-concept (Chapter Nine) or an expanded
set of social relationships (Chapters Two and Three). Nor should it
lead one to overlook the fact that not all the added income can be
retained; some goes for added taxes, child care, additional meals
eaten outside the home, additional transportation, and other expenses.

Summary

This chapter places the individual decision-making and role
changes within the perspective of a changing society, which now
offers more opportunities for maternal employment. The following
conclusions are important.

(1) Women have always been economically productive and
even in paid employment they made a substantial contribution
during the Industrial Revolution and before.

in paid employment were well accepted
iod and throughout the nineteenth and
employment of married women (in sub-
twentieth-century phenomenon, but by
ne in three married women were employed.
ith dependent children have always worked
t it is estimated that just prior to World War
in twelve was in the labor force.
id expansion of the economy after World War
II com.. ow birth rates in the decade and a half prior to
that produced a severe labor shortage, providing a great need for
the labor of mothers and an unusually large number of positions
open to them.

(5) The transfer of much home production to the factory
released much of the time and energy of married women, resulting
in their availability for employment. At the same time, good birth-
control techniques allowed women to limit child-bearing to a few
years following marriage, releasing much time for employment. At
the same time, most tasks were mechanized so that women could
perform them as well as men.

(6) Mothers without husbands or with those unemployed or
earning lower salaries entered the labor force in larger numbers, including more black women because of job discrimination encountered
by black men. However, unemployment is also high now among
young women and those with little education since employers prefer
well-educated women with work experience. Also, women in low-
income families average more children, which increases their problems in combining employee and child-care roles.

(7) Well-educated older women are drawn into the labor
force by numerous openings and salaries much higher than those
offered women with little education. Contrary to popular thought,
these women contribute a larger proportion of the total income of
their families than do those in blue-collar occupations. The income
of these women provides desired extras for the family as well as
intellectual stimulation, additional social contacts, and feelings of
worth and accomplishment.

(8) Much of maternal employment is part-time. Only about
40 percent of mothers are employed more than thirty-five hours

weekly and as much as fifty weeks yearly, especially mothers with children under six years of age. There is also a large flow of women into and out of employment during any given year. About 20 percent leave the labor force each year, with a somewhat larger proportion entering it. After age forty-five, and especially after fifty-five, a declining proportion of women are found in gainful employment.

(9) Comparative analysis of families with husbands employed with those in which the wife is employed also shows that the latter have a higher than average income; but if the average sum earned by a working wife is deducted, those families would have substantially less than average income. The differences are especially great for black couples because the income of the wife provides a greater proportion of the total family income than is true in white families.

2

Psychological Factors

Lois Wladis Hoffman

Chapter One sketched the social changes which seem to have been important in bringing about the increase in maternal employment. Linking these changes to maternal employment are many individual decisions, each made by a single woman or family. Yet these decisions, based on personal and seemingly idiosyncratic factors, have a great deal in common, for the families are part of the same society and subject to similar experiences. Mrs. Jones, her youngest child now in school, may decide to go to work because she is bored staying at home. She does not consider the high degree of mechanization of her household or the availability of commercial services, but the boredom she feels may be intimately linked to these factors nonetheless and, because of them, many other women in her position also feel bored. These same factors can influence the decision to work in additional ways. Another woman, for example, may decide to work as a means of supplementing the family income, but this possibility might not have occurred to her if she were indispensable to the operation of her household.

Study of Motivation

The decision to work usually involves several motivations and takes into consideration certain barriers to employment as well as facilitating factors, but even a single motivation can often be traced to several social factors. Thus, for example, boredom does not result simply from having surplus time. The Protestant Ethic, which has made work the cornerstone of virtue and leisure fraught with anxiety, may also be important. Birth control and the possibility of completing the childbearing period while a mother is still young are yet other possible social factors. Boredom, too, may be tied to the likelihood that a mother is the only adult at home during the day, the husband being at work and no members of the extended family sharing the same household. The possibilities are many. Individual decisions are based on a complex of social factors which are often so interwoven that it is difficult to trace a particular motivation back to its social origins, even when its prevalence suggests such origins. Still, the examination of individual decisions for this purpose should help us understand the functional interrelationships among various relevant social factors. That is, through the analysis of individual decisions a researcher gains insights about the processes by which certain social events have contributed to the increased employment of mothers.

The study of individual motivations may also enable us to predict the effects maternal employment will have in the future, whether it will continue to increase or start to decline, and the functional substitutes which might arise to take its place. In studying individual motivations we often find that two social events, which on the surface appear to be unrelated or even contradictory, are but two alternative responses to the same need. For example, the increase in family size in the forties was often viewed as an opposite trend to that of increased maternal employment. In Chapter Four, however, these are seen as alternative solutions to the same problems. One way to fill time and increase one's sense of contribution is to go to work; another is to have a baby.

In addition, and more germane to the present book, the study of motivations for employment is necessary for understanding the effects of employment on the family for at least two reasons. The first is the methodological problem stemming from the fact that the motivations women have for working differentiate them from non-working women even before their employment. The second is a theoretical concern: the effects of employment may be conditioned by the motives underlying it. Because both these problems, self-selection and the interaction between employment and its underlying motives, come up repeatedly in this book, it is worthwhile to discuss them here.

However, it is as valid to ask why women do not go to work as why they do. In Chapter Six it is noted that the children of steadily employed lower-class women seem in some respects better adjusted than the children of irregularly or nonemployed women. Questions then arise: Who are the employment resisters? Are they ill? Are they less able to find work? Are they less able to cope with dual-role demands? Are their households particularly disorganized? It is important to know why they do not work to understand the etiology of their children's difficulties, particularly since their financial circumstances seem to call for employment.

Self-Selection. In the social sciences one seldom has the opportunity to utilize a laboratory setting with a before-measure, a stimulus imposed by the experimenter, and an after-measure, all under controlled conditions. Rather, the social scientist must be content usually to compare groups of subjects who have selected themselves into the "experimental" or "control" group. This technique always raises questions as to whether differences between the groups are due to the effects of the stimulus (in our example, maternal employment) or merely reflect the previously existing differences that led to "choosing" the given stimulus. Thus, for example, if the children of working mothers show a higher incidence of juvenile delinquency, is their delinquency due to their mothers' employment or to the fact that women who go to work tend to be economically underprivileged, rejecting of their children, or without husbands?

Furthermore, effects of employment can be obscured by selective factors. For example, mothers who seek employment after the youngest child enters school may be the ones who have been most totally involved with their children and who therefore feel the greatest need to fill their time once the children are no longer home during the day. If working were to lessen such involvement, this effect would not be apparent in a comparison of working and non-working women since with lessened involvement the working mothers might be the same as those who were not working.

Almost all the studies reviewed in this volume have tried to deal with the problem of selective factors, which requires an answer to the question of how working mothers differ from nonworking mothers at the point of making their decision about employment. To get that answer, we must understand why mothers work or resist it and what factors make work possible or provide barriers.

Interaction Between Employment and Underlying Motives. The other major reason for considering the factors involved in the employment decision when studying effects on the family involves a problem more theoretical than methodological: the effects of employment depend in part on the meaning it has for the mother and her family. If, for example, employment is motivated by the desire to escape the maternal role, the children may be aware of this motivation and may see their mother's action as rejection, whereas a different motivation might arouse a different response from the children. Or, as another example, the working mother who enjoys her work may feel guilty and try to compensate by overdoing the maternal role, while the mother who does not enjoy work is free of guilt and therefore more likely to withdraw from the maternal role (Hoffman, 1963c). For a further case, work grudgingly engaged in by a woman who sees it as a result of her husband's failure has a totally different effect on the family from work pursued in the belief that the bread-winner role should be shared.

In sum, it may not be fruitful to study the effects of maternal employment per se, but, rather, it may be necessary also to consider the factors involved in the decision to work or not. Maternal employment may be a meaningful variable only when the context within which it takes place is considered.

Data Available. Despite the importance of understanding the factors involved in the decision to seek employment, there has not been a great deal of research on this problem. Most of the existing data are of two kinds: those showing demographic differences between working and nonworking women and those reporting responses of women to direct questions about why they did or did not go to work. The former data exist almost in abundance. It is known, for example, that whether a woman works is related to her education, marital status, and husband's income; to the number of children she has and the age of those children; to her place of residence, race, and ethnic background. Occasionally, two of these variables have been considered simultaneously in relation to maternal employment. For example, the negative relationship between the income of the husband and maternal employment is strongest for mothers of small children. For mothers of older children, financial need seems to be a less salient reason for employment. This finding is borne out also by the figures in Table 7, which show that personal satisfaction was more often given as a reason for employment by the mothers of older children. Almost a quarter of the mothers of children between six and seventeen gave only this reason as compared with 12 percent of the mothers with children under six. Such analyses, in which the relationship between maternal employment and another demographic variable is examined with a third controlled, are much more useful for theory development than simple two-variable correlations. The demographic data, by showing certain correlates of maternal employment, suggest relevant variables that may need to be controlled or considered further but that have not been sufficiently exploited for theoretical purposes.

Data of the second kind, those based on responses of women to direct questions about motivation for employment, often suffer from superficiality. The questions have been simple, and only the first responses given are usually reported. Measuring motivation by the response to a single direct question is inadequate at best. Motives in general, and certainly motives for maternal employment, are not that simple.

An additional complication is that respondents often sense social censure of maternal employment. Therefore, the direct question is likely to put a respondent on the defensive, and, as a result, she may not give her most personal reasons readily. Such a respondent most likely would hold back answers which suggest that she is rejecting her child or working for personal pleasure.

Another reason for the inadequacy of this approach is that the question has an answer that borders on cliché: "Why do you work?" "For money." [1] Indeed, somewhere between 55 and 90

---

[1] Industrial sociologists have noted that inarticulate and unacceptable frustrations and desires on the part of workers often find expression in the form of wage demands. The tendency for women to say they work for money

Table 7.

Most Important Reason Married Women Took Jobs in 1963

Factors	Married women		Stated reason for maternal work (percent)							
	Number (thousands)	Percent	Financial need	Extra money	Husband lost job[a]	Personal satisfaction[b]	Finished school or training	Change in family status[c]	Job offer[d]	Other
Age of children										
Under 6 yrs.	319	43.4	48.1	16.2	8.0	12.1	—	0.6	10.8	4.1
6 to 17 yrs.	254	34.6	39.6	16.8	4.8	24.4	—	0.8	10.0	3.6
None under 18 yrs.	161	22.0	32.1	17.6	8.2	23.9	6.9	—	8.2	3.1
Educational attainment										
Less than 4 yrs. high school	306	41.7	45.2	16.8	7.3	17.5	0.7	0.7	8.9	3.0
4 yrs. high school or more	428	58.3	39.2	16.3	6.6	19.4	2.4	0.5	10.9	4.7
1 yr. college or more	148	20.2	31.3	15.6	4.8	21.8	2.7	—	15.0	8.8
Weekly income of husband[e]										
None or less than $60	142	19.3	59.4	4.5	13.5	3.8	3.0	—	9.8	6.0
$60 to $99	212	28.9	50.3	20.1	7.5	14.1	1.0	—	4.5	2.5
$100 or more	380	51.8	31.1	21.6	3.6	25.5	2.5	0.6	11.8	3.4
Total	734	100.0	41.6	16.9	6.8	18.9	1.5	0.5	9.9	3.8

[a] Includes husbands who were unable to work.
[b] Includes such reasons as just decided to work, have something to do, gain satisfaction, and interested in particular line of work.
[c] Husband died or respondent was divorced.
[d] Includes offered a job by friend, relative, or former employer, or help in family business.
[e] At time wife took job.

Source: Adapted from Rosenfeld and Perrella (1965).

percent of the answers are in terms of money, depending on the particular sample of women being interviewed, the phrasing of the question, whether it is part of a questionnaire or personal interview, and so forth. The answer may be worded simply "the money" or may be somewhat modified: monetary need, money to repay debts, money for the children, money for a specific purchase (such as a home), extra money, personal money, the high pay. If, however, the respondent is encouraged to elaborate on her answer, she usually comes forth with additional reasons. At this point, she often talks about boredom, an insufficiency of work, a feeling of "nervousness" at home, or the positive aspects of her job. Sometimes more specific concerns are added: "The plant was near enough that I could get home before the kids got back from school."

One such study, reported by Rosenfeld and Perrella (1965), involved interviews with a national sample of women who started or stopped work in 1963. Asked the most important reason for going to work, they most commonly responded with financial considerations. The data for married women only are presented in Table 7. Slightly over 72 percent of the mothers of children under six cited a financial motivation as the major reason, while about 61 percent of the mothers of children between six and seventeen did; twice as many of the latter group (24.4 percent) indicated that personal satisfactions motivated them. However, when respondents were asked how they felt about working or under what conditions they would quit, other motivations were involved. Only 25 percent of all women who said they were working out of economic necessity indicated that they preferred not to work. Although the preference for not working was more often indicated by mothers of young children, even among this group only 25 percent spontaneously indicated they would stop working if the money were not needed. When the women who had started working in 1963 were asked what might make them stop working, family obligations, pregnancy, and personal health were the most common responses; and these were also the reasons given for quitting work by those who had left the work force that year.

Some more recent surveys have attempted to ascertain non-

---

may be a similar phenomenon. Money may seem to be a more acceptable reason for employment than the satisfaction of a vaguely felt need.

monetary motives by asking the respondent whether she would continue to work if the money were not needed. A surprisingly high proportion indicate they would. Thus, in one study (Parnes and others, 1970), working women thirty to forty years of age were asked, "If, by some chance you (and your husband) were to get enough money to live comfortably without working, do you think that you would work anyway?" Among whites who were living with their husbands, 51 percent of the mothers of preschoolers and 56 percent of the mothers of older children said they would continue to work; among those currently unmarried, 45 percent with preschoolers and 60 percent with older children gave this response. The age of the child did not make a difference among blacks.

Respondents who said they would continue to work if it were not financially necessary were then asked why; the most common answer for whites and blacks was that they would have "nothing to do" or "be bored." Other answers included liking work, "to get out of the house," the companionship of fellow workers, and the rather vague response that they would be "unsatisfied" if not working. Those who answered that they would not work if they did not need the money were also queried, and they most frequently gave as their reason a desire to have more time with their family.

Although these data are an improvement over those from previous surveys, they do not shed light on the multiplicity of factors that go into the decision to work or not. Intensive interviews are needed in general, and surveys might obtain more information if they presented a list of possible reasons and asked the respondent to rank or otherwise weigh these in terms of their importance for her. Eyde (1962, 1968) used the latter technique in a longitudinal study of college women. Each of several aspects of work motivation—the desire for money; recognition or dominance; independence; achievement; social stimulation; and interesting activity—were assessed by a set of six items. Respondents indicated whether these were important reasons for them to work. The results not only indicate the presence of nonmonetary motives but show them to be stable over a five-year time span. Furthermore, both the Eyde study and the work of Sobol (1963, Chap. 3) indicate that although nonmonetary motivations are less often given, they are more highly related to the commitment to work than are monetary motives. Both these studies are discussed more fully later in this chapter.

Motivations

The decision to be a working mother may be made thoughtfully and deliberately or so subtly that the actors involved—the decision-makers—do not know a decision has been made. Whichever the case, the decision may be considered to have two components, motivations and facilitators. The first are the needs and desires, both conscious and unconscious, that make maternal employment attractive. The second, to be taken up later, are those factors which make it possible.

Money. We have already noted that women give "money" as their major reason for working, and, cliché though it may be, it is undoubtedly a major motivation. For one thing, working women are often supporting dependents and, in fact, are frequently the sole support of their families (Young, 1973). In addition, the relationship between income of the father and employment of the mother has already been mentioned. Besides the size of the income, income satisfaction and perceived financial need are important. Sobol found that wives were more likely to enter the working force when their family incomes dropped from their former level than when they remained stable or increased. This finding was statistically significant for each socioeconomic level.[2] Just as wives go to work to maintain their standard of living, they also take employment to achieve the level of those around them. Thus, if working does not detract from social status, families that strive for upward mobility and take as their reference group families with incomes higher than their own may augment their income through maternal employment. In certain occupational groups, teaching, for example, the actual income is below that necessary to maintain the desired style of life not so much because of mobility strivings as because of education: a school

[2] This finding on work-force entrance was reported by Marion G. Sobol in personal communication. It is based on a panel study of urban families carried out by the Economic Behavior Program, Institute for Social Research, University of Michigan, 1954–1957. She did not, however, find this pattern in a later study (see Chapter Three).

teacher usually hopes that his children can go to college but may not be able to afford this unless his wife works. In each of these situations, where there is financial deprivation relative to a particular standard, a mother may enter the labor force out of what she perceives as financial need.

Sometimes the mother works to pay debts, which may have been incurred by necessity, as for prolonged illness, or credit buying. These situations are like those above, except that here the spending precedes the employment, so that employment becomes a real as well as a perceived necessity. The particular order, spending and then working, may be a function of resistance to employment, poor financial planning, or even good financial planning (for example, when a family engages in deficit spending knowing that the mother will go to work at a later and more convenient date). Consideration of how a family managed to get into debt is important in determining the significance of this motive. The distinction between expensive illness and blatant extravagance is one example. Further, if extravagance accounts for the debt, it might be vital in determining the impact of employment on the family to know which parent was the lavish one or whether both are responsible.

Financial desires are also important. Maternal employment has brought an unprecedented high standard of living to many working-class families. American advertising has succeeded in keeping desires for material goods beyond the ability of people to obtain them. Furthermore, the coveted purchase, perhaps a dryer, a washing machine, a car, the down payment on a house, new carpeting, even a mink coat, is often expensive enough to require extra income, but at the same time it is inexpensive enough to be obtainable without a permanent commitment by the supplementary wage earner and durable enough to make a sustained effort worthwhile. Among a sample of Detroit mothers of elementary school children (Hoffman, 1958), the down payment on a house was mentioned most frequently. Financial desires also may be nonspecific: sometimes a mother works for "pin money," money that can be used for incidental luxuries and spent without family consultation. This is closely akin to "personal money," money a wife controls and can spend independently.

Any of these monetary motivations can be tied in with other attitudes that are important. For example, is the financial motivation related to a feeling that the father is a failure? If so, the mother's employment could symbolize his failure for the whole family. Or a mother's employment could be part of cooperative planning and perceived as a symbol of family unity. Perhaps the working mother is paying penance for her poor management and extravagance, perhaps she wants an independent income because of marital difficulties, or perhaps she has simply a desire for autonomy in an otherwise close and congenial relationship. Clearly, the possible underlying motives are many, and the family climate surrounding employment cannot be automatically inferred from the monetary motive alone.

Money also operates as a motivation for employment in less concrete ways. Because of the availability of jobs, because so many women are working, and because so many have worked at some time in their lives, a woman's time has come to have monetary meaning. The modern woman who bakes her own bread must figure into its cost not only the cost of the ingredients but the cost of her labor. A mother whose children are all in school could spend her day diligently trying to save money by sewing the family's clothes, doing all her own cooking, canning, cleaning, repair work, and redecorating, and still not save enough money to compensate her for her time. If the monetary value of the mother's time is considered, goods can be produced at less cost by mass production than at home, and it may be more economical for her to obtain outside work and use commercial facilities for the needed goods and services. Thus, if her household activities are not intrinsically satisfying, a woman may choose outside employment; even if they are, she may choose employment because then these household activities become akin to leisure and she must acknowledge that she does them for pleasure. The mother who does not work may feel guilty about not working. This seems a switch from the usual view, but as employment becomes increasingly common and increasingly possible, it may become more fruitful to ask why mothers do not work than why they do. The former is also becoming, in some cases, the question that the disapproving neighbors ask. The working mother of adolescent children who does not seem to be neglecting her roles as wife and mother is often admired for "working so hard." The mother of adolescent children who does not work and who can be seen sunning herself in her back yard or visiting with the neighbors is often the object of disapproval. The Protestant Ethic is still with us, and if the roles of mother and wife do not fill the working day, it is increasingly felt that this time should be spent in gainful employment.

The notion that a woman's time represents potential wages has led some young wives to consider their salaries in estimating the cost of having a baby. Although the pattern is changing somewhat, most women leave work during pregnancy or at the time of childbirth. If a wife's wages are a substantial proportion of the family income, this cost is considerable and one that coincides with increased expenses.

Money operates as a motive for employment in still another way. The role of housewife and mother, however important it may be to society, carries with it little opportunity for a sense of achievement, competence, and contribution. The educational system and cultural values have tied feelings of achievement to success in the intellectual or business world. Such satisfactions are intimately linked to money and the increasing size of the pay check, whether it increases because of inflation, union demands, or promotion. The housewife has none of these rewards. As Riesman (1953, p. 300) says: "[The housewife] does not find her work explicitly defined and totaled, either as an hour product or a dollar product, in the national census or in people's minds. Because of the lack of significance attached to her work, the housewife feels she is incompetent and that her contribution is a small one. No one expresses this more clearly than housewives themselves when they answer the inquiry about their occupation with the poignant phrase, 'just a housewife.' Bringing home a pay check, whether it is added to the family budget, saved for a rainy day, or used only as pin money, seems, in contrast, to be a sign of competence and a tangible contribution to the family."

Housewife and Mother Roles. Although the absence of wages may contribute to the feeling of the housewife that her contribution is not great, this is not the whole story. Part of it lies in certain intrinsic aspects of the housekeeping role. Temporarily leaving aside the role of mother and examining only that of housekeeper, one cannot fail to note the lack of creativity it affords. Little skill is demanded, and there is little room for excellence. Cooking is perhaps the most creative of the household tasks. About the time of World War I, a woman came to marriage well schooled in this art, and since it was passed on from mother to daughter and developed through trial and error in private kitchens, each woman had certain dishes that were hers individually. In a small community a woman could become famous for her cherry pie, and since the recipe was not written down and the quantity of the ingredients depended on the size of her hand and the firmness of her "pinch," she usually remained the only person in the community who made pie just like that. Betty Crocker does not depend on the size of a hand; directed precision is the new way: "seven-eighths of a cup of sifted flour." If a guest admires a dish, the generous hostess can say, "page 42 in Betty Crocker"; thus armed, the guest has all the skill needed to reproduce the dish exactly. With the introduction of packaged mixes, even literacy is no longer required, and many a housewife is saddened to learn that with little more than a cardboard box she can make an angel food cake two inches higher than the one she had previously made from one cookbook and twelve left-over egg whites.

If cooking is no longer creative, what is dusting, vacuuming, turning on the washing machine, running the dryer, ironing, making beds, and doing thirty-five hundred dishes each month? Besides, the repetitive nature of these tasks makes the housewife wonder if it is necessary to do them as often as she does, and indeed there is some evidence that it is not. In the Detroit study mentioned above, mothers were asked about the changes that occurred when they started or quit work. A frequent response was that when they were home all day, they were busy doing housework every minute, but when they were working, they could not see what they were leaving undone:

"I think I'm more efficient [when I work] . . .; [I] have a better run home. Who was it that said 'if a woman has an hour to do a job she'll get it done in an hour, but if she has all day, it takes all day'?"

"I'm more relaxed [when I work]. The things that used to upset me don't bother me at all—like the house. I don't like it to be dirty but I don't have to run around picking things up like I did."

"I was driving him [her husband] and Tim [her son] crazy.

I can't stand dirt. . . . My husband was always after me about how much I clean. I'm just that way. I can't stand dirt and when I'm home I do it all the time."

"I did more work in the house that was unnecessary [when I wasn't working]."

"I get more work done [in the house] really when I'm working because I know I have to keep up and I don't waste my time doing foolish things—like dusting that table every time I pass it."

"Sure I clean less thoroughly, . . . but the house is just as clean."

Of the 178 mothers interviewed in the Detroit study, 108 had started or returned to work after a period of not working. This 108 excludes women whose husbands were in the armed services, ill, or unemployed, but includes women who as yet had no children. Asked to report changes in their household, 25 percent reported that they became more efficient in accomplishing household tasks; 46 percent, cleaned less often or less thoroughly; 17 percent, stopped ironing certain items which could be simply folded and put away; 22 percent, spent less time on meal preparation; and 50 percent, baked less. These findings do not mean that the reduced activities were not missed, but they do suggest that much of the work done by the full-time housewife is at least not essential. Studies indicate that despite modern conveniences, the nonemployed housewife—and not the employed—spends as much time doing household work as women in the twenties (Hall and Schroeder, 1970; University of Michigan, 1973; U.S. Department of Labor, 1971; Walker, 1969; Walker, 1970).

Cyrus (1952) expresses vividly what it means to spend the day in labor that is unskilled, repetitive, and partly nonessential. "Modern conveniences plus modern high standards, while freeing women from the back-breaking physical labor of the pioneer woman, have increased enormously her petty cleaning-up tasks. The number of things which modern women have to wash and polish and starch and iron and sterilize, and the number of times they have to do it, have multiplied until many housewives spend most of the time cleaning one thing or another and cannot imagine how the pioneer woman found time to do all she did. If the pioneer woman had spent so much time on the luxury and boredom of cleanliness, she wouldn't have been paying her way, and the modern woman knows in her heart that she isn't paying hers, either" (p. 392).

Work on an assembly line is not fun, but it does have certain advantages. It takes place outside the home. However unattractive the place of work, a change of scenery in traveling between work and home as well as in doing the work adds variety to the day. In addition, outside work usually starts and stops at a specified time, and the job is "done" when the worker leaves the shop. It usually involves interaction with other adults, not only at coffee breaks, which the housewife may also have, but during working hours. Also, outside work often does offer opportunity for creativity and a sense of contribution and competence. These rewards are clearly felt in the professional and social service occupations—teacher, nurse, social worker—and also in many white-collar and skilled-labor jobs. Being judged satisfactory on the basis of performance by persons outside the family who are considered to be more objective and who usually have higher social status adds considerably to a sense of competence. Occupying a particular niche in a large-scale organization, such as that of receptionist or secretary, often makes one feel important. Having contact with important people and distant places, as does the switchboard operator who places calls to foreign countries, adds significance to a job. And for all jobs, even the dullest and most routine, there is at least the pay check, which says, "You have done work which someone considers worth money" and "You are helping to buy a house by your employment."

Weiss and Samelson (1958) asked a national sample of women what activities made them feel useful and important. They found that employed mothers were more likely to mention some aspect of their job than they were to mention either housework or their role in the family as wife and mother; although about 55 percent of the mothers who were not employed mentioned housework as one response, only 36 percent of the employed mothers did.[3] The percentage who mentioned the wife and mother roles, incidentally, was not affected by whether the wife worked. These data

---

[3] Respondents gave more than one response.

support the notion that the outside job is indeed a vital source of feelings of usefulness and importance. They also suggest that whether or not housework is named as a source of these feelings depends in part on whether there are alternative sources.

But is not the mother role the most creative of all? Very possibly, and, viewed from the perspective of a lifetime, most mothers would probably say that here was their most creative endeavor. But, in her day-to-day experience, a mother can easily lose sight of this long-range creativity. Changing and washing diapers, picking up toys, putting on snowsuits, and wiping up footprints do not feel creative when they are being done. To be sure, there are highly creative moments and feelings of being irreplaceable, particularly with a preschool child; and at that stage there is enough work to easily fill the working day. But when the youngest child enters school, the mother is again left with a day full of housework rather than mothering. The Weiss-Samelson data mentioned above also show that satisfactions from "family interrelationships," which include the mother role, diminish when the child enters school: while 58 percent of the nonworking mothers of preschool children mention this source of satisfaction, only 41 percent of the nonworking mothers of school children do so.

Possibly, the greater the joys of mothering, the more empty are the days when the children are all in school. Even women who were satisfied with the housewife role before there were children may not be content to return to it. They have been used to a fuller and, in many ways, richer day, and the housecleaning tasks may seem less important and more boring than ever.

The period when the youngest child enters school is difficult for many mothers. They often feel they are no longer needed, that their major role is over (Birnbaum, 1971). Not only is the child physically absent from the home, but he or she is less dependent on the mother, and for some women this is a great loss. (Just as many women wish to remain dependent themselves, some also wish to have others remain dependent on them.) Mothers may feel, too, that they are growing old or at least that they have lost the vigor of youth. Thus, mothers who return to work when their youngest child enters school may be motivated not only by such practical considerations as their increased dispensability to the household but also by psychological reasons, in particular the dissatisfactions that emerge at this time.

For yet another reason this time may be psychologically appropriate for women to return to work. Having preschool children at home can be frustrating for a mother. In addition to the unrewarding work activities mentioned above, her freedom is often considerably restricted. In fact, in one part of the Detroit study, 217 mothers were asked, "How is a woman's life changed by having children?" The most common response by far was that children meant less freedom, particularly that they restricted the mother's freedom of movement. Forty women gave as their first response that children "tie you to the house," "tie you down," or some similar wording. Most of the answers to this question were negative; four times as many gave totally negative responses as gave totally positive. Only half the respondents gave answers that could, in any part, be considered positive.[4]

Thus, the period when the mother has preschool children may be an extremely frustrating one, a time when she must hold back impulses, defer gratification, and, above all, remain physically in the home. For perhaps twelve years she has had at least one preschool child in the house and been unable to express these frustrations because her role demanded certain behavior, because she felt that to do a good job she should not, and perhaps because she was unable to acknowledge them even to herself. Whatever the reasons, the youngest child's entering school can provide a release for many of the frustrations of the preceding years, and outside employment may be one expression of this release. Such motivation is, in a sense, opposite to the one discussed earlier and characterizes a different group of women. The former involves the notion that the early years of mothering are gratifying and later years are relatively dissatisfying. This view, however, suggests that the early years are frustrating and the later years allow for the release of suppressed tensions.

Other women do not suppress these tensions. For them, the loss of freedom that the preschool child brings is itself a motivation

[4] There was essentially no difference between working mothers and nonworking mothers in the number of positive or negative responses given.

for employment. The gratifying aspects of these years are out-weighed by the dullness of day-to-day routines, by the loneliness and longing for adult company, by boredom with the same physical surroundings, by frustration over the constant requirement to give the child's omnipresent needs priority, by the noise level, and by the overwhelming sense of personal responsibility. In a study of 42,845 employed, college-graduate women, 12 percent of those who were mothers of children under six years indicated that their main reason for working was "to escape household routine." For this group, it was the most common of the nonfinancial reasons. Only 4 percent of the mothers of school-aged children gave this response; their most common nonfinancial reason (21 percent) was "to have a career" (U.S. Department of Labor, 1966).

Personality Factors. It is not meaningful to try to describe the personality characteristics that distinguish working mothers. The pattern is too widespread and the group too heterogeneous. However, comparisons between working and nonworking mothers in the same situation, with comparable education and family incomes, at the same stage in the family cycle, with the same number of children, and with equal opportunities for employment, should reveal person-ality differences. Unfortunately, few such studies have been made, and most of these have concentrated on college-educated women.

In a previous review (Hoffman, 1963a), we considered the evidence bearing on the stereotypic notion that working women have greater needs for power and dominance. With the possible exception of the Eyde study discussed below, empirical evidence does not support the idea that power needs characterize working wives more than nonworking wives. Heer (1963) did not find working and nonworking women significantly different on the trait of dominance as measured by the Bernreuter Personality Inventory Test, nor did Gurin, Veroff, and Feld find power-need differences as measured by a picture projective.[5] Also, Hoffman (1963d) did not find differences on a male dominance ideology scale.

Two variables that have differentiated working from non-working women are their sense of competence and their attitudes

[5] This unpublished finding has been reported in personal communica-tion. It is based on a national sample study carried on by the Institute for Social Research, University of Michigan (1959–1960).

toward the woman's role. A number of studies across social class indicate that working women hold a less traditional notion of sex roles (Birnbaum, 1971; Hoffman, 1963d; Parnes and others, 1970; U.S. Department of Labor, 1971), although whether this is a cause or an effect of employment is not clear. In addition, dislike of housework related to employment status in the across-social-class study of Parnes and his associates (1970), and dislike of the mothering role showed a slight relationship, but only for mothers with young children.[6] With respect to competence, both the Birnbaum study of educated women and a study of middle-class Catholic mothers (Broverman, Vogel, Broverman, Clarkson, and Rosencrantz, 1972) found that working women had a higher sense of competence, although here again the cause-effect relationship is unclear.

Two studies, Eyde (1962, 1968) and Sobol (1963), used a different approach. They did not try to distinguish working from nonworking mothers by virtue of some abstract trait or need, but rather considered which aspects of work the respondents found gratifying. In Eyde's study, respondents were presented with reasons for which women might work for pay, selected to tap the needs for money, recognition or dominance, independence, achievement, social stimulation, and interesting activity. As described earlier, respondents (women who graduated from an Eastern liberal arts college in 1953 and in 1958) ranked the reasons for employment to indicate those important to them. In addition, respondents were asked how long they planned to work and whether they would continue to work through various stages of family life. The women were tested twice, in 1958 and again in 1963. The younger women (college seniors at the time of the first interview) who stressed the dominance-recognition aspect of work indicated the strongest motivation (or commitment) to work, and other aspects were not related. Among the older women, when tested in 1958, five years after college graduation, a need for variety in their activities and for achievement outside the home related to high work motivation.[7] The retest indi-

---

[6] However, among working mothers, those who like caring for children also show higher job satisfaction.

[7] Those alumnae who showed low motivation to work thought that work offered independence (greater autonomy) and a chance to meet people and to be of help to them. Economic values—working to meet financial

cated that these responses were quite stable, that is, both the need-satisfying aspect of work and the indication of work motivation showed consistency over the five years. Stability was somewhat greater for the older women, probably because their life circumstances had changed less during the interval between tests. Even in 1958 many of them were married and had children. Unfortunately, however, the report of the retest did not indicate whether the needs in either time period related to the 1963 work motivation, and actual work behavior was not mentioned at all. However, for the older women, whose responses were more stable (and probably more realistic) than the college seniors, the achievement orientation was important in predicting labor force commitment. This finding ties in well with that of an earlier study by Sobol (1963).

Sobol, in a study of a broader segment of the population, also found that those women who worked to fill a need for accomplishment indicated high motivation, or "commitment" to employment. She found, in general, that although noneconomic reasons for working were less often given, those who gave them indicated a stronger commitment to work. The women who worked to fulfill a need for accomplishment verbalized the strongest commitment, followed by those who worked to "occupy time" or to "meet people."

Birnbaum (1971) in her comparison of educated homemakers and professional women, did not find achievement needs related to maternal employment; however, she used a projective measure that may have been sensitive to *unmet* psychological needs. Thus, professional women in her sample may have been generally characterized by high achievement needs, but because these needs were currently being satisfied by their work, they were not revealed in Birnbaum's measure. Both the Birnbaum study and one by Tangri (1969) suggest that college women with high achievement needs often try to satisfy them vicariously through the achievements of their husbands or children. As suggested in Chapter Six, a woman who has a high need for achievement and who, because of attitudes about her role as mother or the absence of facilitating factors, has no job may express this need in the family to the possible detriment

---

needs—did not differentiate between women with high and those with low desire to work.

of her roles as wife and mother. Perhaps attempts to relate personality traits to employment status will be disappointing and more
valuable research will focus on the interaction of personality and
employment status in its effects on the family.

Because of the paucity of data, it is premature to say whether
or not personality traits differentiate working from nonworking
women within specific groups. Where differences have not been
found, the groups compared were often too heterogeneous; where
differences were clear, usually there has been a question of cause
and effect. The few longitudinal studies have not examined data
germane to this question; and studies of noncollege women are particularly scarce.

Other personality factors besides a need for achievement
have been considered relevant to the decision to work: dominance,
attitudes toward traditional roles, and sense of competence. In a
previous publication (Hoffman, 1963a), we also discussed aspirations for higher status, a drive to realize individual potential, a
desire to use skills for the benefit of society, a high energy level, an
active orientation toward life, the need for social contact, and other
factors. Each has been characteristic of certain working women, and
Sobol (1963) has reported that working women who give such
nonmonetary reasons for employment indicate a more long-term
commitment to their work; but none of these reasons has yet been
found to distinguish employed from unemployed women.

Some studies however indicate that women in a particular
occupational category share certain personality traits or background
characteristics. Thus, for example, highly successful professional
women tend to describe their fathers as supportive and as having
encouraged them in independence and achievement (Ginzberg,
1971). Hennig (1973) studied successful women executives and
found, among other things, that they were first-born children in all-
girl families. In a study of college women, Tangri (1972) found
that those who planned careers in occupations conventionally chosen
by men were more autonomous, individualistic, and internally motivated by high performance demands. Efforts have also been made to
characterize women who have decided to become doctors (Cartwright, 1972), lawyers (Epstein, in press), engineers (Perrucci,
1970), and politicians (Costantini and Craik, 1972). These studies

Psychological Factors

have not revealed dramatic differences, but by concentra[...] more specific and less common occupational patterns, statisti[...] significant differences have been found. For example, both Cart-wright and Costantini and Craik used the Gough-Heilbrun personality scales and found the scores for the professional women they studied different from the norms established for comparable women. The women medical students, according to their self-descriptions, were more "conscientious, deliberate, determined, industrious, persevering, and thorough" (Cartwright, 1972, p. 208). The women politicians were described as more self-confident, dominant, and achievement-oriented.[8]

Personality differences may also influence which women go to work at one stage in the family cycle and which at another, but these differences have not been researched. Further, it was pointed out earlier in this chapter that as maternal employment becomes even more prevalent among certain groups, it may become increasingly fruitful to ask why some women choose nonemployment. In addition, as also suggested above, personality may be important to study in terms of which women should go to work. Certain needs might be more appropriately expressed through a job than within the family, and, indeed, if employment makes a woman's life more satisfying, she may become a better wife and mother. In short, employment may sometimes operate as a safety value to release frustrations that would otherwise be expressed to the family's detriment.

The motivations discussed here have been organized according to three categories: money, social role, and personality. This separation, however, is an artificial one, and the three are in reality highly interrelated. For example, personality factors influence whether the monetary conditions and the social role become motivations for employment. Thus, all three categories must be simultaneously considered in any complete analysis of motivations for employment. Furthermore, in order to understand the decision about employment more fully and to determine whether the motivations

---

[8] There are also a number of studies of personality traits, specific occupations, and job satisfaction geared toward vocational guidance (Kievit, 1972).

...avior, still another group of factors, which
be considered.

Facilitators

...actors operating to facilitate maternal employ-
...een discussed as social trends in Chapter One.
...ed out that the increased mechanization of the
...eater availability of commercial products and
services,   ...ller number of children in the family, and the
relative youth of the mother when the family is complete all operate
to release the mother from household responsibilities and make it
possible for her to combine the housewife and mother roles with that
of wage earner. Changing social attitudes toward maternal employment were also mentioned, and these, too, facilitate employment:
the working mother need no longer face the social censure that she
would have faced in the 1950s. Finally, the discussion in Chapter
One considered the changing nature of available employment—the
shift from jobs that require physical strength to those that emphasize
dexterity and special training—and the increased demand for labor
relative to the supply. These changes in the job market facilitate
employment by broadening opportunities for women. Here, we consider these same issues but focus not upon general social trends but
upon factors which affect families differentially.

Household Demands. Among the many factors that may
facilitate or hinder a mother's employment, an important one is the
extent to which her time is required for the fulfillment of her roles as
housewife and mother. Because the mother is more indispensable
when there is a preschool child in the home, having no preschool
children facilitates employment. We discussed this situation above
in terms of its motivational aspects, but here we are concerned with
it simply as a factor which makes employment feasible. The age of
the children is relevant in two ways: older children require less care,
and they can help with household tasks and the care of younger
children. The number of children is obviously relevant also because
fewer children mean less work. The physical and mental health of
the children is another factor. Not only will the age, number, and
health of the children influence the employment of the mother, but

expectations about these influence both current employment and the degree of commitment to employment. For example, women who confidently feel they will have no more children, either because of subfecundity or experience with effective family planning, can make a more permanent commitment to their jobs.

The extent to which a husband helps with household and child-care tasks is also relevant to the ease with which a mother can work outside the home. Clearly, the "companionship" marriage facilitates maternal employment. The "helping" husband not only lessens the mother's daily household workload but also is a resource in emergencies. And the mother's expectations about how much her husband would help if she found employment are as important as his help prior to this event. Data indicate that husbands of employed women help with household tasks and child care more than do husbands of nonemployed women; yet, the wife still carries the greater share (Hoffman, 1963d; Walker, 1970; U.S. Department of Labor, 1971). Even in the dual-career family, where both husband and wife have a major career commitment, the wife has primary responsibility for these activities (Poloma and Garland, 1970; Rapoport and Rapoport, 1972). However, the gender-based division of labor is probably becoming less rigid, and a husband's assistance, and eventually his equal participation, will be more common in the future (Hoffman, 1973).

Data also show that teen-aged children are a source of household help to the working mother. Walker (1970), for example, found that in families with no younger children, the teen-aged children of working mothers carried out 30 percent of the household work; in families where the mother was employed no more than fourteen hours a week, the percentage dropped to 20. Having teen-aged children in itself does not facilitate employment since the data do not indicate a net advantage over an absence of dependent children. But the data do imply that having the cooperation of children makes it easier for a mother of teen-agers to go to work. No solid evidence indicates that younger children are a source of assistance, although the situation is no doubt easier if they are relatively independent, in good health, and well-adjusted.

The availability of aid from persons outside the conjugal family also enables a mother to seek employment. Thus, extended family ties and physical proximity to relatives are facilitating factors, and working-mother households often include additional relatives, such as a grandmother (U.S. Department of Labor, 1972). Neighbors and other friends are often engaged to help look after the children, and so primary ties of this sort also become functional. Paid household workers also facilitate employment. Paid help may be part of a general style of life or a direct function of maternal employment; in either case, it is more likely to be a middle-class than a lower-class pattern. If someone must be hired to replace the mother, the mother must either be capable of earning more than she pays or she must enjoy her work enough to be willing to work without profit. Domestic help, however, has become increasingly scarce as the ratio of domestic workers to all women workers has declined steadily from .169 in 1940 to .052 in 1970 (U.S. Department of Labor, 1971). The difficulty of finding a housekeeper was the most predominant complaint in a study of Ph.D. women by Astin (1969).

The size of the family residence, the degree of mechanization of the household, and the availability of commercial products and services are also relevant to the time required by the housewife and mother roles.[9] Thus, for example, the urban apartment with laundry appliances would seem maximally facilitative, the rural farmhouse, minimally. In the United States, however, there is a great deal of standardization with respect to these variables. Certain special facilities, such as child-care centers, are more available in urban and industrial locales, but most commercial services and products also have reached even the rural areas.

However, even under optimal circumstances the housewife-mother role and the wage-earner role add up to more than a full-time job. Home responsibilities are the major factor that influences women to leave their jobs or to not seek work even though they

[9] In the Detroit study, working and nonworking women were not different with respect to any of these variables. Furthermore, the only variable mentioned by respondents as a facilitating factor was the degree of mechanization, and that was mentioned by only 5 percent. Greater use of commercial products and services was an important response to employment (for example, 14 percent of the 108 women interviewed about changes reported that they started sending their washing and ironing out), but such facilities were equally available to all subjects in this sample since all lived in the same city.

want jobs (Rosenfeld and Perrella, 1965; U.S. Department of Labor, 1971). Inadequate child-care facilities are another major obstacle to employment: individual arrangements for the care of young children are expensive and difficult, while group care is not yet adequately available. Too, school and employment hours are rarely set for the convenience of the working mother. Outside relatives, helpful neighbors, and hired help are not easy to come by; and while husbands with employed wives help more, they do not help as much as their wives deem necessary (U.S. Department of Labor, 1971). Suburban living and inadequate public transportation have increased the amount of chauffeuring required for children's routine dental and medical visits, for participation in church and community activities, for the use of various facilities, and for the ubiquitous extra lessons. Thus, for most mothers at the present time, there is a conflict about the job decision: one role may not be enough, but two is too many. An absence of commitment to the job or to the pursuit of a career may reflect this dilemma.

Because of the extra requirements of filling the roles of housewife, mother, and worker, it is no surprise that working mothers are statistically more likely than full-time homemakers to consider themselves in good health (Chapter Nine), and ill health is one of the reasons often given for leaving the labor force (Parnes and others, 1970; Rosenfeld and Perrella, 1965). Thus, among the various resources enabling the mother to work is her own physical stamina.

Attitudes. Attitudes and values may sometimes be important as motivational factors, but certain attitudes of the mother, her husband, or her community operate more as facilitators or barriers. Thus, we have already pointed out the relevance as facilitators of attitudes about birth control and about the husband's participation in household tasks. Attitudes about children are also important— for example, views about how essential the mother's constant presence is for the child's development and what the child's share in household tasks should be. The availability of child-care centers is an expression of the community attitude, which has value as a facilitator.

In addition to specific attitudes that operate through their effects on other facilitators, there are general attitudes about the role of women and about whether a mother should work. A great many studies indicate that working mothers are more likely to approve of maternal employment and to report that their husbands do also (Hoffman, 1963a; Morgan, David, Cohen, and Brazer, 1962; Shea and others, 1970; U.S. Department of Labor, 1966).

One recent survey showed that *anticipated* labor-force participation is also related to the attitudes of the husband and the wife. Wives indicated they would be more likely to accept a job offer where positive attitudes toward their working were held by the husband or by the wife (U.S. Department of Labor, 1971). This relationship was obtained for whites and blacks; a more favorable attitude toward employment, however, was held by blacks. These attitudes also predicted labor force participation two years later, although there the relationship was stronger for whites than blacks (Shea, Sookin, and Roderick, 1973). There was an interesting relationship between education and attitudes of the women toward mothers of school-aged children working. For white women, the more education, the more favorable the response to maternal employment. The relationship was linear, and favorable attitudes[10] were held by 17 percent of the women with fewer than nine years of school, and 30 percent of those with college degrees. With the black women, however, the relationship was curvilinear, and favorable attitudes were more often expressed by both extremes of the education continuum; 38 percent of those with fewer than nine years of school were favorable, and 38 percent of the college graduates also were favorable.

The general attitude toward maternal employment need not coincide with the attitude toward the participation of husbands in household tasks. Russo (1971), in a study of the attitudes of college men, found that blacks were more favorable toward their wives' employment than whites, but that they were less willing to help with the household tasks. Both views are important in their effects on maternal employment. The husband's help, as indicated above, is obviously needed, but his general approval is also significant for the solidity of the marriage and the orientation of the family. Maternal employment is not only disapproved in principle by many persons,

---

[10] Attitudes were measured by a scale and scores were tricotomized into "permissive" (or favorable), "ambivalent," and "opposed."

but for some men it may be highly threatening; some men would find their wives' employment a personal and public symbol of failure. This barrier to employment is interesting because the very conditions that might make a husband concerned with failure, such as actually being an inadequate provider, might also make the woman want to work.

There are also group differences in the attitude toward maternal employment, and attitudes prevailing in a women's community, ethnic group, or friendship group operate as facilitators or impediments to her employment. There are few studies of these differences, however. Blacks are more favorable than whites, with educational differences also identified as indicated above, but few other subgroup comparisons have been made. The more generally favorable attitude toward maternal employment in the United States in recent years operates to facilitate this employment in a circular way, for the fact that it is more common also increases its acceptance.

Employment Possibilities. Another group of facilitators concerns the mother's ability to find work, and this depends on jobs available and her qualifications. The availability of well-paying part-time jobs obviously facilitates maternal employment, as do convenience of location and hours, and other particulars. These factors are influenced not only by general economic conditions but also by the conditions of the particular area. Cities like Detroit, for example, where heavy industry predominates, usually have a smaller proportion of women employed than do cities such as Hartford, where white-collar industries are more common, or other New England towns where light manufacturing prevails (National Manpower Council, 1957).

Inexpensive transportation, child-care facilities, and household help are not simply conveniences which make employment feasible, but are also relevant to monetary motivations in that they affect the amount of money maternal employment adds to the household. As might be expected, women will travel farther to work where the pay is higher. Black women travel farther to work than whites, rely more on public transportation, and have higher traveling expenses; whites spend more on child-care facilities (Parnes and others, 1970). Other expenses for working women may include the greater use of commercial facilities for household tasks, higher food costs because of purchasing convenience foods and not having time to do comparative pricing, household help, higher clothing costs, buying lunch at work, taxes, and union dues (Addiss, 1963).

Similarly, both motivations and facilitating factors are involved in the correlation between employment status and education. This correlation is generally interpreted as reflecting the fact that education enables a woman to obtain a job more easily and to find a more interesting and better paid one. In addition, education also facilitates employment since it is more likely, at least for whites, to go along with attitudes favorable to employment and with limiting family size. Education has motivational significance as well, for obtaining an education may reflect the same motivational factors that lead a woman to seek a job.[11] This is particularly true when the woman pursues more schooling than others in her social milieu. Furthermore, the more educated woman may wish to use her knowledge and training, and she is probably more likely to seek the extra stimulation that working affords.

In considering eligibility for employment, one must consider not only the education, training, and skills of the women but whether these might suffer from obsolescence. For example, a woman physicist who has been out of the field for ten years while her children were young might, in some respects, find it more difficult to find work than an untrained woman. If she has not kept pace with new developments, she may be unable to find employment as a physicist and unwilling to accept a position that does not use her training at all. Occupations such as model or stewardess, where age itself is a handicap, present similar difficulties. In general, however, education and training do facilitate employment, and working mothers are usually better educated than nonworking mothers (Waldman, 1970).

Three kinds of facilitators have been discussed: those which affect the housewife and mother roles, specific and general attitudes of the family and community, and the opportunities for employment. These factors distinguish working and nonworking mothers. Working compared to nonworking mothers have fewer children, older chil-

[11] Eyde (1962) found that college seniors who plan to go to graduate school are also more likely to plan long term employment.

dren, husbands who are more active in household and child-care tasks, adult relatives living with the family, attitudes favorable to employment, residence in communities where jobs for women are more available, and higher education. These differences must be considered in any study of the effects of maternal employment on the child. Each of these variables might be independently related to family variables and to child personality. Consequently, group differences between working mothers and nonworking mothers could be the result of these prior factors rather than the result of employment per se. This is the problem of self-selection, and careful empirical controls must be exercised to isolate the working-mother variable.

In addition, just as with the motivational factors, interactions between facilitative variables and maternal employment may influence the effects on the family. Thus, for example, the effect of employment on the child is in part influenced by the husband's attitude toward this employment.

Summary

In this chapter we have pointed to the importance of studying the factors involved in the mother's decision to work. These factors are important methodologically because differences between working and nonworking mothers may be due to their operation rather than to employment itself. They are important theoretically because they may interact with the employment situation and influence its effects on the family.

The monetary motive was given special attention as one which is frequently articulated. It may be based on real or perceived financial need or desire, or it may derive from other motives not truly monetary in origin that become symbolized and expressed in monetary terms.

The significance of the housewife and mother roles for employment motivations was noted. Technological advances have made the housewife role less time-consuming and less satisfying, and, particularly when the youngest child enters school, a mother may look to outside employment to fill her day. In addition, certain frustrating aspects of the maternal role itself motivate some women to seek employment.

Personality variables, such as the needs for achievement and power, a sense of competence, and the attitude toward women's roles were also considered as motivations for employment. At the present time, however, maternal employment is so common that it is not possible to characterize the working woman in terms of personality traits. Recent studies have sought similar traits and background factors for women in specific occupations, particularly those that are still somewhat deviant.

Factors that influence the employment decision by making work more feasible (or more difficult) were also discussed. These facilitators (or barriers) include situational factors affecting the extent to which the mother is needed in the home, attitudes of others operating either indirectly through their effects on the situational factors or directly through their sanctioning of maternal employment, and job opportunities.

3

Commitment to Work

MARION GROSS SOBOL

As Chapter Two demonstrated, the decision to work and subsequent entrance into the labor force may occur for many reasons or combinations of reasons. For a mother, this decision may be one that is frequently subject to review. For example, a study by Lebergott (1958) showed that while 17 percent of married women with children under six years were at work in March 1957, 31 percent had worked at some time during 1956. In long-range terms, 25 percent of all white wives of child-bearing age (eighteen to thirty-nine) were at work in the spring of 1955, yet 70 percent had worked at some time during their married lives (Sobol, 1963).

A study of working women by the U.S. Department of Labor, Women's Bureau (1969), showed that "only 42 percent of the women who worked at some time in 1967 were employed full time the year round. In contrast, 70 percent of all men with work experience in 1967 were full-time year-round workers" (p. 55). Thus women are likely to move in and out of the labor force, and work commitment is a relevant factor for analysis.

This long-range commitment of wives to work is important from many standpoints. The economist, interested in predicting labor supply, must have some notion of the extent of wives' commitment and the factors which influence these decisions. The extent of commitment also has effects on the feelings and behavior of children. (In Chapter Six it is shown that children of steadily employed lower-class women seem in some respects better adjusted than the children of irregularly or nonemployed lower-class women.) Similarly, commitment may also affect the husband and wife relationship (Chapter Eight), division of labor in the family (Chapter Seven), fertility (Chapter Four), and personal adjustment of the employed mother (Chapter Nine).

Before we investigate the factors which influence work commitment, it is valuable to study the trends in work commitment since 1950. The percentage of married women who worked outside the home increased steadily from 25 percent in 1950 to 41 percent in 1971. The increase in full-year (fifty to fifty-two weeks) employment for all women (single and married) who worked full time rose from 37 percent in 1950 to 42 percent in 1967 (U.S. Labor Department, Women's Bureau, 1969). The relative increase in full-year full-time workers has been slow. Even now more than half of all women workers are not working on a full-year, full-time basis. Some of this part-year work is due to the nature of the jobs which women occupy. Teachers and workers in seasonal industries such as canneries, packing plants, and motels, usually work less than fifty weeks per year. However, women generally show less attachment to the labor force than do men. While men usually cite inability to find work as their reason for being out of work, women are most likely to state that they have to attend to household duties. If one looks at part-year workers, more than half of them (29 percent of all employed women) work less than twenty-seven weeks per year. For part-year women workers this percentage distribution for 1967 is not appreciably different from that of 1950.

Since work commitment for women has important effects on the family and since this commitment seems less stable and more difficult to predict than the commitment of men, the factors which influence labor-force attachment need to be analyzed. This chapter reviews modern studies of work commitment. Briefly, the earliest ones—Sobol (1963) and Fogarty, Rapoport, and Rapoport, 1971—measured work commitment in terms of future work plans. Sobol related these work plans to reasons for work and other demographic and economic variables. Such refinements as the distinction between work plans and work wishes have been suggested by Haller and Rosenmayer (1971), while Sobol, in a different approach, measured work commitment on a scale of work behavior and plans, based on interviews with the same women over a ten-year period (1973). A new and different approach to work commitment is offered by Safilios-Rothschild (1970), who feels that a meaningful definition of work commitment should be "based upon the relative distribution of interest, time, energy, and emotional investment in work in relation to other life sectors and notably to family life" (p. 491).

One factor that has been particularly evident in recent studies of work commitment among married women is the large difference between blacks and whites: in every income group, black wives are more highly attached to the labor force than are their white counterparts (Cain, 1966; Parnes, 1971; Kim, 1972). This chapter delves into some of the explanations for that difference. Various extrinsic and intrinsic aspects of a job, job mobility, and social environment are other factors that seem related to work commitment, and these, too, are examined. The first part of this chapter concentrates on measures of work commitment; the second, on race differences, social environment, and job mobility; and the final section suggests some directions for future research.

Measures of Commitment

Future Plans. One of the earliest examinations of work commitment was carried out by Sobol in 1963, using data from the Growth of American Families studies (Freedman and Whelpton, 1955). Considering the responses of 2,713 white married women of child-bearing age living in the United States, Sobol correlated enabling conditions (for example, family status), facilitating conditions (for example, ease in obtaining work), and precipitating conditions (for example, relative dissatisfaction) with future work plans. She made separate studies for women who were and were not working at the time of the interview since each group had been asked a different set of questions.

For women who were working, three variables (type of work, plans to have more children, and reasons for work) related significantly to future work plans. Women employed as operatives were unlikely to plan work in the future, and women pregnant at the time of interview were still less likely to plan future work. The most important variable relating to future work plans was reasons for working.

The relationship between reasons for work and future work plans was rather complicated. Most women initially offered financial reasons for working. Yet well over one-third of the women interviewed did advance reasons other than financial. "Further, the women who offer *only* nonfinancial reasons for work are more likely to plan extended work careers than the women who work for a *combination* of financial and nonfinancial reasons" (Sobol, 1963, p. 54).

In a simple cross-tabulation of the relationship between reasons for work and permanent work expectations, it appeared that work in a family business was most closely related to future work expectation. Second in importance was need for achievement and third was chronic or temporary financial problems. In a more complex multiple-regression analysis which simultaneously studied a number of financial and sociological factors, the standardized regression coefficients indicated that the reason most importantly related to long-term work commitment was need for achievement followed by need to occupy time and to meet people. Reasons for work, in rank order according to their relationship to work commitment (from most committed to least committed to work in the future), are: (1) working to fill a need for accomplishment, (2) working to meet people or to occupy time, (3) helping in a family business, (4) working because the family "needs income," (5) working to acquire assets.

A picture was drawn in the Sobol study of "accomplishers" in contrast to the "financial workers." The accomplisher was likely to be Protestant, active in club activities, highly educated, and generally from a family where the husband's income was high. The reasons most closely related to high labor force attachment or work commitment were similar to McClelland's "need for achievement" (McClelland and others, 1953). Two subsequent studies of women college graduates measured need for achievement and related it to work commitment. In a study of Radcliffe graduates, Baruch

(1966) found a "dramatic decrease in achievement motive between five and ten years out of college" (p. 102). Eyde (1968), however, using a paper-and-pencil test in contrast to Baruch's projective measure, found no such change in the mastery-achievement scores of the Jackson College graduates she tested; their scores remained essentially constant between the fifth and tenth year after college, though there was some change between the senior year and the fifth year after graduation. Further investigation is needed to study this apparent discrepancy. If achievement motive, and hence work commitment, remains constant throughout the life cycle, then prediction of labor-force participation rates can be facilitated. If it does not remain constant, a study of the dynamics of change should be pursued.

Sobol found that, for women not working at the time of interview, the most important variable relating to future work commitment was work experience since marriage. She theorized that job contacts and recent experience would facilitate future employment and that work experience since marriage might indicate a husband's approval of such work. Moreover, she found the influence of a wife's educational level to be overshadowed by work experience since marriage in the determination of commitment to work.

Expectations and Wishes. Haller and Rosenmayer (1971) add a new dimension to the Sobol measurement of work commitment. They suggest that if work commitment is to be measured by the length of time a woman plans to work, then one should distinguish between future work expectation and wishes. The differences in wish and expectation were observed in a study of 1,379 female workers and employees in Austria, married women between the ages of twenty and thirty. This study was carried out by a research group from the Institute of Sociology at the University of Vienna. The questions asked were:

> *1. Do you wish to continue to work during the next ten years or to discontinue? (because of birth of a child, because of having achieved economic target, in any case?)*
>
> *2. Do you expect to work the next ten years or discontinue?*
>
> *3. Would you like to resume work at the age of*

forty or forty-five? (I have this intent; would like; can imagine; no)

In addition to these questions, the Haller study asked two more:

4. Would you work even without financial necessity? (yes, no)
5. What do you think about a married woman/ mother? (she should not work; see work as necessary evil; see work and family as equal; see work as main task).

According to Haller and Rosenmayer, "nonfinancial motivation shows a strong connection with *wishes* for long-term employment. This connection is extremely high for white-collar workers" (p. 504). The Haller data confirm the Sobol statement of 1963: work commitment in terms of wishes is indeed connected with non-financial rather than financial motives. For blue-collar workers, however, financially motivated women often are more likely to expect long-term employment.

In the Haller study, 42 percent of those who expect to continue working also wish to do so. Wishing to continue work is closely related to nonfinancial motives for working. If we compare, for both white- and blue-collar women, those who both plan and wish to continue work with those who plan but do not wish to continue, we find the former twice as likely to be those who "would work without financial necessity."

Haller also relates life-cycle status and work commitment, particularly in the effect of children on work commitment. Sobol (1963) and Fogarty, Rapoport, and Rapoport (1971) found that women with children show higher levels of work commitment than do those without. A later economic study performed at the University of Minnesota confirmed this observation for a sampling of American women (Parnes, 1970). To date, the only published explanation of this surprising finding is the "traditional dream" theory of Bailyn (1964), who hypothesized that women who do not have children idealize motherhood, but after they achieve it they are more likely to want to work. Another possibility is that mothers who work and have grown children expect no further interferences in their work careers and hence express higher work commitment. Yet the Princeton Study showed that many mothers of small children demonstrate a high level of work commitment, though Haller found this true only for white-collar workers; from his data, motherhood does not seem to affect the plans of blue-collar workers.

Haller also found that work experience can affect work commitment. Though it did not for most blue-collar workers, the correlation proved significant for their white-collar counterparts, particularly those with career aspirations or those who judged themselves professionally successful. Among white collar workers with fewer than seven years of work experience, only 20 percent wished for long-term employment, while among those with twelve years work experience, the figure rose to 43 percent. This study of Austrian women suggests that future work wishes depend strongly on occupation.

Although strong work commitment is generally related to occupation, Haller found some exceptions in women employed in the textile industry. These women claimed to work for financial reasons, but showed a high work commitment as measured by future work wishes. Generally, they worked for firms in isolated, small communities. Jobs were passed on through the family, and workers lived in an "occupational community," where they socialized in off-hours with persons in their own line of work. Thus, they developed a high level of satisfaction and commitment, despite objectively bad working conditions. Blauner (1964) found similar results in the textile industry in the United States. Haller points out that textile workers who see work as a continuation of the female role are more likely to wish to continue work. In the clothing industry, "42 percent of those who see many differences between occupational work and household duties would work without financial necessity compared to 74 percent who see no differences" (p. 514). This finding should be investigated for a range of occupations and industries.

Behavior and Plans. Haller and Rosenmayer discuss another interesting concept for measurement of work commitment, the construction of a scalable variable or variate. They suggest such a scale might be based on answers to the attitudinal and expectational

Table 8.

SIMPLE AND MULTIPLE REGRESSION COEFFICIENTS RELATING LABOR-FORCE ATTACHMENT OF 814 WHITE MARRIED WOMEN WITH TWO OR MORE CHILDREN, 1956–1966, TO OTHER SOCIOLOGICAL AND ECONOMIC VARIABLES

Independent Variable	Units of Measure, Assigned Value		Regression Coefficients			Standard Error
			Simple	Multiple	Standardized[b]	
1. Husband's Income 1956	0 Under $3000	9 $10,000 and over	−0.153	−0.1378[a]	−0.1289	(0.04)
2. Husband's Earnings Third Interview (1962–1966)	Same Scale as Above		−0.111	−0.1049	−0.0647	(0.06)
3. Occupational Prestige	0 Low	9 High	−0.054	−0.0148	−0.0012	(0.06)
4. Wife's Perception of Opportunity to Get Ahead	1 Good Chances	7 Poor Chances	+0.014	+0.1063	+0.0680	(0.06)
5. Feelings of Economic Security	1 Low	6 High	−0.132	−0.1438[a]	−0.0921	(0.06)
6. Aspirations for Children's College Education	1 Don't Expect to Go, Depends, Don't Know	7 Would Send Son and Daughter	+0.028	+0.0221	+0.0163	(0.05)
7. Wife's Drive to Get Ahead	1 Low	9 High	+0.034	+0.0622	+0.0442	(0.05)
8. Income of 3 Closest Friends	1 All Lower	7 All Higher	+0.125	+0.1036	+0.0593	(0.06)

Variable	Scale (0)	Scale (9)			
9. Wife's Age at Marriage	0 Less than 204 Months	9 324 months or More	+0.073	+0.1390[a]	+0.1232 (0.04)
10. Expected Family Size	1 Child	9 9 Children	−0.119	−0.3203[a]	−0.1578 (0.07)
11. Income Change 1956–66	2 Up More Than $4000 — Same — Down $4000 or More (8)	8	−0.010	too small to enter	
12. Wife's Education	0 0–8 Years — 1 Year of College	9 More Than 4 Years of College	−0.105	+0.3533[a]	+0.2635 (0.06)
13. Husband's Education	Same Scale as Wife's Education		+0.056	+0.1168[a]	+0.1117 (0.05)
14. Labor Force Attachment (Dependent Variable)	0 Low	9 High			

Notes: The data sample was native-born, white married couples, resident in the largest metropolitan areas, who had recently had a second child and whose marital histories and pregnancy histories were uncomplicated. These wives were interviewed in 1957, again in 1960, and once again between 1963 and 1967. This study was called the Princeton Fertility Study and is described in Bumpass and Westoff (1970, pp. 3–18).

Multiple $R = 0.3312$ (This coefficient relates the dependent variable, wife's labor-force attachment, to the fourteen variables listed above.) Note that the dependent variable goes from 0, low labor-force attachment, to 9, high labor-force attachment.

Constant = 2.94681

Standard error of estimate = 2.5128

[a] Result significant at the 5 percent level.

[b] These are beta coefficients of normalized equations wherein each variable is expressed in terms of its standard deviation. Numbers in parentheses are the standard error of the coefficients.

Source: Sobol (1973).

questions listed above, though they have not yet been able to construct one.

Using data from a Population Institute longitudinal study Sobol based a simple scale on the work behavior and work plans of a group of white married women with at least two children, interviewed three times over a six to ten year period. A scale of labor-force attachment, based on current work behavior and future work plans over the interview period, was related to thirty-four sociological and economic variables by simple and multiple regression analysis. The scale, considered to measure labor-force attachment, was formed as follows: for each of the three interviews, a woman was classified into one of four categories: currently working (4 points); plans to work in the future (3 points); uncertain about future work (2 points); will not work (1 point). The number on each of the three interviews was summed and three points were subtracted from the total, yielding a range from 0 to 9. A woman who had never worked would have a score of 0 and a woman who had worked throughout the period would have a score of 9. This 10-point scale was then used as the dependent variable in a simple and multiple regression analysis. When simple regression methods were used, a wife's labor force attachment seemed primarily related to economic variables. Only six variables in the simple correlation analysis had correlation coefficients of 0.10 or more; these are listed in Table 8.

The economic variables were a combination of dynamic, absolute-income, and relative-security variables. In absolute income, the higher the husband's income in 1956 and 1962–1966, the less likely the wife was to work or plan to work. Feelings of economic insecurity were related positively to labor-force attachment; the more insecure the wife, the more attached to the labor force. Finally, the income of the three closest friends of the family provided another measure of relative security. If the friends' incomes were higher than that of the respondent, the respondent showed much more inclination to work.

A dynamic variable was constructed representing income change between interviews. The scale for this variable measured the extent to which income went up or down between the first and last interview. In her earlier study, Sobol indicated higher labor-force participation for women whose husbands' incomes have recently gone down. No similar significant relationship was found in the present study.The absolute level of income and income relative to that of others was found to have a more important effect on wife's work status than actual changes in income level.

The two noneconomic variables, wife's education and expected family size, are significantly related to labor-force participation. The larger the family expected, the less likely the wife is to work; and the higher the wife's level of education, the less likely she is to work. The relative significance of the two noneconomic variables increases when the multiple regression analysis is performed. Moreover, the education of the wife now is positively correlated with work commitment because the multiple regression takes into account the interrelationship of husband's income and wife's education. At the 5 percent level of significance these two most important variables are: expected family size, $R = -0.320$ (0.070); and wife's education, $R = 0.353$ (0.058). The higher the expected family size, the less likely the wife is to work or plan to work. The higher the wife's level of education, the more likely she is to work. Other variables significant at the five percent level are husband's 1956 earnings, feelings of economic security, and husband's education. Table 8 indicates the direction and extent of these relationships. Thus, although earnings of the husband and feelings of economic security are significantly related to labor force attachment, the relative influence of noneconomic variables is more important than that of economic variables.

The expected family size and wife's education are of utmost significance, when the standardized regression coefficients are studied, in predicting labor-force attachment over a ten-year period, as measured by work behavior rather than by plans to work. This finding holds for women who ordinarily might not be considered likely to work—that is, women who are of child-bearing age and who have at least two children.

Devotion to Job. Thus far we have reviewed measures of work commitment by looking at work history and future work plans. We have related this work commitment to attitudinal factors, such as whether one would work without financial need, reasons for working, and feelings about mothers working. Work commitment may also be measured in terms of the devotion of the woman to her job. If additional time or effort are needed at work, is the woman willing to devote them? Work commitment can be measured by the "relative distribution of interest, time, energy, and emotional investment in family life, work, and other sectors of life" (Safilios-Rothschild, 1971, p. 491). In a study of Greek women, Safilios-Rothschild tried to ascertain the degree of importance a woman attaches to her work obligations rather than to her traditional familial obligations. Safilios-Rothschild measured the degree of work commitment on the basis of answers to seven questions, typical of which are: "If a much better job was offered to you or you were suggested for a promotion that would give you much more money, prestige, and other advantages but would require that you work more hours in the evening, taking more responsibility, or sometimes travel outside Athens: would you accept? If no, why?" (p. 684). "Do you find that your working prevents you from being as good a mother and wife as you could wish? Yes/no; if yes, in what way? and to what extent?" (p. 684). An index of work commitment developed from these questions consisted of six different degrees of commitment. This measure of work commitment was then related to other variables. While degree of work commitment was closely related to education and type of occupation, the relationship was not perfect. Even among high-prestige workers, some women had low work commitment. Three percent of private employees, 40 percent of saleswomen, 6.7 percent of skilled workers, and 12.5 percent of semiskilled workers had high work commitment. Thus work commitment cuts sufficiently across occupation to be a useful variable in analyzing the nature and meaning of work for women.

Safilios-Rothschild also studied family relationships. Perhaps her most striking finding was that women with a high level of work commitment were more likely to report a high degree of marital satisfaction than nonworking women and women with low work commitment. Thus a common notion is contradicted, namely that women work to compensate for an unhappy marriage.

There are also important indications that women who express a high interest in outside work or employment like housework as well, so that it would seem that work is not merely an escape from housework. Parnes (1970) found similar results in a study of American women; Fuchs (1971) also noted in a study of two thousand

German women, that women who express the greatest future work plans are most likely to say they enjoy housework.

This evidence is in agreement with findings about women's attitudes throughout most industrialized Western countries. British, German, Austrian, Swedish, and American wives all stress the non-financial aspects of their work, and those who express long-term future work plans are most likely to indicate that they also enjoy housework.

Black-White Differences

Relation to Socioeconomic and Other Variables. There are important differences in the labor-force participation of black and white wives. In all studies, nonwhite wives have higher labor-force participation rates at a given moment of time (Bowen and Finegan, 1969; Kim, 1972; Cain, 1966; Parnes, 1971). (In a given survey week in 1967, Parnes found that 43.2 percent of white wives were employed and 60.4 percent of black wives were employed. For women with children under six, 26.9 percent of white wives were employed compared with 45.9 percent of black wives.)

This difference does not seem to be due to income differences between the two groups. In a recent panel study, Parnes removed rewards from the picture by asking the question: "If, by some chance you (and your husband) were to get enough money to live comfortably without working, do you think you would work anyway?" Sixty-seven percent of black women said they would work, while 59 percent of white women said they would work. The Cain study (1966) gave similar results.

The Parnes study was based on a national sample of 5,083 women, thirty to forty-four years of age in 1967, who were interviewed in a Bureau of Census survey in 235 areas. The effects of two economic factors, husband's and wife's income, do not explain the higher rates of labor-force participation for nonwhites, although with husband's income, the difference by race narrows. Since white wives' incomes tend to be higher, we would expect them to be even more likely than nonwhite wives to say they would work under these hypothetical conditions.

When black and white women's plans to work were studied (where there is no financial necessity to work), white women in high-level jobs were most likely to plan to continue to work. For black women, there appears to be no relationship to the socioeconomic status of their jobs (Table 9).

Table 9.

PROPORTION OF EMPLOYED RESPONDENTS WHO WOULD WORK
IF THEY RECEIVED ENOUGH MONEY TO LIVE ON WITHOUT
WORKING, BY OCCUPATION AND COLOR, PERCENT

	White	*Black*
Professional and Managerial	74	76
Clerical and Sales	60	62
Blue Collar	45	59
Domestic Service	40	66
Nondomestic	56	74
Farm	57	84
Total or Average	59	67

Source: Reprinted from Parnes and others (1971, p. 174). In a recent communication, the authors indicate that the figures are for non-whites rather than blacks.

In addition to these financial and socioeconomic differences, the presence of young children in the home is less likely to affect the participation of nonwhite than white wives. Some explanations have been offered for this phenomenon. Cain (1966) states, "There is a good deal of evidence that nonwhite women who work are much less likely to have full-time jobs than white women who work," hence, "scheduling time for child care is made easier" (p. 80). Cain further attempts to link black-white work-participation differentials to housing expenditures. Among black families there is greater incidence of doubling-up than among white families. This joint occupancy facilitates baby-sitting; if two husband-wife families occupy a house, one of the wives can baby-sit while the other works. This might explain why the presence of children does not seem as great a deterrent to the black mother's work career as to that of her white counterpart. A variable which measured housing density was significant when children under the age of six were present. The availability of baby-care and labor force commitment should be further examined.

Another explanation of black-white differences advanced by Cain deals with family instability. Excluding women who never married, 41 percent of nonwhite females fourteen to sixty-five years old were either separated, widowed, or divorced in March 1959. In a comparable group of white females, only 22 percent fell in these categories. Cain notes: "Given the relatively high probability that the Negro wife may be without her husband during part of her married life, it seems likely that she would maintain closer ties to the labor force while married" (pp. 82–83). The work behavior pattern of white wives who have remarried and separated is similar to that of black wives. Udry (1966) has shown that the larger proportion of unstable marriages among nonwhites is not "attributable solely to the generally low educational and occupational status of this group, but a characteristic of nonwhite groups of all educational and occupational levels" (p. 206).

Still another possibility discussed in other studies is that the black male's attitude toward a working wife differs from that of his white counterpart. A study of black and white youths graduating from college showed black females more likely than white females to feel that their husbands would expect them to work regularly (Fitcher, 1969). This and other studies (Russo, 1971) indicate greater preference on the part of the black than white college-educated men that wives work regularly.

Axelson's study (1970) further supports the observed differences between black and white males in the acceptance of maternal employment. Axelson found that socioeconomic status and age cohorts do not appreciably change these differences. Kim (1972) found that for black women, husband's and wife's attitudes toward the wife's working are equally powerful in explaining their work behavior; for white women, he finds the husband's attitudes more significant than the wife's in influencing employment.

Intrinsic and Extrinsic Job Factors and Job Mobility. In job satisfaction, Parnes, Shea, and their coworkers (1970) found that the black-white differentials reverse. Seventy-five percent of black and 66 percent of white women said they would work even though they did not need the money, but over 66 percent of white and somewhat less than 60 percent of black women indicated they were highly satisfied with their current jobs. Thus while the black woman is more strongly attached to the labor force, she is less likely to be highly satisfied with her job. Both black and white women seem to prefer their jobs for some intrinsic quality (nature of the work, level of responsibility) rather than for some extrinsic factor (wages, working conditions). "The proportion of black women who believe that extrinsic job attributes ('good wages') are more important than intrinsic attributes ('liking the work') is double that of white women (39 percent versus 20 percent)" (Parnes and others, 1970, p. 180). Also, the black women are less likely than white to express high satisfaction with their jobs (56 percent versus 68 percent) and less likely to register specific job attachment (25 percent versus 39 percent), so that the black woman is more likely to indicate she would change jobs if offered a substantial wage increase.

This study seems to confirm the hypothesis that "other things being equal, black women are more responsive to wage differentials than white women" (Parnes and others, 1971, p. 201), and it may explain why black women seem to be more interested than white women in moving from one job to another. Thirty-nine percent of blacks said they would move for a wage increase of 10 to 50 percent, while only 28 percent of whites expressed the same desire.

The labor force participation rate of black wives has not risen as rapidly as that of white wives. A study by Kim (1972), which used the same data as the Parnes study, measured the change in the weeks of labor supplied by a wife in relation to changes in her wage rate and family income (not including her income). For white women, "a 1 percent increase in hourly wage rates is associated with a 0.61 percent increase in the number of weeks in the labor force as compared with only 0.22 percent in the case of blacks. Thus, the positive elasticity of labor supply with respect to wage rate is almost three times as large for the white woman as for the black" (Kim, 1972, p. 86).

As wage rates for women rise, white women are three times more likely to enter the labor force than are black women. However, as husbands' incomes rise, white and black women are equally likely to stop working. Thus if overall wage rates increase by 1 percent (for women and for their husbands), then there will be a 0.22 percent decrease in the labor supplied by black women because of a rise in the husband's income, and a 0.22 percent increase in the labor of black women because of the rise in their own incomes. On balance, for the black woman, there will be no additional labor force participation. For the white woman, if her wage rates increase by 1 percent, there will be an increase of 0.61 percent in her labor-force participation, and if her husband's income also rises by 1 percent, there will be a 0.29 percent decrease in her labor-force participation. On balance then, for the white woman, if wage rates increase by 1 percent there will be net addition of 0.32 percent to the labor force. Bowen and Finegan (1969) and Cain (1966) find similar effects.

Kim feels that the apparent difference in wage elasticity of labor supply among black and white women is due to differences in the incidence of poverty rather than to the influence of color. He suggests that the effects of public-assistance laws and minimum-wage legislation should be studied. The problem may be related to the relative unavailability of jobs which uneducated women can hold; private household work and farm work are disappearing.

Suggestions for Future Research

Many studies have shown the individual factors that relate to labor-force attachment. Advanced analysis should now be developed by forming composite scales which could be used to study work commitment. Thus many variables could be combined for a thorough study of the factors which lead to high commitment. For prediction purposes, longitudinal studies are desirable to test the stability of commitment to work and the factors influencing commitment to work over the life cycle. For example, changes in achievement motive over the life cycle should be explored. Cross-section studies which utilize cohort analysis should be used to pinpoint the attitudinal and behavioral changes that may be occurring.

As more and more women work, devotion to the job will be an increasingly important variable to relate to the quality of family life. Since the term *work commitment* has been understood to mean attachment to the labor force in the literature of the past decade, perhaps the Safilios-Rothschild concept of devotion to the job should be called job attachment or job commitment rather than work commitment.

The important differences between labor-force participation rates of black and white women require more study. As the black woman and man attain a higher level of education and as the white family structure becomes more uncertain because of increasing divorce rates, will the differences between the participation rates of black and white wives tend to narrow even further? The current social revolution may result in many striking changes in the work commitment of married women in the future.

Summary

Work commitment can be measured by future plans or long-term work histories. Suggestions have also been made to distinguish between plans and wishes, which would seem particularly valuable for blue-collar workers. Further refinements suggest that work commitment be measured by a scale based on responses to attitudinal and behavioral questions. In another fruitful line of inquiry commitment is measured by devotion to the job.

Currently there are important differentials in labor force participation of black and white women, primarily because of differences in culture, family structure, husband's attitudes toward wife's work, and child-care possibilities. Over the years, however, labor-force participation rates for black women have not risen as fast as those for white women.

Among women who are already working, black women seem to be more willing than white women to change jobs because of a pay increase (Kim, 1972). For women who are not currently working, however, white women are more likely than black women to enter the labor market when pay levels rise. This finding could account for the relative increase in labor-force participation of white wives.

4

Employment of
Women and Fertility

LOIS WLADIS HOFFMAN

The employment of women has generally been considered undesirable from the standpoint of the family and society, as indicated in previous chapters. Concern with overpopulation, however, has changed this view somewhat, and encouraging the employment of women has become one of the common and more humane approaches to bringing about a decreased birth rate. Basically the idea is that if women are satisfied with employment they want fewer children and their motivation to practice effective birth control is increased. This argument is bolstered by statistics indicating that in the United States, as in most highly industrialized countries, working women have fewer children than nonworking women. Furthermore, data indicate that females who plan to work plan also to have smaller families (Blake, 1965; Collver and Langlois, 1962; Collver, 1968; Farley, 1970; Hoffman and Hoffman, 1973; Weller, 1971).

Preparation of this chapter supported in part by grant 1 RO1–HD 07412–01 from the National Institute of Child Health and Development. A previous version was published in the *Merrill Palmer Quarterly,* 1974, *20* (2), 99–119.

The negative relationship between maternal employment and family size, however, does not hold under all conditions. The relationship has not been established in the less developed countries, nor where extended family ties are particularly strong (Gendell, 1965; Stycos and Weller, 1967; Safilios-Rothschild, 1969; Zarate, 1967). Furthermore, it is not as firmly established for certain occupations, particularly those in the blue-collar category (Weller, 1971). Thus the nature of the employment-fertility relationship must be more fully understood before it can be translated into an effective population policy. In fact, without understanding the dynamics of the relationship, it is not possible to predict whether the negative association now found in the United States will continue as other aspects of the social environment change. Let us consider the trends in maternal employment and family size that began in this country in the forties.

Social Change after World War II

After World War II, in the late forties and early fifties, two seemingly opposed trends occurred: family size increased and so did the employment of women. Furthermore, both changes were most pronounced for middle-class married women, and both were predominantly voluntary acts. Middle-class women were not only having more babies but they wanted more, and the dramatic increase in employment rates also reflected choice (Nye and Hoffman, 1963). To show how rapidly these changes took place, look at the change in desired family size: Freedman, Whelpton, and Campbell (1959) in a national sample of married women between eighteen and thirty-nine found that whereas, in 1941, 27 percent of the respondents considered four or more children ideal, in 1955 the figure increased to 49 percent. The percentage of mothers employed between 1941 and 1960 more than tripled (U.S. Department of Labor, 1972).[1]

While these two trends seem to be contradictory, both may have been responses to the same social changes: technological and economic events which changed the housewife role and also opened employment opportunities for women.

[1] By 1970, the employment of mothers was still rising but desired family size and actual fertility had begun to decline.

During this period technological advances and commercial food-processing techniques reduced the amount of work involved in housework and cooking and removed a great deal of the household drudgery. However, they also removed much of the creativity and the opportunity to feel that being a full-time housewife was an essential, contributing role. The tasks that remained were the dullest and most uncreative. Areas where a woman could make a special and irreplaceable contribution as a housewife or homemaker have been lost through the greater availability of commercial products. At the same time some interesting changes were occurring in the mothering role. For one thing, medical science was conquering a number of childhood diseases. In the 1930s, for example, many mothers faced the care and entertainment of a child with streptococcal infection, which often went on for weeks or even months and sometimes ended with rheumatic fever. The house was in quarantine, and the books and playthings of the sick child were often burned when he or she became well. With the development of penicillin, the child with a streptococcal infection could return to school in a couple of days. The development of antibiotics and vaccines have greatly diminished the anxieties about physical health and the sheer nursing care that were previously an intrinsic part of motherhood.

While all this was going on, Freudian theory, newly popularized in the media, was putting stress on the importance of the parents, particularly the mother, for developing a psychologically sound human being. Thus, while the housewife role was losing its creative potential, the role of mother was gaining it.

Following World War II, an expanding economy made large families economically feasible and also opened up job opportunities for women. The number of economic opportunities for women was also given a boost by the population distribution; the women looking for jobs were born during the Depression, when the birth rates were down, and they were looking for the conventionally feminine jobs, those that deal with children, such as school teaching and nursing. (Even the rare woman doctor was likely to go into pediatrics.) The children who were available as customers or clients were the children of the baby boom. So the new crop of babies opened up many job opportunities in the conventionally female professions, whereas adult workers were relatively scarce because they had been born at a time of low natality.

The combination of technological advances that so changed the housewife role and made jobs available also made it more economically efficient for the woman to work and use her money to buy a product than to make the same product at home. The full-time housewife without children became a luxury role. The job of housewife as it had been known was gone. What was left of it was repetitive, dull, with compulsive supercleaning, on the one hand, and gourmet cooking and "artsy-craftsy" homemaking on the other. While the latter was creative, it bordered on being leisure because reasonable facsimiles could be purchased and jobs for women were available. So the do-it-yourself homemaker was sometimes troubled by whether she was indeed making a serious contribution to the household. The United States has often been characterized as the land of the Protestant Ethic. That is, most people have an internalized value on productive effort, a need for them to feel that what they do is valuable. Until recently, at least, most middle-class people had a hard time justifying leisure.

The working mother and the mother of four or more children were two responses to the same social changes. The role of nonemployed mother of two school-aged children had ceased to be a full-time job for a young healthy woman who wanted to feel she was an important, contributing member of her family. In short, technology eased the job, and there were two ways to fill it out: more children or paid employment. The increased rates of maternal employment and fertility then were two responses to the changed and no longer fulfilling role of housewife. They were, however, alternative responses; both rates were rising, but the employed mothers had fewer children.

Why Do Working Women Have Fewer Children?

The negative correlation between employment and family size has led some population experts to the view that if employment for women is encouraged, fertility will decrease. Blake (1969, 1971), Davis (1967), and others include jobs for women as a primary means of curtailing population. Blake argues that contraception, even if perfect and adopted by all, will still result in too many children because people really want too many children. The position is that one reason for so many women wanting so many children is that it is the major role for women. If they are encouraged to take jobs, and this choice is facilitated, the desire for motherhood will be reduced. The argument in favor of child-care centers is sometimes given in these same terms: Child-care centers will enable women to work, and working will lead them to cut down their fertility (Farley, 1970).

The increasing employment of women may be inevitable since it reflects a number of other social changes that are discussed in Chapters One and Two. If the role of full-time housewife with no preschool children is not adequately satisfying, even the mother of four well-spaced children eventually faces that problem. If a mother is forty-five when she faces the empty-nest period, she still is too young to cope with retirement. These social conditions are sufficient to justify the need for child-care centers, job opportunities, and equal wages, and the fulfillment of these needs will further encourage and facilitate female employment. However, will they also cut down fertility as has sometimes been suggested? While encouraging female employment as a solution to overpopulation may have a great deal of appeal, is lowered fertility an inevitable result?

A first question to consider is: if employment and fertility are negatively related, which is causal? If this relationship exists only because women who would have few children are more likely to seek outside employment, then encouragement of employment will have no effect. Certainly for some women this is the case; they have few or no children because of either subfecundity or personal preference and turn to employment.

Even if one considers only the women for whom family size results from employment—those who curtail family size because they are working or planning to do so—what aspect of employment leads to curtailment of family size? Does employment provide an alternative gratification to motherhood—that is, does a career compete with motherhood in attractiveness? Or, is family size held down simply because employment and motherhood are to a considerable extent incompatible roles—that is, a working mother at present is under considerable strain because there are inadequate child care facilities and because husbands typically do not share equally in household responsibilities. In addition, even short-term maternity leave usually means a loss in wages, job opportunities, seniority rights, and other employee benefits.

For a large percentage of working women the incompatibilities between motherhood and employment are probably important determinants of the negative relationship between fertility and employment. It has been noted earlier that, in countries where extended family ties make child-care arrangements easy, this negative relationship does not exist, and several papers suggest that the compatibility of the two roles is the crucial explanatory factor (Stycos and Weller, 1967; Weller, 1971). But to the extent that it is the incompatibilities between employment and maternity that explain the lower fertility of working women and not the alternative psychological satisfaction that working provides, we may expect a change as maternity and employment become more compatible. For example, given present trends it is likely that child-care facilities will become increasingly available and husbands will assume more responsibility than in the past for the care of the children. It will thus be more feasible for women to work and have children too. The satisfactions provided by having children have been discussed in detail elsewhere (Hoffman and Hoffman, 1973), and most jobs, particularly blue-collar ones, do not offer equivalent gratification. Thus, as the society moves toward new social norms and legislation to ensure sexual equality, the negative relationship between employment and fertility may disappear for those occupational groups where the job does not supply competing satisfactions. Where there is still a desire for more children and work operates only as a barrier to fertility, working will have less effect on fertility as the roles of worker and mother become more compatible. Only where working women have smaller families because their work provides alternative gratification and thus lessens the desire for children will the encouragement of employment be an effective population policy.

Any gainful employment may offer satisfaction, as indicated in Chapter Two, and, to the extent that a mother has an additional child just to fill out an otherwise empty life, any employment may diminish fertility. However, most occupations are not fully satis-

factory alternatives to motherhood, and the effect may be four children instead of five or three instead of four, but it is not likely that
the joy of work on the assembly line will lead to a two-child family.
In the long run this effect may result only from employment which
is intrinsically gratifying and satisfies some of the same needs that
having children does (Hoffman and Hoffman, 1973). Such employment is more likely to be available to the middle class and the better
educated and is more likely to be challenging and appropriate for the
woman's ability. Although there are skilled blue-collar jobs that
provide a great deal of intrinsic satisfactions—for example, carpentry,
plumbing, and tool and dye making—these have by and large not
been available to women (Tangri, 1972).

Some evidence supports the hypothesis that the more gratifying jobs, even in the short run, are more closely associated with low
fertility. Both Whelpton, Campbell, and Patterson (1966) and
Ryder and Westoff (1971) found that women who worked because
they wanted to expected fewer children than women who worked
because they had to, and Fortney (1972), in a sample of faculty
wives, found that those employed in higher status positions had
fewer children than those employed in lower status positions. In
these studies the working women had fewer children, but within
that group those with the presumably more gratifying jobs had still
fewer. There is also evidence, shown in Table 10, that, for white
respondents, the impact of employment on actual or expected births
is greater for the more educated women than for those who have not
graduated from high school. Furthermore, it can also be seen in
Table 10 that the college-educated, employed women have smaller
expected family size than any other education-employment category
for both whites and nonwhites—2.8 and 2.7 respectively.

The idea that rewarding employment may lead women to
decrease family size but that employment per se may not has been
expressed by Davis (1967), Blake (1969), Chilman (1970), Fortney
(1972), Scanzoni and McMurry (1972), Tangri (1972), and
Hoffman and Hoffman (1973). Some of these writers, concerned
with the issue of overpopulation, have also suggested that if few
lower-class women are likely to settle for the two-child family, the
attainment of "zero population growth" might ultimately rest on
some women choosing to have no children. That is, a national

Table 10.

MEAN NUMBER OF LIVE BIRTHS AND TOTAL EXPECTED NUMBER FOR FECUND WOMEN EIGHTEEN TO THIRTY-NINE YEARS OF AGE BY EDUCATIONAL ATTAINMENT, CURRENT LABOR FORCE STATUS, AND RACE, 1965

	College		*High School, 4 years*		*Less than 4 years High School*	
	White	Nonwhite	White	Nonwhite	White	Nonwhite
	Number of Births					
In labor force	1.4	1.6	1.8	2.3	2.8	3.6
Not in labor force	2.4	1.8	2.4	2.8	3.1	4.0
	Expected Number of Births					
In labor force	2.8	2.7	2.9	3.3	3.7	4.1
Not in labor force	3.3	3.1	3.4	3.7	3.9	4.7

Source: Figures obtained from Table 12 in Ridley (1969, pp. 199–250).

average family size of two could be obtained even though some prefer four children, as long as there were others who preferred none. Blake and Hoffman argue that the group most likely to choose childlessness is the career women since they have the possibility of a highly rewarding life without children. In fact, there is some evidence that highly educated women are more likely to be childless (Astin, 1969), but *voluntary* childlessness in the United States is rare among all groups. In general, the expectation that careers for women will provide alternative satisfactions that fully compete with motherhood has not heretofore been borne out. A number of factors have, until recently, operated to push capable women away from a career commitment and toward motherhood: the failure of women to obtain adequate education, problems encountered in the pursuit of a career, and psychological difficulties resulting from social attitudes and stereotypes about career women, among others.

Education

Although women in the United States are more educated than in the past in an absolute sense, in comparison with the educational levels of the country as a whole, they are not more educated. Consider the same period examined with respect to maternal employment and family size. The data presented in Figures 2 and 3 and Table 11 indicate that although the educational levels of the country as a whole have been increasing since about 1945, the education of women has not kept pace with this trend. After World War II the G.I. Bill provided expenses and financial support for veterans who went to college, which increased the educational level of the country. It provided a pool of educated workers which, in turn, enabled the establishment of higher educational criteria for jobs. But since veterans were far more likely to be males, it also engendered a split in the amount of education that white males and females obtained. Only recently has the gap between white males and females that emerged in the forties begun to be closed.

In this context let us consider the egalitarian marriage that was hailed in the middle class following World War II. The young wife obtained employment in order to help her husband by supplementing the G.I. Bill stipends while he attended college. In the

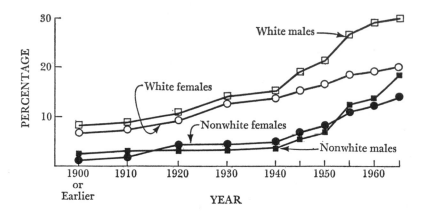

FIGURE 2.   Percentage of population twenty-four to twenty-nine years of age with at least one year of college completed, by sex and color, 1900 to 1965. Adapted from Figure 1 in Ridley (1969).

process, the educational level of the country soared to new heights, but the education of the woman did not. Not only the work she did early in marriage but the work she went back to or considered after her youngest child started school was not a profession or a career but simply a job. If she chose to have another baby instead, at least one of the reasons might be the limited possibilities that faced her on the job market.[2]

The argument thus far is that the lower fertility of the employed married woman might change as motherhood and employment status become more compatible, unless the woman's work offers gratifications that can effectively compete with motherhood. Paid employment has become a part of woman's life because of the technological changes that have so streamlined the housewife role and further removed the functional contributions from the home to the marketplace, as well as the fact that a woman's potentially productive years extend well beyond her child-bearing years. However,

[2] Ridley (1972) points out that although it is often assumed today that the husband will be more educated than the wife, this pattern in the United States started only in the late 1930s and only among whites. Prior to 1930, the average white wife was better educated than her husband just as black wives have continued to be.

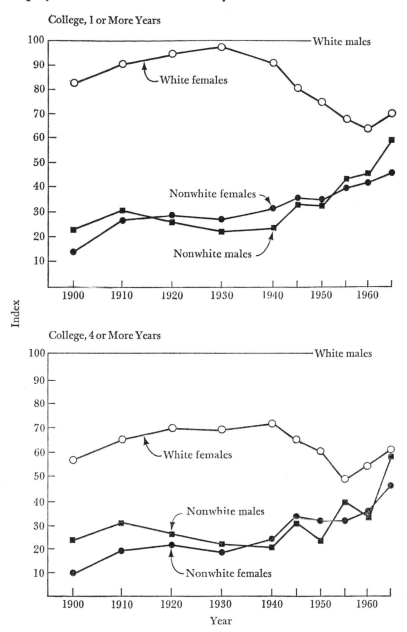

College, 1 or More Years

College, 4 or More Years

Year

FIGURE 3. Indices of college education for white females, nonwhite females, and nonwhite males, twenty-five to twenty-nine years of age, 1900 to 1965. Reprinted from Figure 2 in Ridley (1969).

Table 11.

HIGHER DEGREES EARNED BY WOMEN AS A PERCENTAGE
OF ALL DEGREES CONFERRED, 1900 TO 1970

Degrees[a]

Year	Master's or second professional	Doctorate or equivalent
1900	19.1	6.0
1910	26.4	9.9
1920	30.2	15.1
1930	40.4	15.4
1940	38.2	13.0
1950	29.2	9.7
1960	31.6	10.5
1964	31.8	10.6
1970	39.8	13.3

[a] Does not include bachelor's degrees or other first professional degrees (M.D., D.D.S., L.L.B., B.D., M.L.S., M.S.W.).
Sources: Figures for 1900–1964 obtained from Ridley (1972). Figures for 1970 obtained from U.S. Bureau of the Census (1972).

careers that require education are important as a source of gratification that competes with motherhood. Since 1945 there has been a gap in the amount of education women obtain relative to men.

It might be noted further that education operates as a deterrent to fertility not only because it enables women to obtain satisfying jobs but also because, at present, it delays the time of marriage and the birth of the first child.

Even those women who have obtained advanced degrees, however, have not shown the low fertility desires that might be expected. Farley (1970), for example, presents data that indicate over half of her respondents, all female graduate students at Cornell University in May 1969, wanted three or more children. Levine's data (1968) for graduate women at Yale are consistent with this finding, the majority wanting three or more children, and fully 82 percent of the women in law and medical schools wanting at least three. In the United States there have been both external barriers to career commitments and internal, psychological barriers. These diverse obstacles have pushed women away from full professional commitments and toward motherhood.

Career Barriers

A major deterrent to the career commitment for women is the prejudice and discrimination faced in every profession. Obvious, subtle, deliberate, and inadvertent discriminatory policies against professional women have been documented (Epstein, 1970; Fidell, 1970; Graham, 1970; Roby, 1972; Rossi, 1965; White, 1970).[3] Women have received discriminatory treatment in recruitment and hiring, job assignment, salaries, employee benefits, and promotions. They have not had the same access to their colleagues as men have, and they have been more restricted than men by their family commitments. The pursuit of careers has been difficult and the rewards uncertain. Dropping out has been socially sanctioned, and dropping out for purposes of motherhood has been applauded.

In addition, there is also a psychological problem; if a woman is too achieving, too successful in her academic work or career, she may not feel feminine and may be rejected by men. Horner (1972) demonstrated that college women showed considerable anxiety about academic success. Furthermore, those who indicated anxiety showed poorer performance on a competitive task (particularly when the competition was with men) than when a comparable task was performed alone. The belief that the successful career woman is unfeminine is widely held by men and women alike (Epstein, 1970; Fortney, 1972).

Because of these prevailing stereotypes about the career woman and the prevailing belief that a woman should not be more competent than her husband or boyfriend (Komarovsky, 1973), many highly capable women, including those in the professions, feel that they are under pressure to prove their femininity. And one way

[3] Discriminatory practices that deter women from obtaining an education are discussed by Cross (1971), Roby (1972), and others.

to do so is to have a baby. In a 1971 study of undergraduate women at the University of Michigan, the most common response to an open-ended question about "the most womanly thing you can imagine" was "to have a baby" (Hoffman, 1973). Thus, maternity may provide the career woman with the proof she feels she needs to establish her femininity. It is interesting to note in this connection that in the Levine (1968) study of graduate women at Yale, the women in the professional schools—medical school and law school—indicated a higher desired family size than the women in nursing and teaching, the more conventionally feminine fields. Possibly the former felt a greater need to prove their femininity. Astin (1969) similarly, in a comparison of educated married women, reported that physicians had larger families than Ph.D.s, and among Ph.D.s the women in the sciences had more children than those in arts and humanities or education.[4] Fortney (1972) found in a study of employed faculty wives that those in the predominantly or mainly male occupations were somewhat more likely to have three or more children than those in the more traditionally female occupations. Tangri (1969), however, found that undergraduate women who planned on pursuing more masculine careers wanted fewer children.

The dynamics of deciding between going to work and having a new baby have been discussed elsewhere (Birnbaum, 1971; Hoffman, 1973; Hoffman and Hoffman, 1973; Hoffman and Wyatt, 1960). A common choice point between a new job or another child, one that cuts across educational groups, occurs when the youngest child starts school and the woman experiences a need to fill the resulting void. She may choose employment, or, because this alternative is unattractive, relatively unavailable, or psychologically threatening, she may have another baby instead and thus postpone the diminution in maternal functions. Furthermore, just as employment may sometimes be an escape from maternity, so also can maternity be an escape from employment by offering escape from the pressure or monotony of an unpleasant job.

For the educated woman there may be a particular problem. The success of the marital relationship for this group often requires that both partners perceive the husband to be the more intelligent or

[4] Wives of physicians also have higher fertility rates (Cho and others, 1970).

successful in his career, and this is evidenced even among dual-career couples (Birnbaum, 1971; Garland, 1972; Komarovsky, 1973). Any change in this perception may be a threat to the husband's sense of masculinity, the wife's sense of femininity, and thus to the love relationship. In many cases this threat may come simply from a change in the established equilibrium, such as when the career wife has a success experience or her husband has a failure, or when the nonworking wife considers returning to a career or seeking further education. What could be a better solution than pregnancy? It removes the wife from the achievement-career arena, confirms her femininity, and reestablishes affiliative ties.[5]

Childlessness

As indicated earlier, professional women are more likely than nonprofessional women to be childless. Astin (1969), for example, found that 28 percent of the married women doctorates in her study, women in their early forties, were without children, twice as many as their age cohorts in the general population. But there is no clear indication that this is voluntary childlessness, and the pursuit of a career may have been compensation for subfecundity. Although professional women might choose to have no children because considerable satisfaction is available through their careers, there is little evidence that this has been the case.

Voluntary childlessness in America has, in fact, been almost nonexistent since the early thirties. The percentage at the national level who indicate they do not wish to have any children is usually around 1 percent. In 1973, when the results of the Gallup surveys were indicating a clear decrease in the percentage of Americans who favored large families of four or more children, those who considered the childless family "ideal" still numbered only 1 percent.

The pressures toward having children have already been discussed. In addition, the perception of voluntary childlessness is a particularly negative one. Women who have no children are seen as selfish, sick, cold, and unfeminine (Pohlman, 1969; Rainwater,

---

[5] This "solution" is often an unconscious or impulsive decision, and thus the more liberal views on abortion may mean that such pregnancies are less likely to be carried to term.

1960). In one study, college men indicated that they would be willing to marry a woman who could not have children but not one who would not (Pohlman, 1969). This perception is sufficiently prevalent that many women have not wanted to admit, even to themselves, that they had no desire to be mothers.

Recent Changes and the Future

The situation in general may be changing. The data for 1970 show a decline in the birth rate and in desired family size (Gallup, 1973; U.S. Bureau of the Census, 1973). For lower class or less educated women, this decline is probably a function of the availability of improved methods of birth control. The obstacles to effective contraception by the lower class have been discussed elsewhere (Hoffman and Hoffman, 1973). The techniques that were most frequently used—condom, withdrawal, and rhythm—are unpleasant, inconvenient, and relatively ineffective, resulting in considerable "contraceptive failure." Thus, lower class couples might realistically expect to have four or more children. The number of children a couple say they want is influenced by the number they already have or expect to have and the number most of the people they know have. Thus, as birth control becomes more effective because of improved techniques, actual and expected family size will drop, and eventually so will the family size desired. However, while family size may show a moderate drop generally, it is still expected that for the lower class the relationship between employment and the number of children can be expected to decrease if the roles of mother and worker become more compatible.[6]

On the other hand, the negative relationship between employment and fertility for middle- and upper-class women may be expected to increase. In the preceding sections the following obstacles to this relationship were discussed: women's education has lagged behind that of men; social barriers including discriminatory practices have discouraged women from career commitments; social definitions of femininity and masculinity may have led women to choose

[6] The data for 1969–1973 also indicate that the drop in actual and desired birth rate is less pronounced for the less educated (Gallup, 1973; U.S. Bureau of the Census, 1973).

motherhood to reassure themselves and others of their femininity; and deliberate childlessness has been held in low regard. Each of these—like the birth rate itself—is currently in the process of changing. With respect to women's education, Table 11 shows that in 1970 a higher percentage of the advanced degrees went to women than had been the case since 1930, and the increase between 1964 and 1970 was greater than in any of the previous ten-year periods since 1920. Table 12 presents data based on the educational ex-

Table 12.

HIGHEST DEGREE PLANNED BY ENTERING FRESHMEN

	1966		1972	
	Females	Males	Females	Males
B.A., B.S., associate degree, or none	58.2	42.7	55.0	43.6
M.A., M.S.	32.3	31.2	28.9	26.0
Ph.D. or Ed.D.	5.2	13.7	6.8	10.6
M.D., D.O., D.D.S., or D.V.M.	1.9	7.4	4.3	9.7
L.L.B. or J.D.	0.3	2.5	2.1	6.5
B.D. or M.D.V.	0.1	0.5	0.2	0.6
Other	1.8	2.1	2.7	2.9
All graduate degrees combined[a]	39.8	55.3	42.3	53.4

[a] Excludes "other" category.

Source: Data taken from American Council on Education (1967, 1972).

pectations of a national sample of college freshmen. A comparison between 1966 and 1972 indicates that not only were women's expectations for further education increasing more rapidly than those of men but the percentage of men who indicated they wanted graduate training after the B.A. actually decreased.[7]

[7] Several studies (Hoffman, 1974; Horner, 1973; Horner and Walsh, 1972) have shown that "fear of success," which characterized women but

The career orientation of college women has similarly shown an impressive upswing. Cross (1971) reports data from one college which asked incoming freshmen women every year since 1964 what they would like to be doing in fifteen years. In 1964, 65 percent said they would like to be a housewife and mother. The percentage choosing this life style has declined steadily each year: in 1965, 61 percent gave this answer; in 1966, 60 percent; in 1967, 53 percent; and only 31 percent gave this response in 1970. The percentage wanting to be married career women doubled, going from 20 percent in 1964 to 40 percent in 1970. In discussing this study further, Cross says (p. 148):

> *Most dramatic of all, perhaps, were the responses to a question concerning career choice. In 1964, 57 percent elected a career that would center around home and family; by 1970 the figure had dropped to less than half, 22 percent. The slack was taken up by increases in almost any career area, but especially "academic life" and "professional life." Notice that the size of all of these percentages reflects a conservative student body. These are not "women's lib types." In 1965, for example, when 49 percent of the women at the women's college where these studies were conducted were looking forward to a life centering on home and family, only 26 percent of the women in the national sample were. The career aspirations of college women are rising; the evidence suggests that sex roles are changing very rapidly for young women today.*

Increased career involvement and advanced educational aims on the part of college women have also been documented in the studies reported by Lozoff (1972), which compared college students in the sixties with those enrolled in 1970 and 1971.

The possibility of women pursuing careers has been facilitated also by efforts to combat discrimination in the professions. As barriers to career commitment are lifted and the possibility of appropriate

---

not men in 1965, now is common among college men. Among men, it seems to take the form of questioning the value of academic success and conventional career goals.

rewards in salary and promotions increases, the temptation to drop out because of discouragement and frustration will be less. Furthermore, as careers for women become more common, the stereotype that this is not a feminine role will be weakened, and career women will feel less pressure to prove their femininity through maternity.

Finally, although voluntary childlessness has been both uncommon and widely disparaged in the United States, new evidence suggests this view too may be changing, at least for the well-educated group. In the 1971 Michigan study, 13 percent of 140 women said they planned to have no children; and in a study in 1970 and 1971 of 1800 college students from five different schools, Lozoff (1972) obtained a similar result. The respondents in both studies are almost entirely unmarried women and may change their minds later, but the figures are noteworthy because they are higher than have previously been obtained with comparable samples. For example, Blake (1965) reports a 1961 Gallup survey of 483 college women in which only 2.7 percent of those interviewed favored either one child or none.

There are a number of possible explanations for an increase in voluntary childlessness among college women. Increased career orientation may be related in two ways: (1) the fact that there are more career-bound women means that there is a larger base of women who might opt for childlessness, seeing a career as an adequate fulfillment and motherhood as an unnecessary interference; (2) careers for women are more acceptable and therefore the career-oriented woman does not have to be as defensive as in the past. All women in the Michigan study who said they wanted no children had career plans, and some explicitly indicated that their career interests had affected this decision. But, equally important, because of the widespread concern with overpopulation, voluntary childlessness seems to have become more socially acceptable. There probably always have been women who would have preferred childlessness but who would not admit it since the perception of voluntary childlessness was so negative. The present concern with overpopulation, however, has made it more legitimate for a women to say she wants no children. National sample studies of college populations indicate considerable concern with overpopulation (American Council on Education, 1972), although in the Michigan study this concern was more typically cited as a reason for wanting only two children than for wanting none (Hoffman, 1973).

Thus, the less educated employed women may have a family size closer to that of the nonemployed once employment and motherhood roles are more compatible. For educated women, however, fertility differences between employed and nonemployed may increase. As the successful career woman becomes more acceptable and thus a more attractive image, as rigid stereotypes about what a woman should be and what a man should be break down, the career woman will be under less pressure to assert her femininity through motherhood. Under these conditions, some educated working women may choose childlessness since they are in a position to obtain alternative satisfactions from their careers.

Summary

Because employed women have fewer children than nonemployed women in the United States, it has been suggested that encouraging employment will cut down fertility. But the question of why employed women have fewer children must be considered. If the reason is that women who have few children, either because of subfecundity or choice, are more likely to go to work, then encouraging employment will not decrease fertility. For some women, this may be the case since the role of housewife without young children may not be psychologically satisfying; these women are more motivated to seek employment and freer to do so. But even if we consider those women whose fertility results from their employment, we still need to separate those who find their work so gratifying that they are less motivated for motherhood from those who cut down their fertility only because they cannot find adequate child-care arrangements. With certain changes, such as better child-care centers, husbands who participate more fully in child-rearing and household tasks, and maternity leave without loss of seniority rights, those women whose work does not provide satisfactions comparable to motherhood may be able to have more children without giving up their jobs. These changes are desirable from many standpoints and are likely to come about, but they may not be effective as part of the effort to decrease population growth in the United States. Jobs that typically require education are, in the long run, more likely to diminish fertility because these are more likely to offer the gratifications that compete with motherhood.

The level of education in the United States has been rising, and as a result education is increasingly necessary for access to interesting careers, but women have not kept pace in this area and thus often have not had the credentials for satisfying jobs. Even for educated employed women, however, fertility is not as low as might be expected; many barriers have turned them toward maternity rather than toward a full professional commitment. Because of the stereotype that high-achieving academic and career women are not feminine, many feel a need to prove their femininity through motherhood. In addition, deliberate childlessness has been viewed negatively by Americans. However, these conditions may be changing, with both careers for women and childlessness becoming more acceptable.

5

Child-Care Arrangements

Arthur C. Emlen, Joseph B. Perry, Jr.

When mothers of preschool children take employment, some substitute caregiver must be available, except when the mother can have her children with her while she is employed (5 percent in 1970). Also, many children of school age require some care or supervision since full-time employment usually extends beyond the hours the child is in school.

We here review the arrangements that mothers and their families have made with respect to such variables as whether the child is cared for at home or elsewhere; whether the caregiver is a member of the family or other relative; if nonrelated people care for the child, whether they do so in their own home or in a day-care center; and, if in a day-care center, whether it is permissive, play-centered, or a structured type with emphasis on curriculum.

Extensive need for good substitute care, especially by many low-income mothers who cannot afford its full cost, has led to many proposals for the licensing and regulation of day care and for its subsidization, either partial or complete, by federal and other agencies. These proposals have necessitated the development of criteria for judging what regulation is desirable and what kinds of day care merit support from public funds. This chapter focuses on these facts and issues.

Types

Not until a Children's Bureau survey conducted during May 1958 did information become available on a national basis regarding arrangements made by working mothers for the care of their children under the age of twelve (Lajewski, 1959). A second census conducted in February 1965 reported the arrangements of 12.3 million children under fourteen years of age whose mothers had been employed full or part time for at least six months during the preceding year (Low and Spindler, 1968). The most recent national child care survey was conducted in 1970 by Westinghouse and Westat Corporations (Johns and Gould, 1971), based on an area-probability sample of families with incomes under eight thousand dollars. The results of these three national surveys are shown in Table 13. Though not strictly comparable in population and sampling, they provide us with an approximation of the distributions by type of arrangement for children under six and six to fourteen separately.

Although some form of child care is a corollary of maternal employment, research had assessed the effects of maternal employment without taking the type of care into account. Perry (1963) reports a pioneering study in Spokane, Washington, which was perhaps the first to take informal surrogate care seriously and study the attitudes and behavior involved. In the mid-1960s the Child Welfare League of America reported the most detailed study up to that time of arrangements in six cities and one rural community (Ruderman, 1968). It covered both informal and formal child-care arrangements and compared the sources of satisfaction and dissatisfaction. In 1970 the Council of Jewish Women with an army of volunteers directed a survey of the quality of care (Keyserling, 1972), whose vivid examples of poor care had an impact on conceptions of need. Abt Associates provided a survey and analysis of program elements and costs in a wide variety of exemplary day-care programs across the country (Ruopp and others, 1971, 1973); and

Table 13.

PERCENTAGE DISTRIBUTION OF CHILD-CARE ARRANGEMENTS
OF WORKING MOTHERS BY AGE OF CHILDREN

Child-Care Arrangement	Under 6 Years			6 to 14 Years	
	1958	1965[a]	1970[b]	1965[a]	1970[b]
In own home by	56.6	48.0	49.9	66.0	78.7
Father	14.7	14.1	18.4	15.1	10.6
Other relative	27.8	17.5	18.9	22.6	20.6
Nonrelative	14.2	15.3	7.3	6.8	4.5
Mother worked during child's school hours	—	9.8	5.2	21.5	42.9
In someone else's home by	27.1	30.7	34.5	9.2	12.6
Relative	14.5	14.9	15.5	4.7	7.6
Nonrelative	12.7	15.8	19.0	4.5	5.0
Day-Care Center	4.5	5.6	10.5	0.6	0.6
No special care[c]	11.8	15.7	5.0	24.3	8.3

[a] The predominating and most recent child-care arrangement is given when several kinds of care were used for the same child.

[b] Arrangements on the last day the mother worked.

[c] Child looked after self, mother looked after child while working, or other.
Source: Table compiled by Brookings Institution and adapted. Data from Lajewski (1958, pp. 20–21); Low and Spindler (1968, pp. 15, 71); Office of Economic Opportunity (1971, pp. 175, 178–180). Figures are rounded and may not add to 100.

many state and local surveys were conducted, such as the excellent one in Massachusetts (Rowe, 1972). Reviews were also conducted of federal programs relating to early childhood generally and of the basis in research for the validity of their claims (White and others, 1973).

The data in Table 13 tell several important stories: The proportion of children cared for in centers doubled from 1965 to

1970 but still accounted for only 10 percent of the children under six. Center care includes small owner-operated proprietary facilities, agency-operated group day-care homes with eight to twelve children, large modern proprietary facilities for more than a hundred children, and community-agency centers under either public or voluntary auspices. Head Start programs are also included.

Care in someone else's home by a nonrelative, called family day care, has shown a small but steady growth for care of the under-six child, reaching 19 percent, or twice the number in center care of all kinds; family day care is primarily for younger children and only secondarily for the school-age sibling. According to the Westat survey (Johns and Gould, 1971), 98 percent of family day care is unlicensed and is privately arranged with friends, neighbors, and other nonrelatives who live in the vicinity. The other 2 percent includes both the licensed but minimally supervised homes used extensively by Aid to Families with Dependent Children (AFDC) recipients, some of whom find their own day-care arrangements which then receive special certification; and the traditional agency-supervised family day care.

The percentage of children under six years cared for in their own homes remained stable at about 50 percent from 1965 to 1970. These arrangements do not include "no special form of care," which includes "latch-key" children who look after themselves and those whose mothers tend them while working. Except for Ruderman's survey (1968), almost no attention has been given to the study of own-home child-care arrangements. Unsupervised children have also failed to become objects of systematic research with few exceptions (Glueck and Glueck, 1957; Hirshi and Selvin, 1967; Woods, 1972).

After the parents themselves, nonrelatives are a major child-care resource, competing with kin. Some reasons are to be found in studies of consumer demand and in studies of family day care as a social system. Whatever the reasons, the only large-scale day-care institution operating in the United States is not conventional day care in licensed facilities, but the private, informal child-care arrangement either at home or in other family homes. The caregivers are fathers, siblings, relatives, housekeepers, friends, neighbors, and others. Approximately 90 percent of the children under the age of six from the families of working mothers are in arrangements of this kind. They are more likely to be cared for in their own homes than out, and twice as many preschool children are cared for in the home of a nonrelative (that is, in private family day care) than in a day-care center of any kind—public, voluntary agency, or proprietary.

Legislation

In historical context, the percentages presented in Table 13 reflect vigorous legislative activity in the 1960s and severe institutional constraints that limit the development of federal programs for children.

Federal legislation for day care has been subject to cycles, depending on the crisis of the period. Works Project Administration (WPA) nurseries were set up in 1932 for the children of unemployed teachers, nurses, and others thrown out of work by the Great Depression. By 1937, 1900 nurseries cared for 40,000 children as public funds, both federal and state, were spent for day care for the first time (Steinfels, 1973). The WPA nurseries were allowed to dwindle, but with the advent of World War II maternal employment was needed and this new crisis brought a new expansion of day care. In 1942 the Community Facilities Act (the Lanham Act) provided 50 percent matching grants to operate day-care centers, more than 1100 of them former WPA nurseries (Steinfels, 1973). By the end of the war more than a million and a half children were in day care. Yet, when the war was over, federal funds were withdrawn and few state programs survived, Children's Centers in California being a notable exception.

In the 1960s a new federal expansion of day care appeared. The first advance came with the 1962 Social Security amendments, which authorized federal grants-in-aid to state public-welfare agencies for day-care services. This program permitted the states to develop standards for day care, and Steiner (1970) reports that 43 percent of the four million dollars appropriated for day care in fiscal 1965 was spent on personnel engaged in licensing. A further increase in day-care funds came about as states took advantage of the provisions of Title IV-A of the Social Security Act (amended in 1967) for 75 percent matching funds. In 1971, nearly a quarter of a billion dollars were spent for full-day care to serve an estimated 440,100 children (Parker and Knitzer, 1971). The 1967 amendment also authorized the Work Incentive program (WIN), a manpower program with social services which trained people for permanent jobs and provided child-care services for the trainees.

At the same time that day care was seen as instrumental in reducing welfare rolls, the centers also became a context for compensatory education to remedy the disadvantaging effects of poverty. The Economic Opportunity Act of 1964 authorized grants for day care within community-action programs, the largest and most popular of which was Head Start. Other legislation that provided support for day-care programs included the Elementary and Secondary Education Act of 1965, the Vocational Education Act of 1963, the Education Profession Development Act, and the Manpower Development and Training Act. More than two hundred federal programs exist which affect children (White and others, 1973). Some of the programs to which federal funds were committed include: WIN, Concentrated Employment Program (CEP), AFDC, Child Welfare Services (CWS), Head Start (summer, half day, full day), Parent Child Centers, Model Cities, Aid to Educationally Deprived Children in Low-Income Families, Assistance for Migrant and Seasonal Farm Workers, Assistance for Handicapped Children, Food Services, Health Service, Migrant Health, Pre-School of School Health Program, Staffing Foster Grandparents, Training Educational Professions (Parker and Knitzer, 1971).

The federal level of support for day care and related early childhood programs is shown in Table 14.

Despite the expansion of federal programs, the proportion of children served by them remained relatively small. The number and percentage of children served in licensed day-care facilities doubled between 1965 and 1970; however, according to March 1971 estimates, care in licensed centers and family homes was available for only about 905,000 children (U.S. Department of Labor, Women's Bureau, 1973). The children of working mothers so served was not more than 10 percent. Likewise the WIN program, despite earnest objectives of overcoming the child-care barriers to employment for AFDC mothers, resulted in the employment of only 1.5 percent of the 1.5 million welfare recipients screened for the purpose (Steiner, 1970). The 22,000 employed represent only 7 percent of those

Table 14.

FEDERAL SPENDING FOR DAY CARE AND OTHER PROGRAMS,
FISCAL YEARS, 1970–1973, MILLIONS OF DOLLARS

Program	1970	1971	1972 Estimate	1973 Estimate
Day Care	164	233	404	507
Head Start	330	363	364	369
Preschool programs under Title I	26	92	98	93
Total	520	688	866	969

Source: Table compiled by Brookings Institution and adapted. Data from Senate Committee on Finance (1971, p. 32); *Special Analyses, Budget of the United States Government, Fiscal Year 1972* (1972, pp. 120–121); and *Special Analyses of the United States Government, Fiscal Year 1973* (1973, pp. 123, 144).

regarded as employable and 17 percent of those enrolled in the WIN program.

Head Start is reaching 20 percent of the eligible population of economically disadvantaged children (*Report on Pre-School Education,* 1971), but some caution must be exercised in making assumptions about the eligible population. Of twenty-two million children in the United States under six years in 1970, almost six million had working mothers. Only partly included in this category are two additional populations which became targets of federal programs for day care and related services during the sixties. More than three million economically disadvantaged and two million physically and emotionally handicapped were identified as children to be served by federal programs (Parker and Knitzer, 1971). These are among a variety of partially overlapping populations for whom child-care programs were developed. The vigorous day-care movement, which during the sixties championed day care as a remedy for the disadvantaged, brought under the concept of disadvantaged a constellation of somewhat correlated conditions: poverty, ethnic discrimination, neglect or understimulation in the social-class and home environment, handicapping conditions, and inequities in the delivery of services (White and others, 1973).

Forces Behind Movement. Even though a limited proportion of children were reached by federal programs, a day-care movement was launched during the sixties. It had roots in the two professional traditions of social work and education; each transmitted to day care a distinctive institutional heritage, including an enthusiasm for its own programs, methods, and philosophies and a set of vested interests. Social work concerned itself with licensing, services, and the development of day-care centers. Deriving from the French *creche,* day nurseries appeared in the 1880s and 1890s for the care and protection of the children of seamen, immigrants, single parents, and poor working mothers. Day nurseries were the forerunners of the day-care centers that offer service to problem families (Steinfels, 1973). Agency-supervised day care in family homes also was developed as a placement service patterned after foster family care (Child Welfare League of America, 1969). Kindergarten and nursery schools got their start even earlier than the day nursery; they introduced an educational tradition which later became allied with progressive education and parent cooperatives, and introduced a model of enrichment for middle-class children. In the sixties this tradition contributed to the compensatory educational thrust of Head Start and day-care programs generally.

Head Start then brought together an amalgam of education, health, and social services as part of the War on Poverty at a time when awareness of academic disadvantage among children entering school encouraged use of center care as a context for compensatory education. The popularity of Head Start spread to the onlookers as well and sparked and went hand-in-hand with an enlivened interest in preschool education and the educational potential of day care for any child.

Important forces joined to create a broad day-care movement, going beyond the War on Poverty to give the movement universal scope and purpose. The extent of maternal employment gave day care a degree of universality as maternal employment increased, until one-third of the mothers of preschoolers and half the mothers of school-agers were working (U.S. Department of Labor, 1972). The increasing universalization of maternal employment brought a tolerant attitude toward working and day care. In 1971 child care for working mothers became a substantial tax deduction. The Revenue Act of 1971 allowed up to four hundred dollars monthly deduction for day care and household services (or disabled dependent care). Deductions are reduced for those with adjusted gross incomes over eighteen thousand dollars (Internal Revenue Service, 1972). After the tax revision went into effect in 1972, deductions by working mothers for day care and other household expenses increased sixfold and amounted to $900 million for those with rates up to 20 percent (*Day Care and Child Development Reports*, 1974), an estimated tax break of $180 million for lower- and especially middle-income families.

Business and industry entered the arena as new auspices for day care. Before World War II, business organizations in the United States provided little child-care assistance for the working mother. During the war a few defense plants maintained child-care facilities for their employees but most of these closed at the end of the war. Today a small number of business organizations provide child-care facilities for the children of their employees (U.S. Department of Labor, Women's Bureau, 1971). Most of these programs have been established since the early 1960s, stimulated in part by federal subsidy. Deductions were permitted to businesses for construction and improvement of property for child-care facilities, and Title B of the Economic Opportunity Act provided financial assistance to unions and employers for day-care projects that would serve low-income families (Kleiman, 1973). Some large hospitals have added child-care facilities for the children of their employees (U.S. Department of Labor, Women's Bureau, 1970). Many colleges and universities have maintained nurseries and have responded to demands for day care as a means of securing equal opportunity for education among women students. In addition to small proprietary ventures, large day-care companies and some franchised operations have been established, raising concern about the compatibility of for-profit day care and quality of care (Featherstone, 1970; Roby, 1973).

Research encouraged a period of experimentation and a fresh look at the potentials of day care since effects of maternal employment were not by themselves found to be unfavorable (Herzog, 1960; Stolz, 1960; Caldwell, 1964). Children's Bureau-sponsored demonstrations of center care for infants and toddlers showed that the concepts of maternal separation and institutional deprivation could be separated (U.S. Children's Bureau, 1967). Local and national surveys of need emphasized consumer demand, preferences, and satisfaction with child-care arrangements (Lajewski, 1959; Low and Spindler, 1968; Ruderman, 1968; Johns and Gould, 1971). Children in nonlicensed facilities were counted, and horror stories created some alarm about the informal care (Keyserling, 1972). The Office of Child Development, apprehensive over the possibility of a major expansion of low-quality day care, raced to produce the needed research and to disseminate existing knowledge and experience for use in developing programs (Huntington, Provence, and Parker, 1971; Chapman and Lazar, 1971). The Office of Child Development (OCD), in 1970, convened an interagency panel on early childhood research and development which began a coordination and planning effort (Grotberg, Searcy, and Sowder, 1972). Day care became a context for research in language development, cognitive studies, play, problem-solving, and social-emotional development (Grotberg, 1971; Fein and Clarke-Stewart, 1973; White and others, 1973).

The politics of day care became increasingly strident. The women's movement ushered in egalitarian demands for subsidized day care as a right, justified as a means of giving women equal opportunity with men in education and employment (Roby, 1973). A group of senators and representatives held hearings and wrote several pieces of legislation to support the development of quality child care. The most far-reaching legislation, the Comprehensive Child Development Act of 1971, was passed but was vetoed by President Nixon and failed to obtain the two-thirds majority for an override. The concept of comprehensive day care had become a plank of liberal platforms. The term *comprehensive* was associated with a collection of ideas: (1) that day care would be developmental rather than custodial, meaning that it would contain such components as health care, nutrition, education, social services, and parent participation; (2) that such services would be made available universally to all families and not just to the poor or disadvantaged; and (3) that such services would be subsidized and involve a nationwide federal commitment to a system of quality day-care services.

The alternative to the comprehensive bill was the administration-favored Family Assistance Plan (FAP or HR1) that would restrict a less expensive form of care to a limited population at welfare risk.

Obstacles. In vetoing the Comprehensive Child Development Act of 1971 the President described the bill as "deeply flawed" and objected that "neither the immediate need nor the desirability of a national child development program of this character has been demonstrated" (*Report on Preschool Education,* 1971). The President's veto shocked the day-care movement and brought about a period of reappraisal.

Several obstacles to the expansion of day-care services had to be recognized. There was deep confusion and disagreement about what the goals of day care should be, what constitutes a day-care program, who should benefit, who would pay, and even whether the program could be delivered. The package was expensive and the problems of large-scale service immense. Lacking were the necessary administrative structures, manpower, training, maturity of professional and institutional growth, and even the basic know-how. There was an uneasy feeling that a comprehensive child development program, institutional in form, might bring about significant unanticipated changes in American life in addition to whatever benefits it might bring.

Since early childhood programs did not fit easily into any existing professional-institutional framework—health, education, or welfare—there were also jurisdictional barriers to expansion. The traditional social-work approach to day care was geared better to offering individualized family and child welfare services case by case than to developing a massive system. Early childhood education, however, although increasingly prepared to mount enriched programs for young children, was often at a loss to relate to extramural programs or to deal with parents except as they were ancillary to the educational program. Neither the agency nor the school provided a viable model for early child care.

Research reviews only revealed the complexities of the problems involved and the equivocal results of experiments with early childhood programs (Grotberg, 1969; Hellmuth, 1970; Jencks, 1972; White and others, 1973). An OCD-sponsored "review of the present status and future needs in day care research" (Chapman and Lazar, 1971), richer in the gaps it identified than in its body of findings, raised many questions for research. The report even called for studies of "how the needs of the vast majority of children, those cared for in their own homes or in family day-care arrangements, can be assessed and met. Perhaps the single largest need for demonstrations is the provision of comprehensive, cost-effective service to children in the unlicensed, mother-arranged settings" (Chapman and Lazar, 1971). A shift in attention was beginning to occur as the concept of day care expanded from its narrow focus on group care in centers until it could be described as follows: "The *central* mission of a day-care model is not to promote a particular caregiving arrangement but rather to conceptualize a set of procedures needed to develop optimizing environments in the home, playground, center, and school" (Fein and Clarke-Stewart, 1973).

Consumer Behavior

Impetus for the many day-care surveys came from a desire to estimate need or at least demand for facilities and expanded programs as evidenced in waiting lists, ratings of quality, preferences and expressions of dissatisfaction by users of one form of care who might switch to another, and projections of potential new demand by unemployed women who might go to work if a preferred form of child care were available.

Preference data suggest that most users prefer the type of care they are using (Johns and Gould, 1971); however, much depends on sampling and on the alternatives presented to respondents. Willner (1969) found that private family day-care users in New York City preferred center care, but his sampling was done from center waiting lists—that is, from the ranks of dissatisfied family day-care users. A national survey conducted by Westinghouse-Westat (Johns and Gould, 1971), while based on an area probability sample of families with incomes under eight thousand dollars and children nine years and under, obtained a preference for center care among working mothers by posing the question, "If you wanted to improve the day-care arrangement for your preschool child, what kind of day care would you like best?" Dropped from the analysis were the one-third of the respondents who gave a "don't know" answer (Johns and Gould, 1971). Emlen (1974) found a preference to stay home or to work part-time among users of family day care, options that were not open to them.

Among effective demand factors, cost is powerful enough to override most other considerations (Rowe and Husby, 1973), thus lending weight to the idea that government subsidy of day care would increase the quality of care. While studies of cost suggest that the labor-intensive character of day care appears to make quality expensive in centers, it is not clear that quality can be purchased or how. Abt Associates, in a study of day care in Maryland (Warner and Ruopp, 1974), found a diversity of costs associated with center quality, and it was not true that the more expensive the center, the better the care or the more services provided. Likewise, in private family day care Emlen (1973) found that while the amount paid reflected number of children, hours of care, and to a small extent family income, cost was not related to the consumer's evaluation of quality.

Consumers are probably not free to choose the day care they use solely on the basis of preference. Patterns of usage have been found to be related to other determinants such as income, family size, nonavailability of relatives, availability and accessibility of service, and feasibility of fitting the arrangements into family life. A study in Manitoba, for example, showed large differences based on family size, family structure, income, and parent's occupation between those who pay for commercial day-care facilities and families who use noncommercial subsidized services (Rutman and Chommie, 1973). A disproportionately large number of whites use family day care, 42 percent for whites versus 23 percent for blacks (Parnes, 1971). White-collar workers pay more than the blue-collar, domestic, and nondomestic service workers, and whites pay more than blacks in all occupational categories. Family day care is more expensive than care by relatives either in or out of home, thus it is a more available resource for white-collar whites. Users of family day care also tend not to have relatives available: 94 percent had no relative at home who could be a caregiver and 84 percent had no relative in the vicinity who could give care (Emlen, Donoghue, and Clarkson, 1974). These figures are consistent with the finding that by 1970 three-generational households had declined to 4.4 percent (Mondale, 1974).

Family size is one of the most powerful determinants of the child-care arrangement used. Of the children under fourteen of working mothers (if not cared for by the mother herself), 45 percent are cared for in their own homes if there is but one child in the family, compared with 73 percent at home if there are four or more children (Emlen, 1970b). For reasons of cost and convenience, the large family cannot easily send its children to out-of-home day care of any kind.

Family Day Care as a Social System

A series of studies have provided an understanding of why family day care (out-of-home care by nonrelatives) is used not just as an alternative to center care, but at all. Is it viable? What accounts for its stability and instability? The Portland studies attempted to explain the emergence of family day care as a system of care (Collins and Watson, 1969; Emlen and Watson, 1971; Emlen, Donoghue, and LaForge, 1971; Emlen, Donoghue, and Clarkson, 1974).

A study (Emlen, Donoghue, and Clarkson, 1974) of 116 family day-care arrangements, followed from beginning to the end, focused on characteristics of users and caregivers and on the sources of tension and satisfactions. The dissatisfactions that were disruptive were distinctly different for mothers and sitters. Critical for the mother was the adjustment of the child and critical for the sitter was her relationship to the mother since she herself tended to be happy with the child unless the mother's discipline or other behavior was a matter of concern. Critical for both mother and caregiver was the concern of the other woman for the child. Mutual satisfaction characterized most relationships, and a generally high level of satisfaction was sustained throughout the arrangement, despite some losses of satisfaction on specific issues by the end. However, there was evidence also of mother satisfaction at the expense of sitter dissatisfaction, suggesting some sources of inherent tension and instability in which the caregiver pays a price, such as an increasing feeling that the child is an emotional drain or increasing dissatisfaction with the mother's hours, demands, and lack of planning. The caregiver accommodates at some cost in role strain and emotional drain to the inconsistencies in mothers' schedules.

Arrangements were terminated mostly by the mothers, although caregivers were more likely to be dissatisfied. Some mothers and caregivers tolerated unsatisfactory arrangements for extended periods, and in general satisfaction levels for both mothers and caregivers were high; 80 percent of arrangements were terminated for extrinsic reasons, such as summer vacations and changes in residence, jobs, and marital status, reflecting changes in the circumstances of family life. Thus, a perspective emerged that revealed family day care to be well adapted to short-term purposes, a highly contingent rather than an inherently unstable form of social arrangement, dependent on the purposes for which it was used. It was found, however, to lend itself also to satisfactory long-term arrangements, provided the two families remained in the same location and the mother in her employment.

The degree of friendship or social distance maintained between mother and caregiver was a critical dimension of family day care. An optimal social distance appears to be maintained in which friends become more distant and strangers become closer. Though 75 percent lived within one mile of each other, as in other studies of family day care, only 17 percent were next-door neighbors. Most were in reasonable proximity yet maintained a friendly but definite social distance. Even the friendships that arose tended not to extend beyond the context of the arrangement itself or involve other members of the two families in joint activities.

In going beyond kinship resources, families apparently turned first to friends or prior acquaintances as an easy and useful approach to family day care. However, such relationships are less serviceable for permanent child-care arrangements. The dominant and most successful family day-care arrangement was between strangers rather than between initial friends or those with prior acquaintance. Within the context of a contractual relationship, friendly relations emerged. A tinge of anxiety over sitter possessiveness was usually not allowed to become disruptive; a variety of strains are part of the role.

Those arrangements started between friends, however, tended to be used only temporarily. The task of renegotiating a prior relationship from one of friendship or assumed friendship to one involving exchange of money for services proved to be hazardous either to the friendship or to the child-care arrangement: The arrangement was terminated to save the friendship or the friendship was lost. However, a well-negotiated contractual relationship between strangers was consistent with friendly relations, in which mutual satisfaction bred a special friendship that contributed to an enduring arrangement.

Caregivers tended to be older than working mothers by several years, though there were exceptions, such as a group of young sitters used by older mothers. Yet, even this counter-trend was consistent with a tendency toward a compensating fit in experience. Women with two or more years experience as working mothers used sitters with little experience as caregivers, while mothers who were new and inexperienced as working mothers tended to use experienced caregivers. The family of the working mother was most often a young family at an early stage of development (since it usually involved preschool children), while the caregiver was likely to have a school-age family. An analysis showed that even within family day care there tended to be three types of specialization by stage of family development: the very young child of the new working mother, the full house of preschoolers, and the school-age arrangement. In addition, some arrangements tended to involve large numbers of children, while others specialized in fewer children for longer and more flexible hours.

Almost all (95 percent) caregiver families were intact, while many working mothers were solo parents. The two families differed also in size; caregivers had larger families, partly because most of their families were completed.

The Portland study found caregivers to have sharply different work role preferences from mothers who entered the out-of-home labor force. Five work-role alternatives were posed to mothers and caregivers: full-time job outside home; babysit at home; stay home and not work or sit; part-time job outside; and other work at home. Part-time job outside the home was a first or second work role choice for 76 percent of working mothers but for only 28 percent of the caregivers. Among working mothers, most of whom worked full time, 75 percent gave either working part time or staying home as a first choice. Most caregivers, however, reported doing what they preferred: 45 percent were following their first choice, and 79 percent either a first or second choice among the role alternatives. Thus, the caregivers were homebodies whose preferences were relatively consistent with the roles they were performing.

The differences in family size, age, stage of development, education, and economic circumstances point to an empty-nest hypothesis to explain the phenomenon of family day care. There appears to be a complementary fit between the needs of the young family of the working mother and the older family of the caregiver, whose nest is partially or entirely emptied of young children. Less well prepared educationally for entry into the labor force, deterred by family size, and pushed less by economic need to work outside the home because of husband's income, the caregivers augment a modest family income to the extent of perhaps one or two thousand dollars a year by doing that for which they are best prepared by experience and inclination—raising children.

The Portland group also found extensive match-making by selected caregivers who assisted working mothers in finding other appropriate caregivers. In effect, they provided a service consisting of information and referral as well as recruitment and even protective responses (Emlen and Watson, 1971). These systems of prosocial behavior that initiate and support informal child care were an integral part of the neighborhood ecology of family day care. Together with informal child care itself, the supportive mechanisms formed a basis for a natural system of service delivery (Collins, 1973; Emlen, 1973). The usual success of day care by kith should not obscure the fact that, like all social systems, it generates stresses and strains that lead to the termination of some arrangements. Some failures are due to the pressures on care users and caregivers, others to inappropriate patterns of interaction between them.

Day Care as A Child-Rearing Environment

Evidence is lacking for a comparative assessment of the effects of the several types of day care on the development of the child. In some studies population differences and sampling biases have been problematic. For example, in one study which compared infant development in family day care and center care (Saunders and Keister, 1972) atypical caregivers and other experimental influences could not be separated from child and background differences, so that there was no way of knowing which to attribute the effects on the child to. Diverse populations use different types of day care for many reasons; thus, it is unlikely that research will make much use of random assignment of families in controlling for population differences, and insufficient attention has been given to weaker methods for dealing with population differences.

However, progress has been made in identifying critical dimensions of the day-care environment. Two classes of influences are important. First are those of the setting itself, its social structure and composition, space and architecture, play resources, planned experiences, and behavioral interactions. Second, there are the "external" yet mediating influences of parents, family, neighborhood, which are the context for day care and interact with it. Family circumstances, attitudes, and behavior also mediate the outcome of day care (Heinicke, Strassman, and others, 1973; Hess and others, 1969; Bronfenbrenner, 1970; Rowe and others, 1972; Schaefer, 1970; White and others, 1973). A variety of demonstrations have shown that interventions designed to strengthen parental functioning affect day-care outcomes for the child, whether day care means center care (Heinicke, Strassman, and others, 1973), family day care (Gray, 1970), or home care (Levenstein, 1970). Parent involvement, whether overt or covert and in its many forms, is an integral component of the day-care environment (Hoffman, 1971). Schaefer (1970) emphasizes that parents are the primary educational institution.

Concerns about children's environments have had two emphases: (1) the regulatory one designed to protect the child against harmful conditions or to provide the minimum conditions needed for development (Class, 1968); and (2) setting standards for optimal environmental conditions (Maas, 1971). Early child education and Head Start have been of the second kind. For example, in an effort to disseminate standards for optimal child development in day-care settings, the OCD sponsored a series of seven handbooks, such as *Day Care: Serving Infants* (Huntington, Provence, and Parker, 1971). Efforts to specify standards for children cared for outside the home have been mounted by such groups as the Child Welfare League of America, the American Academy of

Pediatrics, the ocd, and the Federal Panel on Early Childhood (White and others, 1973). Costin (1972), for example, urges certain requirements for the child-care programs, including understanding of individual needs and stages of growth, consistent nurturing, supportive emotional response to children's needs, attention to health and physical progress, and provision of a variety of stimulating experiences which can contribute to the development of the child.

Within the day-care setting, most attention has been given to group size and adult-child ratios, which have been of central concern in licensing and other regulatory efforts. For example, with the approval of a set of standards by the Department of Health, Education and Welfare in 1968, appropriate child-adult ratios for children of different ages became a central issue. The Federal Interagency Day Care Requirements of that date are as follows:

Family Day-Care Home. Infancy through six years: no more than two children under two and no more than five in total, including the family day-care mother's own children under fourteen years old. Three through fourteen years: no more than six children, including the family day-care mother's children under fourteen years old.

Group Day-Care Home. Three through fourteen years: up to twelve children but the child-staff ratio cannot exceed six to one; no child under three. When preschool children are included, the child-staff ratio should not exceed five to one.

Day-Care Center. Three to 4 years: no more than fifteen with an adult and sufficient assistants, supplemented by volunteers, so that the total ratio of children to adults is normally not greater than five to one.

The impact of licensing has been limited. Despite effective work in many areas of the country, licensing requirements frequently are rigid and inappropriate, and agencies understaffed. The average state staff-child ratio required for children under three is one to ten (Chapman and Lazar, 1971, App. F). National surveys of the child-care arrangements of working mothers have been disconcerting in revealing the small proportions of the target population reached or influenced by standards. The Westat survey (Johns and Gould, 1971) found that licensing had reached 90 percent of centers and 2 percent of family day-care homes. About 60 percent of the centers in the survey were proprietary, mostly owner-operated, in neighborhoods of single-family dwellings. One-fourth of all day-care centers were classified as providing developmental care, which involved both an educational program and a range of services. Most of these centers were subsidized, nonprofit, community-agency programs which had ample staff and served low-income families, one-parent families, and minority groups. Approximately 2 percent of the children under six from low- and modest-income families were in traditional day-care centers that might be described as providing developmental day care.

Licensing does not guarantee favorable staff-child ratios. A survey of quality of care (Keyserling, 1972), while inadequate in its sampling, documented the dismal level of quality found, especially in proprietary licensed facilities. Westinghouse-Westat's developmental-care facilities had an average ratio of one caregiver to six children; the others, though licensed, had a mean ratio of one to fourteen.

Family day-care homes stood in dramatic contrast. Of the homes with six or fewer day-care children, 98 percent were unlicensed. Yet the mean number of children in family day-care homes was only 1.6. Unlicensed family day care tends to be "self-regulating" at numbers below regulations, while center care has proved resistant to regulation of adult-child ratios.

Licensing has been criticized by the Pacific Oaks group in Pasadena (Prescott, 1970; Sale, 1972), whose studies of licensing processes suggest that regulation without consultation can be dysfunctional. Moreover, systematic research has yet to establish whether licensing, adequately done, has preventive effects. Surprisingly little research has been done on the licensing function. Its merits have been assumed, but the assumption may be unwarranted.

The family day-care home with many children (seven or more under six) appears to be a deviant phenomenon, not only in the low frequency with which it occurs, but also in the motivations involved (Emlen, 1973). Emlen found that caregivers with more education and with higher SES were those who were likely to take seven or more children under six. A multiple regression predicting total number of children under six in sitters' homes from demographic factors showed that sitters who are better off and mothers who are less well off are the ones who make full-house arrangements.

Thus, we might look to education and not poverty or simple economic need for a theory as to why some caregivers take on an unusual number of children. They become more like the small proprietary center, or what agencies refer to as the group day-care home, with children ranging up to twelve in number.

Most of the agency-developed and proprietary models that use residential homes as settings for day care employ high child-adult ratios compared with private family day care. Even closely supervised family day care homes, which in many places agencies attempt to keep filled to the licensing limit, are a different phenomenon. A difference of two or three children seems to be more than a difference in degree, involving qualitative differences in the activities likely to take place, in the child-rearing experience and skill required, and in the motivations of the caregivers. It is precisely this difference in scale that goes beyond the ordinary child-rearing experiences of the caregivers and calls into play the need for regulation and training emphasized by agencies.

Most of the detailed information about private family day-care arrangements has come from Spokane, Washington; New York City; Portland, Oregon; and Pasadena, California. Perry (1961, 1963) conducted a special exploratory inquiry regarding the caregivers used by employed mothers in Spokane. Willner studied unsupervised family day-care arrangements in New York City (1965, 1969, 1971) and found caregivers to be warm, nurturant, and competent persons. Similar conclusions were reached by Emlen (1973, 1974) in Portland and Sale (1973) in Pasadena. The major exception has been the finding in New York City of substandard housing conditions and lower levels of user satisfaction (Willner, 1969), which may be attributable to the housing conditions and neighborhood environment.

The most detailed comparisons of day care as child-rearing environments are those that were made by Prescott and Jones (1967) at Pacific Oaks College in Pasadena. They have identified and, by means of systematic observations using a Day Care Environmental Inventory, have measured differences in segments of children's activities in four different behavior settings: closed-structure centers, open-structure centers, family day-care homes, and own homes, which are also supplemented part time by nursery school (Prescott, 1974). In closed-structure centers teachers make most of the decisions; in open-structure settings children are encouraged to make choices. These types were associated with center size (Prescott, 1967), the most restricted activity being associated with larger, more routinized centers. Centers of large size (sixty or more children) were characterized by a constellation of conditions, such as philosophy, hiring practices, teacher behaviors, and use of space, that restrict opportunities for play and learning.

The impact of the setting on activities and behaviors within it was found along a number of dimensions. Prescott (1972) found centers offering large-muscle activity and promoting a sense of group membership but restrictive with respect to cross-age experiences, opportunities to observe adults in daily activities, nurturance, and expression of strong emotions. Marked differences were found in how a child gets into and out of activities, with decisions being made by adults 58 percent of the time in closed-structure centers, 20 percent in open-structure centers, 13 percent in family day care, and 7 percent in home care (Prescott, 1974). The difference was between adult pressure and facilitation. Structured activity transitions, such as lining up and waiting, averaged 24 percent of the child's time in closed-structure centers compared with less than 3 percent in either kind of home-based care (1974). Adult-child ratios, the number and kinds of people in settings, numbers of people, kinds of adult input, "softness" of the physical environment, availability of natural materials for play, opportunities for privacy, and variety of adult workers and events to which to respond are among the differences found. Educational experiences were found in all settings, though they were different in appearance, logic, and content.

The differences among types of day care as an interactional environment are theoretically significant for child development. Studies of activities and behavior at least have narrowed the gap in the effort to assess the probable effects of day care on the child.

Summary

In this chapter three histories are examined. One is the quiet, invisible growth of informal child care as the primary resource for supplementary care for the children of working mothers. Ninety percent of the children under age six are in informal modes of care, and half still remain at home. Among varied patterns, a viable substitute for kin and the extended family has emerged. With the use of friends, neighbors, and other nonrelatives who live nearby, child care by kith has become the dominant form of monetized out-of-home care.

Another history is better known: a visible and articulate day-care movement concentrated on the development of licensed facilities and comprehensive services. In the 1960s federal programs had the dual motives of fighting the effects of poverty through Head Start and of removing families from the welfare rolls; and proprietary centers of all sizes competed for the business of middle-class customers. Apotheosis of the day-care center prevailed until a Presidential veto of comprehensive day-care legislation forced a period of reappraisal. The forces behind the day-care movement are reviewed above as well as forces impeding it. Among the latter are high costs, lack of trained personnel and administrative readiness, and a general lack of knowledge on which to base large-scale departures from informal modes of child-rearing.

Throughout these developments, in a third history, research has played a role. Just as early work on the effects of maternal employment tended to ignore the form and quality of child care, research interest in the second half of the sixties shifted to intervention programs but tended to ignore antecedent or mediating effects of family variables. In enthusiasm for the compensatory powers of supplemental experiences in day-care centers and Head Start programs, emphasis was given to education, curricula, training, and cognitive development. Studies of infant day care and a wide variety of demonstration projects gave impetus to experimentation and expanded horizons of what was possible in child-development programing; however, most demonstration and intervention research took place within the context of day-care centers and developed models that would be expensive to deliver on a large scale.

Concern over the need for day care has led to a series of national and local surveys. While needs were never assessed satisfactorily, the surveys did produce findings on the extent of child-care arrangements and fragmented perspectives on preferences, satisfactions, and dissatisfactions. However, the assumption that day-care consumers have free choice is not supported; rather, patterns of usage were found to be related to such determinants as income, family size, and nonavailability of relatives.

Because of the labor-intensive character of formal day care, it is comparatively expensive, but the assumption that more expensive care is of higher quality is not well supported by the evidence. A wide diversity of costs are associated with center quality, and family day-care homes compare favorably by some criteria despite low pay and lack of some program elements.

Family day care is satisfactory to most users as well as caregivers. Caregivers are usually in somewhat better economic circumstances than solo parents who must work, and most of the caregiver's children are in school or have left home. They can remain in their own homes and provide the services they enjoy most, while adding a modest amount to family income. While child care averages a few months in duration, it may extend for years and is usually terminated for reasons extrinsic to the arrangement. Care contracted between strangers frequently results in development of friendship between caregivers and users; however, contractual relationships between friends frequently result in a cool relationship or a break in the arrangement.

Satisfactory research on the effects of different types of day care has not yet been done; however, progress has been made by identifying characteristics of day care that are theoretically significant for child development. The influence of the day-care setting on the activities and behaviors of children and caregivers is dramatic. Yet, since the research on effects of different types of supplemental care on child development is yet to be accomplished, it seems premature to decide that one or another is the best; no one type of care may be the best for all or even most children. More important, there is wide variation in quality of care provided within each type of care. Since several factors, singly or more often in combination, determine the selection and use of different types of care, there is a growing awareness that diversity may be inevitable and even functional.

6

Effects on Child

LOIS WLADIS HOFFMAN

In a previous review of the literature on the effects of maternal employment on the child, we pointed out that the earlier view that maternal employment had a great many effects on the child, all bad, had been replaced by a new outlook—that maternal employment had no effects at all (Hoffman, 1963b). We assumed, however, that maternal employment did have an effect. What the effect was might depend on the nature of the employment, the attitude of the mother, her family circumstances, social class, whether employment is full or part time, the age and sex of the child, the kinds of child-care arrangements, and a host of other conditions. But until the research questions had been properly defined and explored, we were not prepared to concede that there was no effect. While studies of maternal employment as a general concept yielded little, it was suggested that examination of the effects under specified conditions might prove more fruitful. To demonstrate, we tried to show that when the relationships between maternal employment and a child characteristic were examined separately for various subgroups, interesting patterns were seen. Thus juvenile delinquency did seem to relate to maternal employment in the middle class, although it did not in the

A previous version of this chapter was published in *Developmental Psychology*, 1974, *10* (2), 204–228.

lower class. Part-time maternal employment seemed to have a positive effect on adolescent children, although this was not equally true
for full-time employment or for younger children. The lack of consistent findings with respect to the effects on the child's independence
or academic· achievement was tied to the failure to examine these
relationships separately for each sex. And the mother's attitude
toward employment was seen as an important aspect of the situation that would affect her child-rearing behavior and thus mediate
the impact of her employment on the child.

It was hoped that such speculations would give rise to new
empirical investigations, but the intervening years have produced
few studies of maternal employment. About the same time our review was published, three others appeared: Stolz (1960); Siegel and
Haas (1963); and Yudkin and Holme (1963). Perhaps the overall
impression was not that maternal employment required more careful
study but that it should not be studied at all. Most of the more
recent studies reviewed here were only incidentally interested in the
effects of maternal employment on the child, and the few that
focused on this variable were modest in scope. However, segments of
the American population that contributed more than an equal share
of working mothers, blacks and single-parent families in particular,
previously were not studied at all. A few investigators have begun to
fill this gap (Kriesberg, 1970; Rieber and Womack, 1967; Smith,
1969; Woods, 1972).

Moreover, there have been some methodological improve-
ments. Few studies today would lump boys and girls together or fail
to consider relationships separately for each social class. Some have
focused only on one class, the professional mother being a particularly
popular subject (Birnbaum, 1971; Garland, 1972; Hoffman, 1973;
Holmstrom, 1972; Jones, Lundsteen, and Michael, 1967; Poloma,
1972; Rapoport and Rapoport, 1972). These studies have, in turn,
revealed the need to consider both the education of the parents and
the nature of the mother's job. The mother who works as a professional has a different influence from one who works in a less intellectually demanding and less prestigious position. Since jobs often
underuse the talents and training of women, education and the
nature of the job are important singly and in interaction.

Even methodologically, however, the studies leave much to

be desired. Family size and ordinal position were rarely controlled, although these variables relate to both maternal employment and most of the child characteristics studied. Failure to match on these variables may give an advantage to the working mother since her family is smaller, and small family size contributes positively to cognitive abilities, particularly in the lower class (Clausen and Clausen, 1973). The need to control on more than one variable simultaneously is apparent in a number of reports, while the crudeness of the social-class control is a problem in others.

The most distressing aspect of the current research situation is the lack of theory. The typical study uses the sniper approach—maternal employment is run against whatever other variables are at hand, usually scores on intelligence tests or personality inventories. Even when a study indicates a complex pattern of findings or results counter to the accumulated research, no attempt is made to explain the pattern or reconcile the discrepancy.

Furthermore, the typical study deals only with two levels—the mother's employment status and a child characteristic. The many steps in between—family roles and interaction patterns, the child's perceptions, the mother's feelings about her employment, child-rearing practices—are rarely measured. The distance between an antecedent condition like maternal employment and a child characteristic is too great to be covered in a single leap (Hoffman and Lippitt, 1960). Several levels should be examined in any single study to obtain adequate insight into the process involved.

To help counteract the generally atheoretical aspect of so much of the maternal-employment research, the present review tries to organize the data around five basic approaches.

Hypotheses

By what process might maternal employment affect the child? The ideas, whether implicit or explicit, in the research, which we discuss here, can be classified as follows: (1) Because the mother is employed, she and possibly her husband provide a different model of behavior for the children in the family. Children learn sex-role behavior largely from their parents. To the extent that a different role is carried out by the working mother than by the nonworking mother, the child has a different conception of what the female role is. The self-concept of girls is particularly affected. (2) The mother's emotional state is influenced by whether she is employed, and this state affects her interaction with her children. (3) Employed and nonemployed mothers probably use different child-rearing practices, not only because the mother's emotional state is different but also because the situational demands are different. (4) Because of her regular absences from the home, the working mother provides less personal supervision of her child than does the nonworking mother, and it is usually assumed that the supervision is less adequate. (5) Again, because of the working mother's regular absences from the home, the child is deprived, either emotionally or cognitively, or perceives her absence as rejection. These hypotheses are examined in the sections that follow.

The ultimate dependent variables that have been studied—that is, the child characteristics that are the focus of attention—can be classified as follows: (a) social attitudes and values; (b) general mental health and social adjustment and independence or dependence specifically; and (c) cognitive abilities, achievement motivation, and intellectual performance. These are considered throughout the chapter. In addition data on maternal employment and the child's academic achievement are reviewed in a separate section because most of these data are from simple two-level studies in which it is impossible to say what hypotheses are involved.

Working Mother as Role Model

Hartley (1961) observed that one experience common to all children of working mothers is that they "are exposed to a female parent who implements a social role not implemented by the female parents of other children" (p. 42). Since the child learns sex roles from observations of his parents, maternal employment influences his concept of the female role. More importantly, since one of the earliest statuses assigned to the child is that of gender, maternal employment presumably affects the female child's concept of herself and the behavior expected of her.

An impressive array of data supports this theory. Hartley (1961) found that elementary-school daughters of working mothers, compared with daughters of nonworking mothers, were more likely to say that both men and women typically engage in a wide variety of specified adult activities, ranging from using a sewing machine to using a gun and from selecting home furnishings to climbing mountains. They saw women as less restricted to their homes and more active in the world.[1]

That the division of labor between husband and wife is affected by maternal employment is well established. Husbands of employed women help more with household tasks including child care. While considerable traditionalism remains and working women engage in more domestic tasks than do their husbands, the division of household tasks is nonetheless more egalitarian when the mother is employed than when she is not (Blood and Hamblin, 1958; Hall and Schroeder, 1970; Holmstrom, 1972; Kligler, 1954; Szolai, 1966; Walker, 1970b; Weil, 1961). Furthermore, this difference is reflected in the children's perceptions, as seen in the Hoffman (1963c) study of those in the third through sixth grades and the Finkelman (1966) study of fifth and sixth graders. Children five years of age and older whose mothers work are more likely to approve of maternal employment (Duvall, 1955; Mathews, 1933); and King, McIntyre, and Axelson (1968) report that ninth graders whose mothers worked viewed maternal employment as less threatening to the marital relationship. They also found that the greater the father's participation in household tasks, the more accepting of maternal employment were the adolescent boys and girls.

Furthermore, daughters of working mothers view work as something they will want to do when they are mothers, as reported by Hartley (1960) in her study of elementary school children and in four studies of adolescent girls (Banducci, 1967; Below, 1969; Peterson, 1958; Smith, 1969). This attitude was also found in college women (Almquist and Angrist, 1971; Zissis, 1964) and as a background factor among working professional women (Astin, 1969; Birnbaum, 1971). Douvan (1963) and Roy (1963) found that adolescent daughters of working mothers were, in fact, more likely to be already employed than were daughters of nonworking mothers.

----

[1] When asked to indicate which activities women liked and disliked, the daughters of working mothers reported more liking and less disliking of all activities—household, work, and recreation.

Another closely related group of findings concerns the attitudes toward women's roles in general. Are working mothers' children less likely to endorse a traditional or stereotypic view of women than children of nonworking mothers? Douvan (1963) found that the daughters of working mothers scored low on an index of traditional femininity.[2] Vogel, Broverman, Broverman, Clarkson, and Rosenkrantz (1970) studied the relationship between the sex-role perceptions of male and female college students and their mothers' employment. Sex-role perceptions were measured by having subjects describe the typical adult male and female by checking a point along a continuum between two bipolar descriptions. Previous work with this scale indicated which descriptions were more typically assigned to each sex and also which were seen as positive or negative. In general, the positively valued stereotypes about males included items that reflected effectiveness and competence; the highly valued female-associated items described warmth and expressiveness. Both male and female students with employed mothers perceived significantly smaller differences between men and women, with the women being more affected by maternal employment than were the men. Furthermore, the effect of maternal employment was to raise the estimation of one's own sex—that is, each sex added positive traits usually associated with the opposite sex; daughters of working mothers saw women as competent and effective, while sons of working mothers saw men as warm and expressive.

This result is consistent with that of an interesting study by Baruch (1972a). College women were administered a measure developed by Goldberg (1967) in which subjects are presented with a number of journal articles and asked to judge the quality of the article and of the author; half the articles are given female authors and half male authors. Previous research by Goldberg had indicated that college women tended to attach a lower value to articles attributed to women authors. Baruch found that the daughters of employed women were significantly different from the daughters of

[2] This finding should be kept in mind in evaluating studies like Nelson's (1971) that use pencil-and-paper personality inventories. Many of these inventories are biased toward the questionable assumption that traditional femininity is the healthy pattern for girls (Constantinople, 1973; Henshel, 1971; Lunneborg, 1968).

full-time housewives in that they did not downgrade the articles attributed to women. Thus, the daughters of working mothers were less likely to assume lower competence on the part of women authors: "It is women whose mothers have not worked who devalue feminine competence" (Baruch, 1972a, p. 37). Meier (1972) also found among college students that maternal employment was positively related to favoring social equality for women. The most egalitarian ideology was held by daughters of women in high-status occupations.

But the relationship of maternal employment and sex-role ideology is not perfectly clear, particularly when a multidimensional sex-role ideology scale is used. For example, Baruch also developed a twenty-six-item Likert-type scale to measure attitudes toward careers for women. Scores on this scale, which dealt with the desirability of a career orientation in women, the compatibility of the career and family roles, the femininity of the career woman, and women's ability to achieve intellectual excellence, were not related to maternal employment. Rather, a positive attitude toward the dual role resulted when the respondent's mother worked and also had successfully integrated the two roles.

With a comparable sample, wives of graduate students in the Boston area, Lipman-Blumen (1972) found no relationship between employment of the wife's mother and responses on a measure of sex-role ideology. The scale was described in general terms as dealing with whether women belong in the home carrying out domestic duties and child care, with men responsible for the financial support of the family. Earlier, Hoffman (1963d) administered two separate scales, one dealing with husband-wife division of labor and the other with attitudes toward male dominance, to mothers who were less educated than Lipman-Blumen's subjects and represented a broader range of social class. The expected relationship was found on the first scale—working mothers favored a less traditional division of labor than did nonworking mothers—but no relation was obtained between employment and attitudes toward male dominance.

Not only is the role of the working mother different in content from that of the nonworking mother, but the motivation to model the working mother appears to be stronger. Thus, Douvan (1963) found that adolescent daughters of working mothers were more likely than daughters of nonworking mothers to name their mother as the person they most admired; and Baruch (1972b) found that college women with working mothers were more likely than those with nonworking mothers to name their mother as the parent they most resembled and the one they would most want to be like.

The effects of maternal employment considered in this light must be different for males and females. For one, maternal employment might affect all children's concepts of the woman's role, but it should affect only girls' self-concepts unless the mother's working also reflects something about the father. Douvan found that lower-class adolescent boys whose mothers worked full time were less likely than those whose mothers did not work to name their father as the person they most admired. In this class, maternal employment may communicate to the child that the father is an economic failure. McCord, McCord, and Thurber (1963) also found that lower-class boys from intact families whose mothers were employed during the boys' preadolescent years were significantly more likely than were the sons of full-time housewives to indicate disapproval of their fathers. Since these two studies were done, maternal employment has become much more prevalent, so it might be expected these findings would no longer prevail. However, two more recent Canadian studies report the same pattern. Kappel and Lambert (1972), in their study of children nine to sixteen years old, found that the sons of full-time working mothers in the lower class evaluated their fathers lower than did the sons of other full-time working mothers and lower than did the sons of the part-time or nonworking mothers in any class.[3] Propper (1972) found in a predominantly working-class sample that the adolescent sons of full-time working mothers were less likely than were the sons of nonworking mothers to name their father as the man they most admired. The finding by Vogel and his colleagues (1970) discussed previously suggests however that, at least among middle-class males, the father whose wife works may be seen as a nurturant figure, possibly because of his taking over some of the child-care roles. In any case, maternal employment more clearly defines the mother's role change than the father's, and thus the effect on the daughter may be more pronounced.

[3] This finding was obtained from Tables 3 and 5 of the Kappel and Lambert study and was not discussed by the authors.

Nevertheless, there have been few studies of the effect of maternal employment on the daughter's self-esteem, and they have not always had the expected results. Baruch (1972b) found no relationship between maternal employment and the self-esteem of college women, as measured by the Coopersmith Self-Esteem Inventory. The daughters of working mothers with positive career attitudes tended to have higher self-esteem, but this relationship was not statistically significant. Kappel and Lambert (1972), using a semantic-differential-style self-esteem measure with 3,315 Canadian children nine to sixteen years old, found that the daughters of nonworking mothers were lower in self-esteem than were the daughters of part-time working mothers but higher than the daughters of full-time working mothers. The daughters of full-time working mothers had higher self-esteem than did those of the nonworking group, however, when any one of the following conditions existed: the mother worked for self-oriented reasons, was satisfied with work, or was a professional.

Despite the inconclusive findings on self-esteem, for girls, maternal employment seems to contribute to a greater admiration of the mother, a concept of the female role that includes less restriction and a wider range of activities, and a self-concept that incorporates these aspects of the female role. Douvan (1963) found the adolescent daughters of working mothers to be relatively independent, autonomous, and active, and other studies suggest that this may be true for younger girls as well (Hoffman, 1963b). For boys, maternal employment might influence their concept of the female role, but what the effects are on their attitudes toward their father and themselves depends very much on the circumstances surrounding the mother's employment.

The daughter of a working mother, then, should have higher academic and career aspirations and show a higher level of achievement than the daughter of a nonworking mother. Considerable evidence for this assumption comes from studies of college women. Almquist and Angrist (1971) found that career-oriented college women were more likely to be the daughters of working women, and Tangri (1969) found that college women who aspired to careers in the less conventionally feminine areas were more likely to be the daughters of working women. In studies of highly educated professional women, both Ginzberg (1971) and Birnbaum (1971) found maternal employment a significant background factor.

Studies of the achievement motivation or academic success of younger children provide neither overwhelming support nor clear refutation of the role-model explanation. The data are consistent with such a theory, but the investigations have not been designed to pinpoint the process by which the independent and dependent variables are linked. Many studies have not examined the relationships separately for male and female subjects, an essential step for applying the results to the role-model hypothesis. For example, Powell (1963) obtained projective-test measures of achievement motivation from subjects four times, at ages nine, ten, eleven, and twelve. The children of working mothers had higher achievement motives, but the relationship was significant only at age nine. However, the data were not reported separately by sex. Jones and coworkers (1967), using a similar measure, compared sixth-grade children of professionally employed mothers with a matched sample whose mothers were full-time housewives. The children of professional women showed a higher achievement motive, but the difference was not statistically significant. The relationship might have been stronger in these two studies if the girls had been examined alone.

In some cases the predicted child behavior may not be found because there is a counter-influence at work. For example, the study by Kappel and Lambert (1972) suggests that when maternal employment involves conflict and difficulties, as it does sometimes with full-time employment, the daughter's self-esteem is not enhanced.

In other cases, the empirical data seem to support the role-model rationale, but other processes could also explain the result. For example, the study by Jones and coworkers (1967) showed that children of professional mothers were better readers than were the children of full-time housewives. Although their subjects were matched by socioeconomic status, the professional mothers were better educated than the housewives, more time was spent with the child in reading activities, and their homes included more books. One wonders whether the process involved was modeling or the more stimulating home environment that the professionally employed mothers provided. In short, while the parental roles in the employed-mother family may exert influence in a particular direction, other factors associated with maternal employment might exert influence in the same direction. The conceptual gap between maternal employment and a child trait is too great to be covered in simple two-level studies. A better test of the hypothesis would involve examination of the many intervening steps in the modeling process: the content of the roles, the attitudes toward the roles, the child's motivations to model various aspects of the roles, and the development in the child of the skills needed to implement the appropriate behaviors.

Nevertheless, it does seem clear that when a mother works she provides a different model of behavior for the children in the family, particularly for the girls. Further, the hypothesis that this difference is important for the daughter's concept of sex roles and thus presumably for her self-concept makes sense. Traditional sex-role stereotypes in the United States assign a lower status to women than to men and include the view that women are less competent. Maslow, Rand, and Newman (1960) described one effect: "The woman in order to be a good female may feel it necessary to give up her strength, intelligence, or talent, fearing them as somehow masculine and defeminizing" (p. 208). Another effect has been empirically documented by Horner (1972)—that women who dare to achieve do so with anxiety and ambivalence about their success. The role of working mother is less likely to lead to traditional sex-role stereotypes and more likely to communicate competence and the value of the woman's contribution to the family. She may have higher status in the family and appear to her daughter as a person who is capable in areas that are, in some respects, more salient to a growing girl than are household skills.

To summarize: From the standpoint of the role-model theory, the data indicate that maternal employment is associated with less traditional sex-role concepts, more approval of maternal employment, and a higher evaluation of female competence. These in turn should imply a more positive self-concept for the daughters of working compared with nonworking mothers and better social adjustment, but there are only indirect data on this. The idea that daughters of working mothers are more independent because they model their more independent mothers finds some support. Evidence also suggests that daughters of working mothers have higher achievement aspirations, but it has not yet been demonstrated that the abilities of the child are affected by the different role model provided by the working mother.

Mother's Emotional State

Morale. The assumption that the mother's emotional state is influenced by whether she is employed and that this affects her adequacy as a mother underlies several different approaches. One type of hypothesis, for example, relies on the commonly accepted belief that good morale improves job performance. Since this theory has validity in the industrial setting (Roethlisberger and Dickson, 1939), why not in the home? In fact, there is some support for it. Yarrow, Scott, DeLeeuw, and Heinig (1962) examined child-rearing patterns by interviewing four groups of mothers of elementary school children: mothers who worked and preferred to work, mothers who worked and preferred not to work, nonworking mothers who preferred to work, and nonworking mothers who preferred not to work. Among the nonworking mothers, satisfaction with their lot made a significant difference. The satisfied nonworking mothers obtained higher scores on a measure of adequacy of mothering. However, satisfaction did not differentiate the working mothers. One should keep in mind that when this study was conducted it was more socially acceptable to say, "Yes, I am working, but I wish I could be home all the time with my children" than it was to say, "Yes, I am home all day with my children, but I wish I were out working," so that some workers may not have been as dissatisfied as they indicated. By the same token, the dissatisfaction of the homemaker may have been more extreme, and her dissatisfaction more closely linked to the mothering role itself—that is, the very role with which she was indicating dissatisfaction included mothering. Of all four groups, the lowest scores on adequacy of mothering were obtained by the dissatisfied homemaker; the highest, by the satisfied homemaker. When the motives for choosing full-time homemaking were considered, those women who stressed duty as the basis for the choice had the lowest scores of all.

The real issue may be: Would the working mother who enjoys her work be dissatisfied as a full-time homemaker? The data of Yarrow and coworkers (1962) suggest that the satisfied working mother may not be as adequate a parent as the satisfied nonworking mother but she is more adequate than the dissatisfied nonworking mother. Birnbaum (1971) compared professionally employed mothers with mothers who had graduated from college "with distinction" but had become full-time homemakers—that is, women who had the ability to pursue professional careers had they so chosen. Both groups were about fifteen to twenty-five years past their bachelor's degree at the time they were interviewed. The professional women were clearly higher in morale. The nonworking mothers had lower self-esteem, a lower sense of personal competence—even with respect to child care skills—felt less attractive, expressed more concern over identity issues, and indicated greater feelings of loneliness. The nonworking mothers were even more insecure and unhappy in these respects than professional women who had never married. Asked what they felt was missing from their lives, the predominant answer from the two groups of professional women was time, but for the housewives it was challenge and creative involvement.

The mothers were also compared with respect to orientation toward their children. In response to the question "How does having children change a woman's life?" the full-time homemakers stressed the sacrifice that motherhood entailed significantly more often than did the professional women, who answered more often in terms of enrichment and self-fulfillment. Although both groups mentioned the work and the demanding aspects of motherhood, the homemakers stressed duty and responsibility to a greater extent, indicated more anxiety about their children, especially the children's achievements, and stressed their own inadequacies as mothers. In response to a projective picture showing a boy and his parents with a crutch in the background, the homemakers told more dramatic, depressed, and anxious stories. The professional women responded positively to the growing independence of their children, while the homemakers indicated ambivalence, regret, and seemed to be concerned about the loss of familiar patterns or their own importance.

The Birnbaum (1971) study includes no direct data on the children themselves, but the pattern of the able, educated, full-time homemakers suggests that they would have shortcomings as mothers, particularly as their children approached adolescence. At that time, when the child needs a parent who can encourage independence and instill self-confidence, the anxieties and concerns of these women and their own frustrations might operate as a handicap.

There are additional studies suggesting that when work is a source of personal satisfaction for the mother, her role as mother is positively affected. Kligler (1954) found that women who worked because of interest in the job were more likely than were those who worked for financial reasons to feel that there was improvement in the child's behavior as a result of employment. Kappel and Lambert (1972) found that the nine to sixteen-year-old daughters of full-time working mothers who were working for self-oriented reasons had higher self-esteem and evaluated both parents more highly than did either the daughters of full-time working mothers who were working for family-oriented reasons or the daughters of nonworking mothers. In this study the measures of the mother's motives for working and the child data were obtained independently. In the studies by Yarrow and coworkers (1962), Birnbaum (1971), and Kligler (1954), the mother was the source of all the data. Woods (1972) studied fifth graders in a lower-class, predominantly black urban area, where almost all the mothers were employed, and found that mothers who reported a positive attitude toward employment had children whose scores on the California Test of Personality indicated good social and personal adjustment.

Role Strain. Another dimension of morale focuses on the strain of handling the dual roles of worker and mother. The general idea is that whatever the effect of maternal employment under conflict-free circumstances, the sheer pressure of trying to fill these two demanding roles can result in a state of stress that, in turn, has a negative effect on the child. The main thrust of the argument of Kappel and Lambert (1972) is that part-time employment, and full-time employment when it involves minimal conflict, have a positive effect; however, full-time employment under most conditions involves strain and therefore has adverse effects. In Douvan's (1963) study of adolescent children in intact families, the only group of working-mother children who had adjustment problems were those of full-time working mothers in the lower class. This group of working mothers was the one for whom the strain of the dual role seemed to be the greatest.

In contrast, Woods (1972) found the children of full-time

workers to be the best adjusted; her sample, however, was lower class, from a population in which most mothers were employed and which included many single-parent families. Under these circumstances, the full-time employed mothers may have been financially better off than were the others and may have had more stable household arrangements to facilitate their employment. The mother's positive attitude toward employment was related to the child's adjustment, but her satisfaction with child-care arrangements also contributed to a positive attitude toward employment. In a sense then, although full-time employment of lower-class mothers did not seem to have adverse effects on the child, strain, as manifested in dissatisfaction with child-care arrangements, may have exerted such an influence.[4] To some extent, the attitude toward employment generally may reflect the mother's feeling of role strain.

Guilt. Still another possible emotional response to employment is that the working mother feels guilty about her work because of the prevailing admonishments against maternal employment. While this may result in some appropriate compensation for her absence from home, it may also be overdone.

Working mothers are concerned about whether or not their employment is "bad" for their children, and they often feel guilty. Even the happy professional mothers in Birnbaum's (1971) study indicated frequent guilt feelings. Kligler (1954) also notes that working mothers experience anxiety and guilt and try to compensate in their behavior toward their children. The research by Hoffman (1963c) provides some evidence for guilt on the part of the working mother and its effects on children. Third- through sixth-grade children of working mothers were studied, with each working-mother family matched to a nonworking-mother family on father's occupation, sex of child, and ordinal position of child. The data included questionnaires filled out by the children, personal interviews with the mothers, teacher ratings, and classroom sociometrics. The working mothers were divided into those who indicated that they liked working and those who disliked it. Working mothers who liked work, when compared with the nonworking matched sample, had

---

[4] The study does not indicate whether the woman's satisfaction reflected the objective conditions; the mother's perceptions and the child's report of the situation were significantly but not highly related.

more positive interaction with the child, felt more sympathy and less anger toward the child in discipline situations, and used less severe discipline techniques. However, children of these working mothers appeared to be less assertive and less effective in their peer interactions. Their intellectual performance was rated lower by teachers, scores on the school intelligence tests were lower, and they helped somewhat less in household tasks than did the children of nonworking mothers. Thus, the overall pattern seemed to indicate that the working mother who liked work not only tried to compensate for her employment but may have overcompensated. These data were collected in 1957, when popular sentiment was opposed to maternal employment. As a result the women may have felt guilty about working, and in trying to be good mothers they may have gone too far since the children's behavior suggested a pattern of overprotection or "smother love."

The mothers who did not like work showed a different pattern. They seemed less involved with the child; for example, they indicated less frequent disciplining and somewhat fewer positive interactions compared with nonworking mothers. The children helped with household tasks to a greater extent than did the children of nonworking mothers and were more assertive and hostile toward their peers. Their school performance as rated by their teachers was lower, but they did not perform more poorly on the school intelligence tests. The total pattern suggested some neglect of these children in comparison with those in the nonworking matched sample. The working mothers who disliked work had less reason to feel guilty since they were working for other than self-oriented reasons.

Effects on Child. A complicated picture is presented if the working mother's emotional state is considered in relation to the child characteristics most often linked to maternal employment: the child's attitudes, mental health and social adjustment (independence-dependence specifically), and cognitive abilities and orientations. There are some indications that the tendency of children of working mothers to have a positive attitude toward their mothers' employment is enhanced when the employment is accompanied by a minimum of conflict and strain for the mother (Baruch, 1972a; King and coworkers, 1968).

When maternal employment is satisfying to the mother, either because it is more easily incorporated into her activities or because it is intrinsically gratifying, the effects on the child may be positive. The effects are more clearly positive—as indicated by various measures such as an "adequacy-of-mothering" score, the child's self-esteem, the child's adjustment score on the California Test of Personality, and attitudes toward parents—for mothers satisfied with their work compared either with full-time housewives who would prefer to work (Yarrow and others, 1962) or with mothers whose employment is accompanied by strain and harassment (Douvan, 1963; Kappel and Lambert, 1972; Woods, 1972). When children are approaching or into adolescence or when the mother is particularly educated and able, the working-mother role may be more satisfying than the role of full-time housewife, making the working mother less anxious and more encouraging of independence in her children than the nonworking mother (Birnbaum, 1971). However, the working mother with younger children who likes work might feel guilty and thus overcompensate, with adverse effects for the child in the form of passivity, ineffectiveness with peers, and low academic performance (Hoffman, 1963c). Thus the data about the mother's emotional state suggest that the working mother who obtains satisfaction from her work, who has adequate arrangements so that her dual role does not involve undue strain, and who does not feel so guilty that she overcompensates is likely to do quite well and, under certain conditions, better than the nonworking mother.

Child-Rearing Practices

Is the child of a working mother subject to different child-rearing practices and how do these practices affect the child's development? In discussing the different role models presented in the working-mother families, we have indicated that the child-rearing functions are more likely to be shared by both parents. The fact that the child then has a more balanced relationship with both parents has generally been viewed with favor. The active involvement of the father has been seen as conducive to high achievement in women, particularly when he is supportive of independence and performance (Ginzberg, 1971; Hoffman, 1973), and to the social adjustment of boys (Hoffman, 1961), as well as to the general adjustment of both boys and girls (Dizard, 1968).

Data also indicate that the working mother's family is more likely than the nonworking mother's to include someone outside the conjugal family who participates in child care (Hoffman, 1958; U.S. Department of Labor, 1972). This situation undoubtedly operates as a selective factor since the presence of the grandmother, for example, might make it easier for the mother to go to work; but the effects of this pattern have not been widely examined. The specific issue of multiple mothering and frequent turnover in baby-sitters is discussed later, primarily in terms of effects on the infant and the young child, for whom these issues are most meaningful.

Considerable evidence indicates that working mothers, particularly in the middle class, try to compensate for working. This compensation is made explicit by respondents in some studies (Jones and coworkers, 1967; Kligler, 1954; Rapoport and Rapoport, 1972), while in others it is revealed in the pattern of working-nonworking differences obtained. As examples of the latter, Yarrow and her colleagues (1962) found that the college-educated working mothers compensated by having more planned activities with children, and the professional mothers in Fisher's (1939) early study spent as many hours with their children as did the full-time homemakers. Mothers employed as professionals spent more time reading with their sixth-grade children than did nonworking mothers, though this attention was part of a generally greater stress on educational goals, not just compensation for employment (Jones and coworkers, 1967).

When the working mother tries to make up for her employment, she often makes certain implicit judgments about what the nonworking situation is like. These judgments may be quite inaccurate. The working mothers in Hoffman's (1963c) study who required less household help from their children than did the non-working mothers are a case in point. And, in general, the nonworking mother is not necessarily interacting with her child as much as is imagined or as pleasantly. There is a great deal of pluralistic ignorance about the mothering role, and many mothers may be measuring themselves against, and trying to match, an overidealized image. Because the nonworking mother may spend relatively little time in direct positive interaction with her child, the working mother's deliberate efforts might add up to more total positive interaction time. Comparisons indicate that the nonworking women spend more time in total child care (Robinson, 1971; Walker and Woods, 1972). These reports, however, are geared toward other purposes and are not helpful in providing information about parent-child interaction. In most cases, working and nonworking women are compared without regard to whether they are mothers. Obviously the nonworking women include more mothers so that they do, as a group, spend more time in child care. Even when only mothers are compared, the number of children in the family and their ages are not considered, and the kind of child care is often not specified. There is an unfortunate gap in our knowledge about how much of the day the nonworking mother spends interacting with her child.

Independence Training. Several studies have focused on whether the working mother encourages independence and maturity in her children more than does the nonworking mother. The answer seems to depend on the age of the child and the social class or education of the mother. In the work of Yarrow and her colleagues (1962), the working mothers who had not gone to college were more likely to stress independence training and to assign the children a greater share of the household responsibilities. The college-educated working mothers did not show this pattern and in fact showed a nonsignificant tendency in the opposite direction. The subjects in this study were similar to Hoffman's (1963c) respondents in that the children were elementary school age; and the college-educated working mothers in the Yarrow study exhibited a pattern similar to the working women who liked work in the Hoffman study. Burchinal and Lovell (1959) report that working mothers of older children were more likely to stress independence than were nonworking mothers, and stress on independence and responsibility can be inferred as more characteristic of the working mothers in the national sample study of adolescent girls reported by Douvan (1963), although the data rely more on what the girl is like than on parental child-rearing practices. Birnbaum's (1971) study of professionally employed mothers with children of various ages also suggests encouragement of independence. The study by Von Mering (1955) is often cited as evidence that professional mothers stress independence training in elementary school children, but since there were only eight mothers in the sample such conclusions do not seem justified.[5]

[5] Propper (1972) found that the adolescent children of working

A longitudinal study of lower-class boys from intact families, begun in the 1930s, suggests that the relationship between maternal employment and independence training is contingent on the family milieu (McCord and coworkers, 1963). With boys between ten and fifteen, in families judged to be stable by a composite index, working mothers were less overprotective and more supportive of independence than were nonworking mothers. These differences were not obtained for unstable families, and the sons of the working mothers in this group proved to be the most dependent subjects in the entire sample. Because their mothers did not seem to be the most encouraging of dependency, their dependent behavior was interpreted by the authors as a response to feelings of rejection rather than to parental patterns of independence training.

The data are quite sketchy, but the general picture is that except for working mothers who have younger children (elementary school age) and who are educated or enjoy work and possibly except for working mothers in unstable families, working mothers stress independence training more than do nonworking mothers. This is consistent with what one would expect. It has already been indicated that the more educated working mothers try to compensate for their employment. Thus they would be expected to avoid pushing the younger children into maturity, stressing the nurturant aspects of their role to make up for their absence at work. As the child grows older, independence is called for. To the nonworking mother the move from protector and nurturer to independence trainer is often difficult. For the working mother, however, the child's growing independence eases her role strain. Furthermore, the psychological threat of becoming less essential to the child is lessened by the presence of alternative roles and sources of self-worth.

The evidence for the effect of this pattern on the child is not definitely established. Two studies—Hoffman (1963c) and McCord and coworkers (1963)—examined data at each of three levels: employment status, child-rearing behavior, and child characteristics;

---

mothers were more likely to report disagreements with parents but were not different from the children of nonworking mothers in feelings of closeness to parents, parental interest, and support. The overall pattern may indicate more tolerance of disagreement by the working mothers rather than a more strained relationship. This interpretation fits well with the general picture of working mothers' encouraging independence and autonomy in adolescent children.

but the findings are ambiguous. Hoffman did not directly examine the relationship between maternal behavior and the child characteristics; McCord and her colleagues did but failed to find a significant association between independence training and independence. Other relevant maternal employment studies did not obtain separate data on the child-rearing patterns and the child characteristics. But several child-development studies that have no data on maternal employment have found that parental encouragement of independence was related to high achievement motivation, competence, and achievement behavior in both males and females (Baumrind and Black, 1967; Hoffman, 1972; Winterbottom, 1958).

Household Responsibilities. Most data indicate that the child of the working mother has more household responsibilities (Douvan, 1963; Johnson, 1969; Propper, 1972; Roy, 1963; Walker, 1970a); the exceptions are younger children whose mothers are more educated or who enjoy work. Although working mothers may sometimes deliberately avoid giving the child household responsibilities, such participation by children has generally been found to have a positive, not a negative, effect (Clausen, 1966; Johnson, 1969; Woods, 1972). Obviously, this does not mean overburdening the child; but expecting the child to be one of the effectively contributing members of the family seems conducive to the development of social adjustment and responsibility.

Parental Control. What other effects of maternal employment on child-rearing practices might be expected? One hypothesis might be that the working mother leaves her child more often without care or supervision. This is the focus of the next section, but by and large, there is little evidence that this is the case. Another hypothesis is that because of the demands imposed by her dual role, the working mother in contrast to the nonworking mother might be stricter and impose more conformity to a specified standard. That is, just as reality adaptation might lead her to encourage the child to be independent and to take on household responsibilities, she might also demand more conformity to rules so that the household can function smoothly in her absence. Some evidence for this pattern exists among the less educated groups. Yarrow and others (1962) found that the children of working mothers in their noncollege group were generally under firmer parental control than were the children of nonworking mothers. Woods (1972) found more consistency between principles and practice in the discipline used by the full-time working mothers in her lower-class, predominantly black sample, although Yarrow and coworkers (1962) found greater inconsistency in her college-educated working mothers.

Still another possibility is that the working mother is milder in discipline because of conscious efforts to compensate or because of higher morale. Hoffman's (1963c) working mothers, especially those who liked work, used less severe discipline and indicated less hostility in the discipline situation than did nonworking mothers. The focus in this study was however not on the content of the discipline but on its severity. Thus the data do not indicate whether the children were under more or less firm control but only that the discipline was milder.

A few studies, such as those that compared the child-rearing views of working and nonworking mothers and found no meaningful differences (Kligler, 1954; Powell, 1963), are not reviewed here, but most of the available data on maternal employment and child-rearing practices have been included. It is surprising how few investigations of maternal employment have obtained data about child-rearing behavior. Most of the studies have simply related employment to a child characteristic and then later speculated about any relationship found. If the daughters of working mothers are found to be more independent or higher achievers than daughters of nonworking mothers, one cannot tell whether these attributes are products of the working mother as model, the fact that the father is more likely to have had an active part in the girl's upbringing, the fact that the father in working-mother families is more likely to approve of and encourage competence in females, or because the girls were more likely to have been encouraged by their mothers to achieve independence and assume responsibilities. All these intervening variables have been linked to female independence and achievement (Hoffman, 1972, 1973).

Maternal Absence and Supervision

The most persistent concern about maternal employment has to do with the absence of the mother from the home while she is

working and the consequent fear that the child then lacks supervision, love, and cognitive enrichment. Earlier research on maternal
employment and juvenile delinquency often was based on this hypothesis: The mother was working, the child was unsupervised, and
thus the child would be a delinquent. There is some support for this
theory, despite the fact that maternal employment and delinquency
do not relate as expected. In the study of lower-class boys carried out
by Glueck and Glueck (1957), regularly employed mothers were no
more likely to have delinquent sons than were nonemployed mothers.
However, inadequate supervision seemed to lead to delinquency
whatever the mother's employment status, and employed mothers,
whether employed regularly or occasionally, were more likely to provide inadequate supervision. McCord and McCord (1959) also
found a tie between supervision and delinquency in their longitudinal
study of lower-class boys (which, unlike the Glueck study, included
only intact families), but there was little difference between the
working and nonworking mothers as to adequacy of supervision
(McCord and coworkers, 1963). Furthermore, the tie between the
adequacy of supervision and social adjustment conceptualized generally is not conclusively established. In the study by Woods (1972)
of lower-class fifth-grade children, inadequate supervision did not
have a statistically demonstrable adverse effect on boys, although
unsupervised girls showed lower school-adjustment scores on tests of
social relations and cognitive abilities.[6] Delinquency was too rare in
the Woods sample for any comparison, and the relationship between
maternal employment and the adequacy of supervision was not examined.

Even less is known about the linkage of maternal employ-

---

[6] The sex differences in the Woods study are both intriguing and
difficult to interpret. In most child-development studies, the girls show ill
effects from too much supervision or control, while the boys typically suffer
from too little (Becker, 1964; Bronfenbrenner, 1961; Hoffman, 1972). This
finding may reflect the higher level of control generally exercised over girls,
so that the low end of the scale for girls is not as low as for boys, either
objectively or subjectively. However, there have been few child-development
studies of the lower class, and lack of supervision possibly is more extreme
here than in the typical child-development sample. Thus the middle-class
girl who is unsupervised relative to other middle-class girls may not be at
the same level of neglect as that encountered by Woods.

ment, supervision, and delinquency in the middle class. Although middle-class working mothers express concern about finding adequate supervision for their children and a number of publications stress the inadequacy of supervision in families in which the mother works (Low and Spindler, 1968), it is not clearly established that the children end up with less supervision in either social class. Furthermore, although the adequacy of supervision seems related to delinquency in the lower class, this relationship is not established for the middle class. Nye (1958), for example, found a curvilinear relationship, both high and low supervision moderately associated with delinquency. It seems that these three variables should be linked in both the middle and the lower class, but there is little empirical documentation.

If we ignore the issue of supervision, what is the relationship between maternal employment and delinquency? In a previous review, we suggested that there seemed to be a relationship between maternal employment and delinquency in the middle class (Hoffman, 1963b). This relationship was found by Nye (1963), using a self-report measure of delinquent behavior, and Gold (1961), who used police contact as the measure; in both studies the relationship was obtained for the middle class and not for the lower class. In two other studies (Brown, 1970; Riege, 1972) no relationship was found between maternal employment and juvenile delinquency. Since there was no separate examination by social class or attention to relevant mediating variables, however, these studies are not illuminating in this discussion. Glueck and Glueck (1957), studying only lower-class subjects, found no tendency for the sons of regularly employed women to be delinquent despite the fact that their sample included broken homes, a variable that relates to both delinquency and maternal employment. They found sons of the "occasionally" employed women to be delinquent, but this group was clearly more unstable than were those in which the mother worked regularly or not at all. They were more likely to have husbands with poor work habits and emotional disturbances, poor marriages, or to be widowed or divorced. The Gluecks saw the occasionally employed mother as working "to escape household drudgery and parental responsibility"; but, in another view, the question is not why they went to work, since their employment was obviously necessary, but why they resisted regular employment. The delinquency of their sons seemed to be linked to family instability, the inadequacies of the father, or characteristics of the mothers reflected in their not being employed regularly rather than to maternal employment.

Two studies already mentioned supplement these ideas. McCord and others (1963) found no tendency for maternal employment to be associated with delinquency when the family was stable, but in the unstable families the sons of working mothers had a higher delinquency rate. The higher frequency of delinquency was clearly not due simply to instability; family instability was related to delinquency, but maternal employment in the unstable family further increased the risk.

Woods (1972), who included in her study results of psychological tests and information gathered from teachers and school and community records, found that the full-time, steadily working mother seemed to be a positive factor in the child's social adjustment. The subjects were 142 fifth graders, all the fifth graders in the school, 108 of whom had working mothers. In this context, in which maternal employment is the common accepted pattern, its meaning to parents and children is quite different. The author suggests that full-time maternal employment is a requirement of family well-being considering their economic circumstances and, as such, is respected and appreciated. This interpretation is consistent with our own earlier hypotheses about the meaning of maternal employment particularly among blacks (Hoffman, 1963b) and with other data (Kriesberg, 1970). A basic theme throughout both the earlier review and the present one is that the context within which maternal employment takes place, the meaning it has for the family and the social setting, determines its effects. In addition, the positive influence of full-time maternal employment in the lower class raises the question again of why some lower-class women resist full-time employment when their situation obviously calls for it. What characterizes these nonworking or irregularly employed mothers? They may have less ego strength; less competence because of their physical or emotional health, training, or intellectual ability; or more children. The data of the Gluecks (1957) indicate that the occasionally employed mothers were the most likely to have a history of delinquency themselves. In short, in addition to the value of the mother's employment to the family, the differences may reflect selective factors, and the employed mothers in these circumstances may be healthier, more competent, or in better circumstances with respect to family size.[7]

Consistent with the interpretation of Woods (1972) is the fact that the children in the study with extensive responsibility for household tasks and the care of siblings showed higher school achievement.[8] Like their mothers, they were meeting realistic family demands. The author is aware, however, that the causality might be reversed, that mothers give competent children more responsibilities. There are also other interpretations: For example, first-born children, particularly in lower-income families, usually have higher academic performance and are also those more likely to be given household tasks.

To summarize, the hypothesis that maternal employment means inadequate supervision has been invoked primarily to predict higher delinquency rates for the children of working mothers. There are data, although not very solid, that, in the lower class, working mothers provide less adequate supervision for their children and that adequacy of supervision is linked to delinquency and social adjustment, but there is not evidence that the children of working mothers are more likely to be delinquent. The data suggest instead that full-time maternal employment in the very low social classes is a realistic response to economic stress and thus, because of selective factors or effects, may be correlated with socially desirable characteristics in the child. Adequacy of supervision has rarely been studied in the middle class, although there is some evidence for a

---

[7] There are data that indicate that children from large families, particularly in the lower class, show lower school performance than do children from smaller families (Clausen and Clausen, 1973). Perhaps, then, it is not that full-time employment has a positive effect but that the full-time employed mothers have fewer children and the positive effect is a function of smaller family size.

[8] These findings seem somewhat inconsistent with Douvan's (1963) suggestion that the lower-class daughters of full-time working mothers were overburdened with household responsibilities. Douvan's subjects were older, and thus it is possible that they were more heavily burdened than were the fifth graders and more resentful of their duties. The Douvan sample was also white, while Woods's was predominantly black.

higher delinquency rate among children of working mothers in this group.

Maternal Deprivation

School-Age Child. For school-age children, little empirical evidence links maternal employment to maternal deprivation. Although Woods (1972) suggests that full-time employment may be interpreted as rejection by the middle-class child, there is no evidence in support of this interpretation. Instead, the evidence suggests that the children of working mothers tend to support the idea of mothers' working. Furthermore, as maternal employment becomes the norm in the middle as well as the lower class, it seems even less likely that the fact that a mother is working would lead to a sense of rejection.

The evidence as to whether the working mother does reject the school-age child has already been covered. Generally, the working mother, particularly in the middle class, makes a deliberate effort to compensate the child for her employment (Hoffman, 1963c; Jones and coworkers, 1967; Kligler, 1954; Poloma, 1972; Rapoport and Rapoport, 1972; Yarrow and coworkers, 1962), and the dissatisfied mother, whether employed or not and whether lower or middle class, is less likely to be an adequate mother (Birnbaum, 1971; Woods, 1972; Yarrow and coworkers, 1962). The idea that maternal employment brings emotional deprivation to the school-age child has not been supported (Hoffman, 1963b; Peterson, 1958; Propper, 1972; Siegel and Haas, 1963; Yudkin and Holme, 1963), perhaps in part because the working mother is often away from home only when the child is in school. In addition, if her work is gratifying, if she does not feel unduly hassled, or if she deliberately sets about to do so, she may even spend more time in positive interaction with the child than does a nonworking mother. While this compensation can sometimes be overdone and turn into overcompensation (Hoffman, 1963c), it may also be one of the important reasons why maternal employment has not been experienced by the school-age child as deprivation. In drawing conclusions from the research, one must keep in mind that the absence of negative effects does not mean that the mother's employment is an irrelevant variable; it may mean that mothers have been sufficiently concerned to effectively counter-balance such effects.

Infancy. More recently attention has been focused on the possible adverse effects of maternal employment on the infant and the young child. The importance of attachment and a one-to-one relationship in the early years has been stressed by Spitz (1945), Bowlby (1958, 1969), and others (Yarrow, 1964). Although most of this research has been carried out on children in institutions, with the most dramatic effects demonstrated among children whose infancy was spent in grossly deprived circumstances, it nevertheless seems clear that during critical periods cognitive and affective inputs can have important ramifications that affect an individual through-out life. Concern has been generated about this issue because of increased employment among mothers of infants and young children and new interest in day-care centers for preschool children. Here evidence is reviewed on both sides of this issue, although we really know very little.

Research suggests that without a one-to-one relationship with an adult, the infant may suffer cognitive and affective loss that can, in extreme conditions, never be regained. The importance of re-ciprocal interactions with an adult has been particularly stressed (Bronfenbrenner, 1973). There is some evidence of a need for cuddling (Harlow and Harlow, 1966) and a need for environmental stimulation (Dennis and Najarian, 1957; Hunt, 1961). These studies are often cited as evidence for the necessity of the mother's full-time presence in the home when the infant is young.

Extending these findings to the maternal-employment situa-tion may be inappropriate, however. Not only were the early Bowlby (1953, 1958) and Spitz (1945) data obtained from studies of extremely barren, understaffed institutions, but later research suggested that the drastic effects they had observed might be avoided by increasing the staff-child ratio; by providing nurses who attended and responded to the infants' cries, smiles and vocalizations; and by providing a stimulating visual environment. Further, age, duration of institutionalization, and previous and subsequent experiences of the child also affect the outcome (Rheingold, 1956; Rheingold and Bayley, 1959; Rheingold, Gewirtz, and Ross, 1959; Tizard, Cooper-man, Joseph, and Tizard, 1972; Yarrow 1964). Most important, however, institutionalization is not the same as day care, and day care is not the same as maternal employment. The inappropriateness of extrapolating findings on institutionalized infants to infants whose mothers are employed has also been noted by Yudkin and Holme (1963), by Yarrow (1964), and by Wortis (1971).

In addition, there is no evidence that the caretaker has to be the mother or that this role is better filled by a male or a female. Some evidence indicates that the baby benefits from predictability in handling, but whether this is true throughout infancy or only during certain periods is not clear, nor is it clear whether different handling has any long-lasting effects. Studies of multiple mothering have produced conflicting results (Caldwell, 1964). Child psychologists generally believe that there must be at least one stable figure to whom the infant forms an attachment, but this theory is not definitely established; and we do not know whether the periodic absence from the infant that is likely to accompany maternal employment is sufficient to undermine her potential as the object of the infant's attachment.

Nevertheless, a number of child-development studies suggest that within the normal range of parent-child interaction, the amount of expressive and vocal stimulation and response the mother gives affects the infant's development (Emerson and Schafer, 1964; Kagan, 1969; Lewis and Goldberg, 1969; Moss, 1967). Furthermore, although attempts to increase cognitive performance through day-care programs have not been very successful, efforts to increase the mother-infant interaction in the home appear to have more enduring effects (Bronfenbrenner, 1973; Levenstein, 1970, 1971). While there is no evidence that employment affects the quantity or quality of the mother-infant interaction, the voluntary employment of mothers of infants and young children has not been common and has rarely been studied. It is therefore important to find out whether the mother's employment results in less (or more) personal stimulation and interaction for the infant.

In addition to the importance of stimulation and interaction and the issue of emotional attachment for the infant, there are less fully explored questions about the effects on the mother. Bowlby (1958) and others (Hess, 1970) believe that the mother-child interaction is important for the development of the mother's "attachment," that an important source of maternal feeling is the experience of caring for the infant. Yudkin and Holme (1963), who generally approve of maternal employment, stress this as one of the real dangers of full-time maternal employment when the child is young (pp. 131–132):

> *We would consider this need for a mother to develop a close and mutually satisfying relationship with her young infant one of the fundamental reasons why we oppose full-time work for mothers of children under three years. We do not say that it would not be possible to combine the two if children were cared for near their mothers so that they could see and be with each other during the day for parts of the day, and by such changes in households as will reduce the amount of time and energy needed for household chores. We are only stating that this occurs very rarely in our present society and is unlikely to be general in the foreseeable future and that the separation of children from their mothers for eight or nine hours a day, while the effects on the children may be counteracted by good substitute care, must have profound effects on the mother's own relationship with her young children and therefore on their relationship in the family as they grow older.*

The issue of day care centers is not discussed in this chapter in any detail; however, our ignorance is almost as great here. While the cognitive advances expected from the Head Start day care programs were not adequately demonstrated (Bronfenbrenner, 1973), neither were there negative effects of these programs (Caldwell, Wright, Honig and Tannenbaum, 1970). Obviously, the effects of day-care centers for children of working mothers depend on the quality of the program, the time the child spends there, what happens when the child is not at the day-care center, and the alternatives.

Proponents on each side of the issue often use data from studies of the kibbutzim in Israel since all kibbutzim mothers work and, from infancy, the child lives most of the time in centers. Some investigators have been favorably impressed with the development of these children (Kohn-Raz, 1968; Rabkin and Rabkin, 1969),

while others have noted at least some deleterious consequences
(Bettelheim, 1969; Spiro, 1965). In fact, however, these data are
probably irrelevant. According to Bronfenbrenner (1973), kibbutzim
children spend more time each day interacting with their parents
than do children in the more conventional nuclear family arrangement, and the time they spend together is less subject to distractions.
The entire living arrangement is different, including the nature of
parental work and the social context within which interaction takes
place. The mother participates a great deal in infant care, breast-
feeding is the norm, and both parents play with the child daily for
long periods and without other diversions, even as he matures. Thus,
the Israeli kibbutz does not provide an example of maternal deprivation, day-care, or maternal employment as it is experienced in the
United States.

Few direct attempts have been made to study the effects of
the mother's employment during the child's infancy. These few have
had to cope with two special problems: (a) observed differences in
infancy are difficult to interpret in terms of long-range adjustment;
and (b) because the pattern of going to work when one had an
infant was previously unusual, there were often special surrounding
circumstances that made it difficult to ferret out the effects of employment per se. One way to handle the first problem is to compare
older children with respect to their mothers' earlier employment.
For example, Burchinal (1963) examined intelligence scores and
school adjustment for a large sample of children in the seventh and
eleventh grades. Children whose mothers had been employed when
the child was three years old or younger were compared with children whose mothers were employed only when the child was older
or whose mothers were never employed. Few statistically significant
results were obtained.

The second problem plagued the intensive longitudinal study
by Moore (1963), who compared children of elementary school age in
Great Britain on their mothers' employment history, with particular
consideration given to the nature of child-care arrangements. However, the groups contrasted were different in ways other than whether
the mother was employed at certain points in the child's life. For
example, the children who had been left by their mothers from early
infancy showed more dependent attachment to their parents than

did any other children in the study, and they also exhibited other symptoms of insecurity, such as nail-biting and bad dreams. However, Moore also indicated that the mothers who started work early in the child's life did not themselves seem as attached to the child. While this latter observation could have been a result of lack of close contact with the child, it is also possible that these mothers were different from the start and the child's disturbance reflected this difference more than the mother's employment. Since these mothers had sought employment when few mothers of infants worked, they may have been a more psychologically distinct group than one would now find. Indeed, Moore's case studies reveal patterns of emotional rejection; and, in some cases, the mother explicitly went to work to escape from the child. Furthermore, the mothers who went to work full time before their children were two years old often had difficulty finding good mother substitutes, and the data indicate that the stability of child-care arrangements was an important factor in the child's adjustment.

Obviously the effects of maternal employment on the infant depend on the extent of the mother's absence and the nature of the substitute care—whether it is warm, stimulating, and stable. However, while studies of maternal employment and the school-age child offer reassurance to the working mother, we have little solid evidence concerning the effect on the younger child.

Academic Achievement

Probably the child characteristics that have most often been examined in relation to maternal employment are those pertaining to academic achievement. These are reviewed separately since in most cases the data are too skimpy to be interpreted in terms of the five approaches discussed above. Included are studies of academic aspirations (usually whether the child plans to go to college), achievement motivation, intelligence test scores, and school performance. Most of the studies lack a guiding theory or even post hoc interpretations; the investigator rarely tries to explain why his data are consistent or inconsistent with other studies. The result is a hodge podge of findings. The more recent studies have analyzed the data separately for sex and social class, and this has resulted in complex patterns, but there is no apparent order in these patterns. Until this issue is tackled with more theoretical sophistication, there will be little illumination.

College Plans. Why would one expect college plans to be affected by the mother's employment? Possibly extra money in the house would make it easier for children of employed women to plan on college. In fact, mothers often indicate they are working to help finance their children's college education. Possibly, daughters, modeling active, occupation-oriented mothers' would be likely to seek college. This second hypothesis might be affected by the kind of work the mother did, particularly in relation to her education, and also by how she felt about her employment. None of these necessary additional pieces of data are available in the pertinent studies, so an interpretation of the results is impossible.

Roy (1963) found that among rural high school students, the children of working mothers were more likely to plan to go to college than were the children of nonworking mothers. This finding held for both sexes, although a general impression from Roy's tables is that the relationship is stronger for girls. (The report does not indicate whether this sex difference was statistically significant.) However, the children of working mothers in a "town" sample were less likely to go to college. (Here the difference for girls appeared slight.) The research supported the investigator's point that even within the same generally rural area, residence in the town or on farms was a meaningful distinction, but the data are insufficient for interpreting the results.

Banducci (1967) also examined the relationship between desires and plans for college and maternal employment, reporting the data separately by sex and father's occupation. His sample consisted of 3,014 Iowa high school seniors living with both parents. Three occupational levels were considered—laborer, skilled worker, and professional—presumably representing socioeconomic levels generally; "professional" in this study did not necessarily connote high educational achievement. For most subjects, males and females, maternal employment was positively associated with desires and plans for college. But for the group classified as professional, the opposite relationship prevailed; the daughters of working mothers were significantly less likely to expect to go to college, and the sons were less likely to expect or to aspire to go, the latter relationship being significant. How can we interpret this curious pattern of findings? Did the presence of a working mother indicate the lower socioeconomic end of the professional group? Were the working mothers employed in a family business, and thus the family was less education-oriented? The sons of these women also had lower grade-point averages, so there was something different about them, but whether an effect of maternal employment or some other peculiarity of this particular subsample was uncovered, it is impossible to say with the available information.

The several studies of college and professional women that associate maternal employment with ambitious career goals have already been cited (Almquist and Angrist, 1971; Birnbaum, 1971; Ginzberg, 1971; Tangri, 1969).

Achievement Motives. Two studies of children's achievement motives in relation to maternal employment measured achievement motives by scoring projective responses according to the scheme developed by McClelland and Atkinson (Atkinson, 1958). Powell (1963) obtained achievement motivation scores and maternal employment data longitudinally for subjects at nine, ten, eleven, and twelve years. The children of employed mothers showed higher achievement motivation at each age level, significantly for age nine. Several years after the Powell study was published, Jones and his coworkers (1967) carried out a similar study with sixth graders; they found a parallel but nonsignificant relationship. No mention was made of the earlier study. How valuable it would have been if they had replicated Powell's work by presenting data for nine, ten, eleven, and twelve year olds! Neither study analyzed the data separately for boys and girls, although a "modeling" hypothesis would suggest that the relationship might have been stronger for girls than for boys.

I.Q. Scores. Two studies of the lower socioeconomic class indicate that maternal employment and I.Q. scores are positively related. Woods (1972) in her study of fifth graders found that full-time maternal employment was associated with higher intelligence test scores as measured by the California Test of Mental Maturity, and Rieber and Womack (1967), studying preschoolers, found that more of the children of working mothers fell in the highest quartile on the Peabody Picture Vocabulary Test. Both these studies included blacks and single-parent families; the latter also included families of Latin American background.

The relationship between maternal employment and intelligence test scores in middle-class samples is more complex. Hoffman (1963c) found that, in a sample of white intact families, the children of working mothers who liked work had lower I.Q. scores than did matched children of nonworking mothers. Children of working mothers who disliked work, however, were no different from the nonworking matched group.

Rees and Palmer (1970) present a particularly interesting and complicated analysis of longitudinal data from a number of different studies. Their samples varied, but represented a generally higher socioeconomic group than the above three studies. Important differences appeared in data analyzed separately for boys and girls. In general, maternal employment related to high I.Q. in girls and low I.Q. in boys. Using as the independent variable the mother's employment status when the child was fifteen, they found that the daughters of working mothers had higher I.Q.s at age six and around age fifteen, although there was no relationship at age twelve. Was the working mother of the fifteen-year-old also working when the child was six? We do not know. The relationships for the boys were the opposite. The data were interpreted as reflecting a general association between nontraditional femininity and higher I.Q. in girls: the working mother represented to her daughter a less traditional view of femininity.[9] This theory, suggesting a negative relationship between traditional femininity and achievement in girls, has been discussed in detail by Maccoby (1966) and by Hoffman (1972), and data tying maternal employment to nontraditional femininity were discussed earlier in this chapter.

Academic Performance. Hoffman (1963c) found that the elementary school children of working mothers showed lower school performance than did the matched sample with nonworking mothers, using teacher ratings of performance to measure the dependent vari-

---

[9] Another finding of their analysis consistent with this interpretation is that girls who had a brother either just older or just younger also had higher I.Q.s.

able. Nolan (1963) found no difference for rural elementary school children and a difference favoring the children of working mothers in high school, but that study did not even control on social class. Neither study reported the data separately by sex.

Two more recent studies of elementary school children were directed to whether the mother was employed in a professional capacity. The reading achievement of the sixth-grade children of professionally employed mothers was compared with that of children with mothers at home matched by social class, sex, age, and I.Q. (Jones and coworkers, 1967). The children of the professional mothers were more proficient, perhaps because these parents spent more time in reading activities with the children, had more plans for their education, had more books in the home, and the mothers were better educated. The data were not analyzed separately for boys and girls. One implication of this study is that matching on social class is not the same as matching on education, and matching on the father's occupation is not the same as matching on income or life style.

The difference between employed mothers and professionally employed mothers is indicated in the study by Frankel (1964) of intellectually gifted high school boys. High and low achievers matched on I.Q. scores were compared. The low achievers were more likely to have working mothers, but the high achievers were more likely to have professional mothers. Although the socioeconomic status as conventionally measured did not differentiate the groups, education of the mothers (and possibly both parents) did. While the higher achievement of the children of professional mothers is easily interpreted, it is not clear why the low achievers tended to have nonprofessional working mothers. Frankel describes these women impressionistically as dissatisfied and hostile. This judgment may or may not be valid, but it would be worthwhile to compare women working at various levels of jobs on both selective factors and the effects of employment on the mother's psychological state. In Levine's (1968) study of women's career choice, the mother's education was found to be more important than whether she worked; Tangri (1969) found the mother's employment the more important.

Moving into the high school age, most studies found no differences in school achievement. Thus neither Nye (1963) nor Nelson (1969) reported significant differences, nor did Keidel (1970) in a comparison that matched on academic ability. In Burchinal's data (1963) one of the few relationships that remained significant, despite controls introduced on socioeconomic status, was the lower school grades of the eleventh-grade boys whose mothers were currently working. Roy (1963) also found that adolescent sons of working mothers had lower school grades, although only in his town sample. Banducci also reported that sons of working mothers in the "professional" socioeconomic class had significantly lower grades than did the sons of nonworking mothers, but in the "skilled-worker" class the opposite relationship prevailed: the sons of working mothers had significantly higher grades than did the sons of the nonworkers. No other differences in school grades were significant. Of the several comparisons by Banducci (1967) of scores on the Iowa Tests of Educational Development, a standardized achievement measure, the sons of working mothers in the lowest socioeconomic group, laborers, had higher scores than did the sons of nonworking mothers in that class. Brown (1970) found lower scores on the California Achievement Test for middle-class eighth- and ninth-grade sons of working mothers.

Farley (1968) compared self-reported grade-point averages of students in an introductory sociology course at Cornell University. The males who indicated their mothers were employed also reported significantly higher grades; there was no relationship for females, and no variables were controlled. If the data were solidly established, they would be interesting since several studies indicate that maternal employment is prevalent in the backgrounds of women who pursue professional careers, but whether their college grades are better has not been established.

Summary. Although there are some indications that maternal employment is positively associated with college plans of high school children, the opposite relationship has occasionally been shown. Per capita family income has not been controlled in these studies however, and maternal employment may sometimes reflect low income as well as augmented income.

There is evidence, however, that college-educated daughters of working mothers have higher career aspirations and achievements than do college-educated daughters of nonworking mothers. In one study daughters of working mothers obtained higher intelligence test scores at six and fifteen years of age. Two hypotheses, the modeling theory and the idea that independence training is stressed by working mothers, are particularly pertinent to the achievement of girls, and both predict higher achievement for the daughters of working mothers.

However, sons of working mothers may not fare so well (Hoffman, 1963b). This view receives a modest amount of support, and data suggest that the sons of working mothers in the middle class have lower academic performance. In the lower class, however, better academic performance is associated with maternal employment for both sexes.

Summary

The research reviewed in this chapter has been organized around five general hypotheses that seem to be implicitly involved in the expectation that maternal employment affects the child. These hypotheses are not mutually exclusive, and the various processes in fact interact, sometimes reinforcing one another, sometimes counteracting. The social scientist interested in this topic should ascertain the conditions under which one process or another operates and how these processes interact. It is important to understand the effects of maternal employment at this level so that predictions and action implications are meaningful for a changing society.

The first hypothesis is that maternal employment affects the child, particularly the daughter, because the role models provided by working and nonworking mothers differ. Although no single study has adequately investigated the hypothesis, accumulated findings provide considerable support. In general, maternal employment is associated with less traditional sex-role concepts and a higher evaluation of female competence. Daughters of working mothers compare positively with daughters of nonworking mothers, particularly with respect to independence and achievement-related variables. The effects of maternal employment are much less clear for sons, perhaps because the modeling theory is less direct for them and depends on how maternal employment affects the father's role.

The second hypothesis deals with the effects of the mother's emotional state on the child. Three different states were considered as mediating variables which tie the mother's employment status to the child's behavior: morale or satisfactions from employment status, emotional stress because of dual-role demands, and guilt about the child. There is some evidence for the occurrence of all these processes. Data support the idea that when the mother is satisfied with her employment status, she does a better job; and the full-time mother who avoids employment because of her "duty" to the child in one study obtained the lowest scores on "adequacy of mothering." However, mothers of young children and better educated working mothers may mar employment satisfaction by too much guilt. Role strain is more often a lower-class pattern since the working mother in the lower class is less likely to work by free choice and has more role conflicts because of large family size and more difficulty in making adequate child-care arrangements. The data, on the whole, suggest that the working mother who obtains personal satisfactions from employment, does not have excessive guilt, and has adequate household arrangements is likely to perform as well as the nonworking mother or better; and the mother's emotional state is an important mediating variable.

The third hypothesis is that maternal employment affects the child through its influence on child-rearing practices, but few studies considered the relationships between each of the three levels. Thus, in some studies, maternal employment increased the father's participation in child-rearing, while in others the active participation of the father had a positive effect on the child. But until an investigator measures all three levels and examines the relationships among them, we can not be certain that there is a direct connection or even that the father's activities that result from maternal employment are those that have a positive effect. As another case in point, with certain exceptions, as when the child is young, working mothers seem to stress independence training more than nonworking mothers and give their children more household responsibilities. Both these patterns have been linked to independence, achievement, and responsibility in children, but these relationships were not examined in the maternal employment studies.

There is evidence that working mothers, particularly in the middle class, deliberately try to compensate for their employment by planning specific activities and times for the child; whether this attention matches that of the mother who is not employed is unknown. Finally, data indicate that among the lower class, working mothers tend to exercise firmer controls.

The fourth hypothesis is that the working mother provides less adequate supervision. This hypothesis has often been the basis for the prediction that the children of working mothers are more likely than the children of nonworking mothers to be juvenile delinquents. The accumulated findings suggest that the children of lower-class working mothers are not more likely to be delinquent, although these mothers may provide less adequate supervision and this less adequate supervision is linked to delinquency. In the middle class, however, maternal employment has not been linked to inadequate supervision nor inadequate supervision to delinquency, but there is some indication that maternal employment and delinquency are related.

The fifth hypothesis is that the working mother's child is a victim of maternal deprivation. Studies of the school-age child offer no support for this hypothesis. Almost no research, however, has been carried out on the effects of maternal employment on the infant and preschool child. Child-development research indicates the importance of the early mother-child interaction, but no data are available on whether maternal employment affects the amount of stimulation and person-to-person interaction available to the infant, whether the mother's absence interferes with her serving as the stable adult figure needed by the infant, or whether the attachment of the infant to the mother or the mother to the infant is jeopardized. These questions are extremely important to investigate since a rapidly increasing percentage of mothers of infants are seeking employment.

The data on maternal employment and the child's academic achievement were reviewed separately because most of these data are from simple, two-level studies where it was impossible to say what process was involved. The findings constitute a kaleidoscope, but even if every study had produced the same empirical results they would not have been useful. If, for example, the data uniformly indicated that the children of working mothers had higher cognitive abilities, but did not indicate the process by which this effect occurred, we would be unable to say whether the effect would continue as other aspects of the situation changed. If, for example, the relationship existed because the working mothers were conscientiously making up for their absence, then as working mothers adopted a casual attitude about their employment, this effect might disappear. Over-eagerness to demonstrate that maternal employment is good, bad, or has no effect, may result in misleading conclusions.

7

Effects on Power and Division of Labor in the Family

STEPHEN J. BAHR

Power and division of labor appear to be two of the most central concepts for describing familial behavior. When any group is formed a power structure evolves, and work and privileges are divided up among members in some fashion. The power structure and division of labor affect emotional as well as interactional patterns within a family. This chapter examines the effects of female employment on power and division of labor within the family.

Power

Power is considered by some as one of the central concepts in social science (Russell, 1938; Cartwright, 1965; Jacobson, 1972). For example, Jacobson (1972, p. 2) asserts that "the totality of human interaction can never be understood without power's pervasive role." However, the ambiguities of the concept prompted Dahl

(1957) to call it a "bottomless swamp," while several family scholars have suggested that no additional studies should be conducted on family power until conceptualization is improved (Turk and Bell, 1972; Olson and Rabunsky, 1972). One aim of this chapter is to improve conceptualization through an analysis of the existing empirical knowledge regarding the effects of the mother's employment on power. Furthermore, we agree with Cartwright (1965, p. 4) that power is not a "bottomless swamp," although it does have its "soggy spots."

In many studies power has not been defined explicitly; investigators have apparently assumed that we all know what it refers to. When an explicit nominal definition has been presented it is usually similar to the following: "Power may be defined as the potential ability of one partner to influence the other's behavior" (Blood and Wolfe, 1960, p. 11). In most existing studies decision-making has been assumed to be an indicator of power, and the two terms have been used interchangeably (Safilios-Rothschild, 1970b, p. 539).

A variety of concepts seem to be implicit in the term *family power* as used in the literature, yet these various dimensions have not been explicitly delineated and examined empirically. One conclusion of recent research is that since power is multidimensional, it may be inappropriate to examine the relationship between power in general and other variables (Safilios-Rothschild, 1970b). What is needed is a typology identifying a few basic dimensions of power. In this chapter, in addition to discussing power on a general level, we discuss the distinction made by Blood (1963) between internal and external power and categorize power within five family roles.

Relevance of Wife's Employment. The resource theory of Blood and Wolfe (1960) is often used to explain why the wife's employment is relevant to family power. The assumption is that because of her employment the wife is able to contribute economic and other resources which may meet the needs of her husband. Blood and Wolfe outline the essence of the resource theory (1960, p. 12): "The sources of power in so intimate a relationship as marriage must be sought in the comparative resources which the husband and wife bring to the marriage, rather than in brute force. A resource may be defined as anything that one partner may make available to the other, helping the latter satisfy his needs or attain his goals. The balance of power will be on the side of that partner who contributes the greater resources to the marriage." A resource need not have objective reality, although it must be perceived as such. If either one's needs or ability to provide decrease, one's power over the other decreases (Wolfe, 1959).

The resource theory is a social-exchange model in which power results from resources and needs. Alternatives (Thibaut and Kelly, 1959) are not explicitly discussed by Blood and Wolfe, but appear essential in understanding marital power. A power imbalance occurs when the alternatives of one partner are more abundant than those of the other. For example, the husband may enter into an exchange because it is his best alternative, even though it may be unsatisfactory. The wife may find the exchange rewarding, but may also have other rewarding alternatives available. Thus, the wife has power over her husband because she has considerable control over the resources he needs, while the resources she receives from him could be obtained elsewhere if necessary. Waller and Hill (1951, p. 191) refer to this exchange as the principle of least interest: "That person is able to dictate the conditions of association whose interest in the continuation of the affair is least."

This social-exchange model helps explain how and why the employment of wives affects family power and division of labor. The exact nature of these effects depends on the need priorities of the family. If the value of the employed mother's economic resources appears greater than the value of her forgone household services, she tends to have greater overall power than her nonemployed counterpart. One would expect the wife's power over internal affairs to be less if she works since the resources she contributes internally are probably less than those contributed by the full-time housewife. Similarly, if the wife becomes employed, her external power may increase, particularly with regard to economic decisions, since income is a primary contribution from her employment.

One would naturally expect division of labor to be affected by employment in a similar way. If the employment of the wife decreases her contribution of resources to the internal household, then it may be necessary to seek alternative sources to fill these needs. The husband, children, maid, or a service establishment may be required to perform household tasks previously performed by the wife. Another possibility is that the standards of the household become somewhat relaxed. A third alternative is that the wife becomes more efficient, enabling her to maintain simultaneously her contribution to the household and her economic contribution from employment. In the last case the wife's employment would increase her external power without decreasing her internal power, and the internal division of labor would remain essentially the same. If the contribution of her employment is valued more than her household chores, the cleanliness standards within the household may become relaxed without any marked change in division of labor. All three changes occur, as indicated in Chapter Two, but increased household performance by husband or children or both is probably the most common. In this exchange, the husband gains increased power within the household and performs more household tasks, unless children perform these household tasks. In this case, the children have greater participation in household tasks and probably gain increased influence concerning these affairs.

The employment of the wife might also provide opportunities and alternatives that the housewife does not have. Through employment, women may become more involved in activities and social relationships outside the family than the housewife. The husband's resources may be just as important to the wife, but her alternatives may increase and become more rewarding, which would tend to decrease the relative power of the husband.

Employment might also induce some change in the wife's perceived needs. The interaction with those outside the family may socialize women to become less satisfied with their current marital exchange. As the wife's needs change, the power relationship with her husband changes, unless he is able to contribute further resources to balance his wife's changing needs.

In summary, a model of social exchange for the family seems to be a fruitful framework because it helps to explain how and why the wife's employment affects power and division of labor. Using this framework a number of relationships between employment, power, and division of labor have been suggested.

Measurement of Power. Studies that have examined the relationship between the wife's employment and family power have used several different indicators of power. The most common measurement procedure has been a self-report of which spouse makes certain decisions. The instrument developed by Blood and Wolfe (1960) has probably been the most frequently used self-report measure of family power; it asks who usually makes the final decision about eight important family matters. This measure or a similar decision-making measure has been used by other investigators (Aldous, 1969; Bahr, 1972; Blood, 1967; Buric and Zecevic, 1967; Centers, Raven and Rodrigues, 1971; Kandel and Lesser, 1972; Kligler, 1954; Lamouse, 1969; Lupri, 1969; Michel, 1967, 1971; Oppong, 1970; Safilios-Rothschild, 1967, 1969a, 1970a; Silverman and Hill, 1967; Weller, 1968). The eight decisions chosen by Blood and Wolfe are what job the husband should take; what car to get; whether to buy life insurance; where to go on a vacation; what house or apartment to take; whether the wife should go to work or quit work; what doctor to have; how much money the family can afford to spend per week on food. Other researchers have augmented and refined this list to fit the needs of their particular investigation.

The outcome of conflicts is another method sometimes used to measure power. A review of the literature uncovered only five studies on employed wives in which conflict was explicitly used as the basis for measuring family power. Heer (1963a) asked who usually wins when there is an important decision on which the couple disagree. Scanzoni (1970, p. 148) used a variation of the Heer technique and asked what the couple disagree about most often and who usually gets his way when they disagree about that particular item. Bahr and coworkers (1974) used two general questions similar to those of Heer (1963a) as well as several specific questions concerning disagreements over the spending of income, religion, child discipline, and furnishing the home. Bahr (1972) examined contested decision-making on five major family matters delineated by Nye (1970)— child socialization, child care, income provision, housekeeping, and recreation. For each area, respondents were asked who made the final decision when there was disagreement. In the fifth study, Middleton and Putney (1960) used a modification of the Strodtbeck (1951) Revealed Difference Technique to measure power. Husband and wife filled out a questionnaire individually and then a second time jointly. The number of disagreements on the individual question-

naires was tabulated, and the proportion of disagreements which
were resolved in the favor of the position originally taken by the
husband was computed. This is one of the few observational studies
of the relationship between the employment and power of wives.

Two other important studies have measured power in a
somewhat different way. Blood and Hamblin (1958) asked respondents whether the husband's or wife's initial idea was accepted for
each of eighteen decisions. This measure appears symptomatic of
conjugal power, for the one who initiates the act is intentionally
changing the other's behavior.

A study by Hoffman (1963d) measured power by the extent
to which one parent decided the other's behavior. Third- through
sixth-grade children were asked which parent decided and which parent performed thirty-three household activities. The child's report was
assumed to indicate the power of the parent who made the decision.
Hoffman also used the decision questions to measure a related concept which she called "activity control." The activity-control score
for each spouse differentiated major from minor actors and took into
account the exclusiveness of the deciding vote.

In almost all studies power was measured by self-reports of
the respondents. Usually the data were obtained from the wife, although in several instances responses were obtained from both husband and wife (Bahr, 1972; Centers and coworkers, 1971; Heer,
1963a; Lamouse, 1969; Middleton and Putney, 1960; Safilios-
Rothschild, 1967, 1969a, 1970a). Two studies (Hoffman, 1963d;
Bahr and coworkers, 1974) relied on children's perceptions of power.

The fact that power is a relatively imprecise concept has
hampered the development of cumulative knowledge in this area
(Safilios-Rothschild, 1970b; Olson and Rabunsky, 1972; Turk and
Bell, 1972; Sprey, 1972). Nevertheless, existing limitations do not
preclude the possibility that valuable information regarding the
effects of employment on power can be obtained from available data.
It is assumed here that measurement error is sufficiently small that
meaningful trends can be observed. Even though this assumption
can be challenged, it allows us to examine the substantive findings
regarding power without becoming involved in excessive methodological detail. Such a strategy has been used by Rodman (1972) and
appears useful in developing substantive theory.

A number of consistent findings regarding the effects of the wife's employment on power have emerged from empirical research. Thus, despite methodological and conceptual limitations, her employment appears to be consistently related to marital power. These findings require further empirical verification, particularly as methodological refinements become available.

Empirical Data. Employed wives tend to have greater power than nonemployed wives. This tendency has been found in several studies in the United States (Bahr, 1972; Blood, 1963; Blood and Wolfe, 1960; Glueck and Glueck, 1957; Heer, 1963a; Kligler, 1954; Scanzoni, 1970) as well as studies in Denmark (Kandel and Lesser, 1972), France (Michel, 1967, 1971), Germany (Lamouse, 1969; Lupri, 1969), Yugoslavia (Buric and Zecevic, 1967), Japan (Blood, 1967), Greece (Safilios-Rothschild, 1967, 1970a), Puerto Rico (Weller, 1968), and Ghana (Oppong, 1970). In addition, anthropological studies of Navaho Indians (Hamamsy, 1957) and primitive African tribes (Faller, 1965; Oberg, 1938) give evidence of a positive association between the wife's employment and her bargaining power.

Several other studies suggest that this general finding requires qualification. Middleton and Putney (1960) observed that families in which the wife worked were more patriarchal than families with nonemployed wives. Survey studies by Safilios-Rothschild (1969a, 1970a), Centers and coworkers (1971), Blood and Hamblin (1958), and Hoffman (1963d) showed no significant differences between the overall conjugal power of employed and nonemployed wives. However, as we shall see, when these findings are analyzed by decision area, rather than by treating power as a global phenomenon, they appear generally consistent with the earlier cited studies.

Middleton and Putney maintain that they measured minor family decisions comparable to many that couples make daily. In their discussion of findings they state: "A possible interpretation of our findings would be that husbands whose wives do not work tend to leave minor family decisions largely to the wife. Husbands of working wives, on the other hand, almost necessarily participate to a much greater degree in home life and might, therefore, be expected to play a greater role in minor family decisions" (1960, p. 609).

When broken down by decision area, their data showed

working wives to be less dominant than housewives in child-rearing and recreation, while the dominance of the two groups was not significantly different in the area of purchases and living standards. Blood (1963) notes that these findings are consistent with other research which suggests that housewives relative to working wives are more powerful in internal household affairs, while working wives have relatively greater external power, particularly with regard to economic affairs.

Blood and Hamblin (1958) found that working wives averaged a greater percentage of adopted suggestions than housewives, but the difference was not statistically significant. Perhaps if analyzed by the internal and external categories, the data might have shown that employed wives were significantly more powerful in the external decisions and less powerful in the internal area. This same explanation also may be applicable to the studies of Centers and coworkers (1971) and Hoffman (1963d) since neither analyzed their power data with this distinction. Hoffman (1963d) found: "working mothers made fewer decisions about routine household matters than nonworking mothers, and their husbands made more."

Safilios-Rothschild's (1969a) data appear generally consistent with this interpretation. Although there were no significant differences between employed and nonemployed wives in global power, such differences did exist in several economic decisions. The employed wives made more decisions with respect to the purchase of clothes, furniture, and other household items, and the budgeting of money; they also made more decisions regarding child-rearing.

These studies illustrate the value of examining various spheres of power or decision areas in addition to the standard global assessments of power. The most consistent finding from the studies in which various decision areas were examined is the positive association between the wife's employment and her power concerning financial matters. The Detroit Area Study (Blood, 1963) showed that employed wives, compared with nonemployed wives, made significantly more major economic decisions (what car to buy, what house to choose, whether to buy insurance, and whether the wife should work); the decision of what doctor to call was made less by employed wives, while there were no differences concerning the choice of the husband's job. Decisions about where to spend vacations tended to be more egalitarian in families with employed wives, while housewife families were more husband- or wife-dominant, depending on the level of income (income and social class differences are examined later in this chapter). Weller (1968) found that employed wives had greater influence concerning "buying things" and "food expenditures," as well as for having and rearing children, holidays, and place of residence. In her German study, Lamouse (1969) found that working wives gained more influence in those decisions which had some connection with financial problems. Kligler (1954) found decision influence regarding major purchases, loans and savings, and investments to be greater for employed wives. Safilios-Rothschild (1967, 1969a, 1970a) showed that decision-making concerning purchases of clothes, furniture, and other household goods, and concerning budgeting and use of money was related to the wife's employment status. Buric and Zecevic (1967) found similar results in Yugoslavia, except that the housewife appeared to have the advantage with regard to budgeting. The employment of wives was related to paying bills and borrowing money in a study by Aldous (1969).

Oppong (1970) found no significant difference between the power of working wives who made a low contribution to domestic expenses and the power of housewives. However, large differences existed between the power of working wives who contributed significantly to domestic expenses and the power of housewives.

The one contradictory finding was evidenced in Michel's (1971) French data. She found that working wives had greater decision-making power concerning holidays and the wife's employment status, while monthly expenses and purchases of electrical appliances were not significantly related to female employment.

The employment of wives also increases their power with regard to having and raising children. Weller (1968, 1971) showed that the wife's employment is associated with her greater influence in decisions about having additional children, and this increased influence is associated with her lower fertility. Safilios-Rothschild (1970a) and Buric and Zecevic (1967) also found female employment and having children to be related, although this relationship was relatively weak in the Buric and Zecevic data. In another survey by Safilios-Rothschild (1967) no significant relationship between the wife's employment and decisions about family size was evident. Bahr and coworkers (1974), Weller (1968), and Safilios-Rothschild (1967, 1969a) all found the wife's employment to have a positive association with her decision-making in the realm of child-rearing.

Types of Employment. Wives enter different occupations for a number of different reasons and with varying degrees of commitment. Relatively few studies have examined these different types of employment. Sussman (1961) and Safilios-Rothschild (1970b) suggest that grouping all employed women in one heterogeneous category may account for some of the inconsistent findings.

Some researchers have refined the traditional employed-unemployed dichotomy by changing it to a trichotomy: nonemployed, employed part time, and employed full time (Lupri, 1969; Bahr and coworkers, 1974). The results showed that part-time workers were between housewives and full-time workers in family power, as may have been expected.

Kandel and Lesser (1972) in their study of American and Danish urban families, categorized the wife's employment into five categories: full time out of home, full time in home, part time out of home, part time in home, not employed. They found that "when the wife is employed out of the home, whether full time or part time, her husband has less power than when she is not employed" (p. 136). The families with the greatest husband power were those in which the wife was either not employed or was employed full time in the home. (These two groups have similar power scores. There were too few cases of women working part time in the home to discern meaningful results.)

In urban Greece, Safilios-Rothschild (1970a) examined work commitment in an attempt to gain increased understanding of types of female employment. She categorized employed wives into those with high work commitment and those with low work commitment. Those with high work commitment valued work for its own sake and expected to continue working regardless of financial affluence. Safilios-Rothschild found that employed wives (both those with low and those with high work commitment) were more likely than nonemployed wives to report wife-dominated decision-making. Egalitarian rather than husband-dominated decision-making was more frequent among high-work-commitment women than among either low-work-commitment or nonemployed wives. Women with low work commitment appeared slightly more egalitarian than the nonemployed. The husbands of wives with high work commitment gave in to their wives during disagreements more often than did husbands of wives not highly committed to their work. Furthermore, Safilios-Rothschild (1970a, p. 686) states that the less committed wives tended to give in to their husbands to an even greater extent than the nonemployed wives did.

Work commitment is related to type of occupation, income, and education of the wife, and the effects of these variables on conjugal power also depend on the husband's occupation, income, and education. A fairly large number of studies have examined the relationship of the husband's occupation and income to power, as well as the relationship between comparative husband-wife education and power. Few studies, however, have examined the relationship of the wife's occupational prestige and income and her power. Lupri (1969) found that the wife's power was positively associated with her income. She was considerably more powerful if she earned more than her husband than if their incomes were equal or the husband's was greater.

Bahr (1972) used the Duncan occupational status index to compare occupations of husband and wife. The wife's occupational status was subtracted from that of her husband and if the wife was not employed her score was assumed to be zero. The power of wives tended to increase as their occupational status relative to that of their husband increased. Two different measures were used, the decision-making index of Blood and Wolfe and a measure based on contested decisions on six family matters (Bahr, 1972).

Related Variables. Perhaps the greatest weakness of many existing studies is that adequate controls have not been employed. The wife's employment may be related to variables such as the husband's occupational status, family size, and age of children, among others. The studies by Hoffman (1963d) and Heer (1963a) are two of the more sophisticated attempts to examine related variables. Hoffman found that, with no controls, working women have greater power than those who do not work. However, a subsample of eighty-nine working and eighty-nine nonworking wives matched on husband's occupation, number of children under thirteen, and age of oldest child showed no such relationship. Furthermore, Hoffman suggested that the prevalence of male-dominance ideology might under certain conditions neutralize the effect of the wife's employment. Hoffman's research is significant because of the controls employed, the hypotheses suggested for future research, and additional findings that indicated that the effect of employment on power might depend on the interaction with existing ideologies and personalities. Perhaps the major question regarding her research is: Would the results have differed if power had been analyzed with attention to the internal-external distinction elaborated earlier?

Heer (1963a) found that when controlling for family size the relationship between the wife's employment and conjugal power continued to exist but was not as strong, perhaps, as he suggests, indicating causation in the reverse direction. Wives who are more powerful may tend to have fewer children and enter the labor force more easily. Heer also controlled for what he calls a generalized trait of personality dominance, which was found to be unrelated to the fact that working wives have more influence than housewives.

Social Class and Ethnic Group. Working-class wives gain more power through employment than middle-class wives. The Lupri (1969) German study found that wives of the lower class gained substantially more power by employment than did wives of other classes. This finding was the same using the husband's income, his occupation, and an interviewer rating of social class. The difference between the power of employed and nonemployed wives decreased as the husband's occupation and income increased. The Heer (1963a) study indicated a similar difference by social class. When family size was controlled, the difference between the power of employed and nonemployed wives was over twice as large in the working as in the middle class.

Scanzoni (1970) used level of education as an indicator of class in his examination of conjugal power. In the lower class, the findings from husbands and wives were similar, but they differed among the more educated. According to the perceptions of wives, the power of the wife was greater when she was employed; this finding held among all educational levels. Those husbands without a high school diploma perceived their wives as having more power when they worked, while husbands with at least a high school education felt that employment decreased the wife's power (Scanzoni, 1970).

There has been little study of black and white differences in the relationship between female employment and family power. When Aldous (1969) compared 122 lower-class whites with 46 lower-class blacks, employed wives participated to a greater extent in decision-making than did nonemployed wives. Among white couples the differences were small, while for the black couples employed wives were significantly more powerful than the nonemployed. In both groups, employed wives made significantly more decisions in borrowing money, paying bills, and whether the wife should work—findings consistent with those of studies cited earlier in this chapter. Other decisions showed small differences for whites and significant differences for blacks.

Bahr (1972) examined the conjugal power of 216 couples on income provision, housekeeping, recreation, child care, and child socialization. Couples were asked who made the final decision if there was disagreement. The power of the wife concerning her occupation was greater for employed than nonemployed wives (average correlation = 0.38).[1] This relationship was considerably stronger in the blue-collar than white-collar families. In the blue-collar group the average rank-order correlation between the wife's employment and power concerning her occupation was 0.50. In the white-collar group the comparable correlation was .21. Among small families (one or two children) the relationship between the wife's power and her employment was strong (correlation = 0.80), and it was moderately small (0.30) in families with three or more children. When the youngest child was of preschool age, a statistically nonsignificant relationship between employment and power existed, while a moderate relationship existed when the youngest child was in school. (The sample was chosen from school records of third-grade children,

---

[1] The correlations reported in this section are gamma, a rank order measure of association. Average correlation is the mean of the correlation computed using the husbands' perceptions and the correlation computed using the wives' perceptions. This procedure was chosen for ease and clarity of exposition and does not change the basic finding in any way.

and thus all families had a third-grade child.) Among those families in which the oldest child was a teenager a positive relationship between the wife's employment and her power existed.

With regard to husband's occupation working wives tended to be slightly more powerful than nonemployed wives, although this relationship was weak because a substantial majority said the husband had this power regardless of the wife's work status. The relationship appeared to be slightly stronger within the blue-collar than white-collar group.

The data also showed that while wives may lose some power in the housekeeper role by their employment, in the blue-collar group employed wives tended to have slightly more power in the housekeeper role than did nonemployed wives. In the blue-collar group a small positive correlation existed between the wife's power in recreational decisions and her employment, while in the white-collar group this relationship was small but negative. In child care husbands in the white-collar group reported that wives tend to have less power when employed (correlation $= -0.36$), while the wives' data showed no such tendency. Power over child socialization showed no consistent relationship to the wife's employment.

Although only suggestive, these data imply that, except in income-provision decisions, employment may decrease the power of wives with white-collar husbands. However, the power of wives with blue-collar husbands appears to increase in all areas when she becomes employed. Perhaps white-collar husbands of employed women increase their activity in housekeeping, child socialization, child care, and recreation, but in blue-collar families the wife does it all by continuing to fully enact these activities in addition to her share in income provision. This explanation seems worthy of future empirical investigation.

Summary. Considerable cross-cultural and subcultural evidence suggests that the employment of wives increases their power. However, this tends to be primarily in "external" decisions regarding finances and the provider role. A working wife tends to have less power within the household arena, although within the lower class her employment might increase her power in these "internal" decisions. Overall, the effect of her employment on power within the child care, socialization, housekeeper, and recreation roles appears to be relatively small. The effects of employment appear to vary according to certain structural and normative patterns, although there is relatively little empirical data regarding such variation. The existing data indicate that the effects of her employment may be more pronounced in the lower class, in small families, and in families without preschool children. The effects of employment may exist in large, middle-class families with preschool children, but counterforces might lessen or neutralize such effects.

Division of Labor

Division of labor refers to task division. In marriage, as in any other group, some division of the work takes place. Some tasks are performed solely by the wife, some solely by the husband, others are undertaken jointly, or husband and wife may alternate their labor, or the task may not be performed by anyone.

Certain tasks are normatively assigned to one sex or the other. Traditionally, the provider of income for the family through outside employment has been the man; and sometimes proscriptions prohibit employment of the wife outside the home, particularly if the couple has small children. The wife has usually been assigned the task of caring for the children, cooking meals, and cleaning house. In America, changes have occurred in some of these norms, but the wife is still considered to have primary responsibility for the house and children, even if she is employed. Similarly, men have not had the freedom to become househusbands, even if they so desire. Other essential tasks may be optional, in that norms do not assign them to one particular spouse. They must be done, but either spouse can perform them. Organizing family recreation appears to be one such task.

There is a general consistency among the studies on the effects of the wife's employment on division of labor within the family. A basic finding is that when the wife is employed the husband's household labor increases while that of the wife decreases. Blood and his associates (Blood, 1963; Blood and Hamblin, 1958; Blood and Wolfe, 1960) provided some of the first empirical data regarding employment and division of labor. Their data showed that husbands of working wives did more housework than husbands of housewives.

An examination of specific tasks revealed the following (Blood, 1963, pp. 287–288):

> [*The employment of wives produces*] *substantial decreases in the number of wives who carry sole responsibilities of getting the husband's breakfast, doing the evening dishes, and straightening up the living room when company is coming. Working wives also tend to do less household repairing and do less grocery shopping by themselves (especially in the lower-income group, where the main shift is to joint shopping). The only task which working wives maintain as active an interest in is the economic one of "keeping track of the money and bills." Here the wife's lessened time is offset by an increased sense of involvement in the family finances—so no significant change occurs.*

A study of over four hundred Japanese families produced similar results (Blood, 1967).

The studies by Hoffman (1963d), Nolan (1963) and Powell (1963) add additional insights. In the Hoffman study, children reported that employed mothers performed fewer tasks in four household task areas; Nolan found that working mothers used commercial services more. Husbands of employed wives participated more in the conventionally feminine activities such as cleaning and child care. The Powell study included data on the family life cycle. With children in the preschool and school-age stages husbands of employed wives were more involved in the house than were husbands of nonemployed wives. However, when the oldest child was an adolescent, husbands of employed wives participated in fewer home activities than did husbands of nonemployed wives.

In her German study, Lamouse (1969) reported that division of labor was less traditional in families with working wives and formerly working wives than in families with housewives. However, the families of formerly employed wives exhibited a division of labor more traditional than did families of currently employed wives.

A study of Russian women (Kharchev and Golod, 1971) showed that even though husbands of employed wives did more household tasks than husbands of nonemployed wives, these tasks were still primarily the responsibility of the wife. Additional data supporting this point are reported in Chapter Six. In the Russian study, husbands' participation appeared to be greater in child care than in other household tasks; similar findings were reported in a Polish study by Piotrowski (1971), who also noted that the husband's help was greater in families where the children were small.

The Safilios-Rothschild (1970a) Greek study provided data regarding work commitment, employment, and division of labor. Husbands were more likely to help their wives in household tasks if the wife had low rather than high work commitment, and working wives with high work commitment were more likely to receive help from their husbands than were nonemployed wives. Division of labor may have been less important for the wives with higher incomes because they could hire help—more of the high than low work commitment group had maids.

Silverman and Hill (1967) reported that division of labor was more egalitarian early in marriage, especially if the wife was employed. They also found that a traditional division of labor was associated with a traditional pattern of decision-making. The French findings of Michel (1971) are similar to many of the above studies. Over twice as many working than nonworking wives received help in their housework, especially in white-collar families.

Epstein (1971), who studied twelve wives who were law partners to their husbands, found that the wife had the major responsibility for the house and children, but among younger couples it was typical for the husband to do some housework. She also found that division of labor in their law practice tended to occur along traditional male-female lines.

Holmstrom (1972) conducted a study of twenty middle-age couples in which the wife had obtained her doctorate and was employed in a professional position. She found that professional wives received considerable help from their husbands, but many relied on hired help. The following were trends in the division of labor of specific household activities: "The tasks most likely to be done by the husband were emptying the garbage and trash, repair work, and heavy yard work. Tasks most likely to be shared equally between husband and wife were cooking breakfast and washing dishes. Financial tasks tended to be randomly allocated; for example, keeping track of the money and paying monthly bills were two tasks as likely to be assigned to one spouse as the other. Tasks most likely to be hired out were ironing, vacuuming, and general cleaning" (p. 68). Holmstrom also notes extensive interchangeability of tasks even though there was a tendency for one partner to perform certain tasks. Rarely did the professional couples give ideological justification for allocation of tasks; availability, skill, interest, and enjoyment were the major reasons for the pattern of task allocation.

These data provide a fairly clear picture of the relationship between division of labor and the wife's employment. When a wife becomes employed she has less time for housework and consequently is likely to get at least some help from her husband. Nevertheless, working or not, it appears that housework is still primarily her responsibility. Husbands of employed wives get particularly involved in child care, although they also do considerably more housework than husbands of nonemployed wives. Division of labor appears to be more balanced early in marriage. The wife's employment may produce little change in the involvement of the husband in household tasks if they have adolescent children to perform the tasks. In general, employment tends to increase practical considerations, such as availability and skill as factors in task allocation, and lessen the influence of role prescriptions which assign tasks as "women's" and "men's" work. As one husband put it, "I help because there is no other feasible way of running the menage without a twenty-four-hour-a-day household staff" (Holmstrom, 1972, p. 59).

Conclusions

This chapter has examined the relationship between the wife's employment and power and division of labor within the family. Social-exchange theory provided a basis for answering the question of why the wife's employment is relevant to family power and division of labor. Such employment alters the exchange relationship within the family by producing changes in resources, needs, and alternatives. Various methods of measuring family power were then examined briefly, and empirical data were reviewed.

In general the wife's power tends to increase when she becomes employed, although power is contingent on other factors, and more powerful wives are more likely to become employed. Specifically, employment increases a wife's power concerning finance, while her power tends to decrease within the household arena. Although employed wives tend to remain primarily responsible for household tasks, their husbands perform significantly more of them than do husbands of nonemployed wives. These trends appear more pronounced for wives employed in the professions than for those in less prestigious jobs. However, wives highly committed to their work (who would work regardless of financial need) receive less household help from their husbands than do wives with low work commitment, presumably because the husband feels more constrained to help out around the house if his wife is working to fulfill a financial need rather than merely because she wants to.

The effects of the wife's employment are influenced by existing normative and structural conditions. Lower-class wives gain more power through employment than do middle-class wives. In large families the wife appears to gain less power by employment than in small families, presumably because the cost of a mother's leaving the home for employment is much greater in a large family. Norms about what roles the husband and wife should play may also modify the effects of employment, as Hoffman's (1963d) research showed. The employment of the wife appears to have relatively small effects on internal family matters; in the lower class it increases her internal power slightly while decreasing it slightly in the middle class. Income provision was the only area where important effects were found, primarily with regard to the wife's occupation.

Existing studies have a number of methodological and conceptual limitations, and therefore the findings presented here should be viewed as tentative approximations. Methodological and conceptual refinements necessary to advance our knowledge beyond the present state should be forthcoming.

8

Husband-Wife Relationship

F. Ivan Nye

Two related questions are explored in this chapter: Are the husband-wife relationships different in families in which the mother has a paid-employee role? If they are different is the difference or any portion of it attributable to behavior or feelings related to the paid employment of the mother? The first question is an empirical one which has been studied by almost a dozen research teams, operating independently. There is a broad although not complete consensus on the facts of the matter, but whether the differences are causal or selective is a difficult question.

Early Perspectives

Psychoanalysts took a dim view of women earning part or all of the income for a family. Many viewed the intrinsic nature of woman as being dependent, nurturant and unaggressive. Child-bearing, child-care, and supportive activities (in relation to the husband) were viewed as being in harmony with the physiology and psychology of women. Extensive participation in paid employment was seen as encouraging the nonfeminine aspects of personality—aggression, competition, and dominance (Lundberg and Farnham, 1947). This line of thinking viewed men as needing to be dominant and assumed that any sharing of the provider role would result in damage to the male ego and to conflict between spouses.

A number of sociologists also expected conflict and negative affect in marriages in which the mother was employed full time. There are obvious conflicts between the child-care, socialization, and housekeeper roles of mothers and their enactment of the provider role. Most full-time paid employment requires the mother to leave her house for eight or more hours daily. Preschool children must be placed in the care of others. Usually the mother cannot be home when children are dismissed from school, so that some other arrangement, or none, is made for an hour or so after they are out of school. Likewise, the preemption of forty hours weekly changes the ways in which a woman can enact the housekeeper role. Because of these factors, the working mother cannot fully, personally enact these traditional roles. Accordingly, sociologists often assumed that these mothers would not perform as well, an assumption which is frequently unwarranted. However, the interruption in role enactment and the necessity of delegating responsibilities led to the hypothesis that maternal employment results in an increase in conflict between spouses.

Sociologists generally expect major role changes to be initially characterized by increased conflict because of confusion, lack of predictability of behavior, and different perceptions of the social norms. This conflict is assumed to be transitory, persisting only until a new consensus is reached. Kirkpatrick (1952) points to an additional cause of initial conflict. His research disclosed that when new role combinations occur, each person tends to expect the rewards but to reject any new responsibilities.

Finally, two sociological perspectives were contributed by a child psychologist, Susanne Lloyd (personal communication). She suggests that the addition of another role for the mother increases the number of behaviors and possibilities of conflict. The other perspective involves changes in conflict from a covert to an overt level. Lloyd suggests that housewives frequently disagree with their spouses without verbalizing their opposition because of their dependence on their husbands. Employment may lessen such dependence and allow covert conflict to be expressed.

However, Bott (1957), Rainwater (1965), and Dizard (1968) state, and others imply, that role-sharing is related to close, warm, rewarding relationships between spouses, while role segregation is associated with social distance and a lack of positive affect. Dizard makes a connection between role-sharing and the employment of wives, pointing to the fact that husbands of employed wives are more likely to participate in child care, child socialization, and housekeeping tasks than are husbands of nonemployed wives. This role-sharing provides a rationale for the possibility that the employment of wives may result in an increase in marital happiness. Nye (1963) approached role-sharing a little differently: "Employment increases the family level of living, the prestige of the mother, the appreciation of her by her husband, and the amount of democratic decision-making in the family; moreover, she enjoys some of the social contacts connected with her job" (p. 264).

Orden and Bradburn (1969) hypothesize greater marital happiness for those wives who take employment voluntarily because such opportunity extends their freedom of choice. Contrariwise, being "forced" into taking employment reduces their autonomy and results in lessened marital satisfaction.

Criteria of Marital Success

Early studies of marital success frequently conceptualized it as marital adjustment. More recent researchers feel that concept to be too broad and ambiguous, and have utilized permanence, happiness, conflict, and satisfaction as specific criteria (Burgess and Wallin, 1953; Nye and MacDougal, 1959). Bowerman developed a set of Guttman scales which, besides the above content, included a dimension termed *general goal fulfillment* (Bowerman, 1957). Blood (1963) and Orden and Bradburn (1969) suggest that going out together "just to have a good time" is a dimension of marital success. Still others utilize as a measure of marital success the number of positive and negative comments checked or volunteered about the spouse.

Even these diverse measures of the husband-wife relationship do not exhaust the indicators which have been employed. However, this diversity apparently is less problematic than it might appear. Nye and MacDougal (1959) showed that four of the most common indicators—conflict, satisfaction, happiness, and permanence—all measure a single dimension of the husband-wife relationship.

Recreation. Blood (1963) and Orden and Bradburn (1969) considered joint recreation crucial to the husband-wife relationship, but data bearing on the effects of maternal employment on joint recreation are limited. Recreational data were included in a study of two thousand Washington mothers by Nye (1963). This study disclosed almost identical patterns for housewives and full-time employed women with respect to dancing, movies, tennis, water sports, bowling, parties, and visits to relatives. Only playing cards is a less frequent recreation for the full-time employed woman. Orden and Bradburn (1969), using a large random sample of husbands and wives, constructed a sociability score which included recreational behavior. Housewives had higher sociability scores than wives employed "by necessity" but lower scores than those in the labor force "by choice" (Table 15). When all employed women are combined and a weighted score is obtained, housewives have the same scores as wives employed full time but lower scores than those employed part time. Husbands of housewives had lower sociability scores than those with wives employed either full or part time.

Carlson (1973) found that employed mothers were much more likely to say they would like to have more recreation with their family than they have. Since they have as much as housewives, this finding suggests that mothers who have other interests and who are not tied to their children and households around the clock appreciate interaction with their families more and welcome more family-centered recreation.

Conflict and Dissolution. In the popular literature of the 1950s and early 1960s frequent assertions were made that the employment of wives was a major cause of the high divorce rate. Some statistical evidence could be advanced to support this idea. Divorcees (but also young widows) are found in the labor force in disproportionate numbers. In 1969 about 40 percent of women married and living with their husbands were employed, but 72 percent of those divorced were working (U.S. Department of Labor, Women's

Table 15.

ᴇᴍᴘʟᴏʏᴍᴇɴᴛ Sᴛᴀᴛᴜs ᴏғ Mᴏᴛʜᴇʀ ᴀɴᴅ Mᴀʀɪᴛᴀʟ Aᴅᴊᴜsᴛᴍᴇɴᴛ

Criteria of Marital Adjustment[a]	*Not Employed*		*Employed Full-Time*	
	Number	Percent	Number	Percent
Conflict				
Argued	183	45.8	103	51.6
Quarreled[b]	30	7.6	26	13.4
Permanence				
Lived apart[b]	46	11.6	33	16.7
Considered divorce[b]	178	46.6	133	60.1
Happiness				
"Was unhappy"	80	20.7	52	26.8
Satisfaction				
"Was dissatisfied"	110	28.9	56	28.3
Total	400		199	

[a] Categories presented are from the lower end of the marital success distribution: arguing: sometimes or oftener in four or more areas; quarreling: fairly often or more frequently; lived apart: one or more times following a quarrel; considered divorce: all responses except never; happiness: partly unhappy, unhappy, and very unhappy; satisfaction: partly or less satisfied.

[b] Statistically significant.

Source: Nye and Hoffman (1963b, p. 268). Permission to reprint this table is granted by *Social Problems*.

Bureau, 1970). These statistics could suggest that employed women are more likely to be divorced, but they could also mean that divorced women, lacking sufficient financial support, take employment as a result of the divorce.

Gianopulos and Mitchell (1957) studied 134 couples from a marriage counseling clinic and compared the frequency of conflict among couples in which wives were not employed with two categories of those who were employed: those whose husbands approved of the employment and those whose husbands disapproved. They found much more conflict among couples in which the husband disapproved of the wife's working. However, the greater conflict was concentrated in areas substantively related to her activity in the provider role, including sharing household tasks, wife working,

financial matters, husband's work, children and household management. The conflicts centered on matters related to employment
rather than in all areas of the husband-wife relationship.

In the Nye study of two thousand Washington mothers,
among the employed mothers presently married, 13 percent had
been married previously. Of those married women who were not
employed, 11.9 percent had been married previously, a nonsignificant difference. However, Hoffman (1958) found a greater proportion of remarriages among employed than nonemployed mothers.
Her sample included largely blue-collar families, while Nye's was
predominantly white collar. With the exception of one study (Blood
and Wolfe, 1960), employment of mothers seems more stressful in
blue-collar families.

There is evidence of more conflict, arguing, quarrelling,
living apart, and consideration of divorce among the employed
mothers (Table 15), but not necessarily more divorces or permanent separations. Despite more conflict, no more employed mothers
than housewives are dissatisfied with their marriages. Apparently,
the advantages associated with employment compensated for the
higher levels of conflict characteristic of their marriages. This
balancing of positive and negative elements has been conceptualized
and measured by Orden and Bradburn (1969) and is explored
below.

Happiness and Satisfaction. Happiness and satisfaction are
not precisely the same thing, yet they are closely related and frequently are treated interchangeably. They scale on the same
dimension, and several researchers have utilized one or the other, or
both.

Locke and Mackeprang (1949) studied the marital adjustment of employed wives in two samples: 542 divorced and 404
happily married couples, and 41 couples in which the wife was employed full time and 51 in which she was a housewife. In the latter
sample, employed and nonemployed were approximately matched
by age, education of the wife, and income of the husband. In neither
study was there a difference in marital adjustment between couples
in which the wife was employed and those in which she was a housewife. This study was of employed wives, however; some, but not all,
were mothers.

Blood (1963), with a sample of 582 mothers in the Detroit metropolitan area, studied the satisfaction of employed wives and housewives with respect to companionship, love and affection from husband, and overall. With respect to satisfaction of the wife with companionship of the husband, employed wives were more likely to be satisfied, especially those in the low-income category. With respect to husband's love and affection, there was little difference except that the least satisfied were housewives with husbands who had earnings in the lower-income category. On the composite score of satisfactions, working wives of the low-income group and non-working wives of high income ranked highest in marital satisfaction. Blood felt the high satisfaction of the working wives of low-income husbands could be explained by their relatively more important contribution to the family income. However other data have shown that employed wives in higher-income families earn a larger proportion of the income than do wives in lower-income families. "For example the earnings of working wives contributed 24 percent of total income in those families with incomes under three thousand dollars, but 28 percent of total income in families with incomes of ten thousand dollars or more" (U.S. Department of Labor, Women's Bureau, 1971, p. 10).

Feld (1963) included marital happiness in her analysis of data from a national probability sample of mothers aged twenty-one or older. In her initial comparison of full-time employed women and housewives, only slight, nonsignificant differences were found. However, working wives had higher family incomes and averaged more education, two characteristics positively related to marital happiness. When she standardized her working and housewife samples on education and family income, the negative relationship between employment and marital happiness became significant. The differences favoring the nonworking wife were much greater in her subsample of wives with no more than grade school education, than they were in the high school or college population (Table 16).

Nye (1959) compared employed mothers and housewives on self-rated satisfaction and happiness as single items and on a Guttman-type scale which included conflict items and also separation and thoughts of divorce, in addition to the happiness and satisfaction items. These samples were matched by occupation of husband, ed-

Table 16

EMPLOYMENT STATUS AND MARITAL UNHAPPINESS, PERCENT

EMPLOYMENT STATUS AND EDUCATION

Marital Unhappiness	Grade School		High School		College		Total	
	Working	Non-working	Working	Non-working	Working	Non-working	Working	Non-working
Not too happy	10	7	2	3	0	0	3	4
Just average	60	47	28	26	36	25	35	31
Little happier than average	20	17	30	23	18	23	26	21
Very happy	10	29	40	48	46	52	36	44
Number	10	98	40	223	11	56	61	377

Note: Tau—employment status, marital unhappiness, education = 0.054.

Source: Feld (1963).

ucation of wife, number of children, presence of preschool children, and previous marital status. No significant difference was found employing the single satisfaction and happiness items (Table 15). However, when the scale was utilized as the criteria, a small but significant association was found between employment and evaluation of the marriage, with a larger proportion of the employed mothers making a negative evaluation.

Several test variables were introduced to refine the above analysis. Comparisons were made within subsamples of large and small families, older and younger children, occupation levels of the husband, length of time the wife had been employed, education levels of the wives, and previous marital status of the wife. Of these, only the educational level of the wife and her previous marital status modified the small negative association between being employed and evaluation of the marriage. At the minimum education level of the wife there was a substantial difference between the housewives and the fully employed mothers. In this low-education-level category, 49 percent of the housewives gave a positive evaluation of their marriage compared with only 21 percent of the fully employed women. In contrast, among the college-educated mothers the difference favoring the housewives was 39 compared with 32 percent for the fully employed mothers. The results of this study are consistent with those of Feld in that most of the differences between housewives and employed mothers were concentrated among less educated women.

When the attitude of employed wives toward working was correlated with their evaluation of their marriage, there was a slight difference favoring those who liked working, but it was not statistically significant. Nye also found, as had Gianopulos and Mitchell (1957), that more of the wives whose husbands approved of their working gave a positive evaluation of their marriage than did those whose husbands disapproved. An element of tautology is involved here since conflict related to the decision to work would also be measured in the evaluation of the marriage. However, Nye also compared the evaluation of the marriage when the wife was not working and the husband approved of her not working with that when she was employed and the husband approved, and found a difference favoring the nonemployed mothers. Previous marital status provided an unexpected finding. No relationship was found between employment status and evaluation of the marriage among the remarried, so that their elimination from the sample increased the association between being employed and negatively evaluating the marriage.

The Feld (1963) and Nye (1959) studies found the greatest differences in the evaluation of the marriage at the lower socioeconomic levels, specifically among women with no more than eighth-grade education who had husbands in the blue-collar occupations. In contrast, Blood (1963) found that employed mothers in his lower-income category compared more favorably with housewives than did employed mothers in families with high incomes. These findings seem to be contradictory, although education, occupation, and income are not perfectly correlated and are not precisely equivalent measures of social class.

Nye had offered the post hoc hypothesis that the conditions and rewards for employment were more attractive at the higher socioeconomic levels and that those wives probably had more help with their housekeeper and child-care duties than did the women with less than high school education. Gover (1963) employed data from a random sample of 361 white married women living with their husbands in Greensboro, North Carolina, to test these ideas. He found that middle-class working wives were more likely than blue-collar wives to enjoy high prestige in their jobs, work much shorter hours, and have help with their housework. He was unable, however, to find a relationship between these conditions and the evaluation of the marriage by the wife. Therefore, he found no support for these as intervening variables, although his findings added evidence that the marital satisfaction of employed middle-class women compares more favorably with that of housewives than is the case among lower-class women.

Feldman (1965) studied the relationship between employment status of the mother and her marital satisfaction, employing a middle-class sample of 852 families, and found no significant differences. However, Feldman and Feldman (1973), utilizing the same measure of marital satisfaction with 1,325 poverty-level families who were or had been on welfare, found that the employed women had a significantly lower satisfaction level. This finding was confirmed by asking the women how much of a problem or a source of satisfaction they found the marriage. The nonemployed responded with a higher level of satisfaction. On another set of questions the wives indicated how satisfied they thought their husbands were with them in five areas. "The employed wives thought that the husband was less satisfied with their functioning than did the nonemployed. Employed wives reported the husbands were less satisfied with the meals served, with the time spent with the husband, and with the employment status of the wife. . . . To explore marital conflict, subjects were asked to state the main areas of disagreement. . . . Her work was one of the two items where there was a significant difference between the two employment groups with the employed reporting more conflict in this area (14 versus 7 percent). Sex, as an area of conflict, was also more often mentioned by the employed (14 versus 7 percent)" (p. 15). In this study, all significant differences in marital satisfaction favored the nonemployed women and their husbands. Although families were roughly matched for socioeconomic level, the employed women averaged a higher education level, had fewer children, had considerably higher family incomes and a higher proportion owned their homes, but the amount of income from sources other than the wives' income was less than in families in which the wife was not employed. These differences would usually be associated with higher marital satisfaction. Yet, like almost all other analyses of maternal employment and marital satisfaction in the lower class, the level of marital satisfaction was less in couples in which the mother was gainfully employed.

Axelson (1963), believing that evaluation of the marriage by the husband had been neglected, collected data from a random sample of 122 married men living with their wives in a small western city and evaluated the marriages on the Nye-MacDougal scale, which is composed of items measuring conflict, permanence, happiness, and satisfaction with the marriage. His data showed substantial differences, indicating that a larger proportion of husbands whose wives did not work (61 percent) evaluated the marriage positively, compared with 38 percent of the husbands whose wives were employed full time. Axelson was not able to match his two groups of husbands by socioeconomic class, family size, or other social variables.

Orden and Bradburn (1969) took another approach to marriage evaluation. They point to the fact that marriages include both satisfactions and tensions, which they view as not merely opposite ends of a single continuum but as separate and independent dimensions. (This multidimensional view of marital adjustment may seem to conflict with the Nye-MacDougal finding that satisfaction, conflict, happiness, and thoughts of divorce can be scaled on a single dimension. However, the indicators and even the concepts are different. Orden and Bradburn took a number of behaviors and from these compute a score which they conceptualize as satisfactions. Nye and MacDougal asked each person how satisfied or dissatisfied she was with her marriage. The Nye and MacDougal evaluation presumably produced a response which took into account both tensions and positive satisfactions, while Orden and Bradburn include only positive elements in their measure of satisfactions and only negative elements in the measure of dissatisfactions.) Orden and Bradburn utilized two measures of satisfactions (companionship and sociability) and one of tensions (1968, p. 719). Thus, a marriage may be high in satisfactions and low in tensions, high in satisfactions and tensions, low in satisfactions and high in tensions, or low in both. In their comparisons of the husband-wife relationship they computed and analyzed scores for tensions, companionship, sociability, happiness, and a Marital Adjustment Balance Scale (MABS) computed by subtracting tension scores from satisfaction scores (Table 17).

Orden and Bradburn distinguished between women who were in paid employment by their own choice and those who had to work because of economic necessity. They asked both wives and husbands, "Would you [or your wife, if the respondent was a man] work if you [or she] didn't need the money?" They inferred that those who said they would work even if they didn't need the money (55 percent of the women) were not working primarily for income, while those who replied in the negative received few, if any, nonmonetary rewards. We cannot tell from replies to this question whether the women were free to leave employment, but we do have a measure of whether they liked their work. It is in this sense that their findings are presented and discussed.

Orden and Bradburn found a consistent relationship between the wife's enjoyment of work and her evaluation of her marriage. Those employed women who would not work except for the income averaged high on tensions and low on satisfactions (Table 17). Except on companionship, appreciable differences favored the

Table 17.

AVERAGE RIDITS ON MARRIAGE-ADJUSTMENT MEASURE CONTROLLING FOR WIFE'S WORK STATUS AND FULL-TIME VERSUS PART-TIME EMPLOYMENT

Wife's Work Status	Marriage Adjustment Measure					
	Happiness	Tensions	Companionship	Sociability	MABS	N-NA
Husband						
Labor market by necessity						
Full time	0.43	0.63	0.47	0.39	0.34	90
Part time	0.44	0.65	0.52	0.44	0.36	27
Labor market by choice						
Full time	0.49	0.47	0.47	0.45	0.48	99
Part time	0.51	0.46	0.60	0.43	0.54	36
Home market	0.47	0.54	0.50	0.38	0.40	487
Wife						
Labor market by necessity						
Full time	0.36	0.56	0.40	0.33	0.33	102
Part time	0.41	0.59	0.41	0.36	0.33	36
Labor market by choice						
Full time	0.46	0.51	0.46	0.42	0.45	110
Part time	0.52	0.51	0.50	0.48	0.47	51
Home market	0.47	0.56	0.46	0.38	0.38	600

Note: A ridit "measures the probability that a person chosen at random from a particular subgroup of the sample will be better or worse off on a measure than an individual chosen at random from an identified reference distribution" (Orden and Bradburn, 1969, p. 398).

Source: Adapted from Orden and Bradburn (1969, p. 403).

women who enjoyed their employment compared with those working only for income. The difference between housewives and women who enjoyed their paid employment was less; three of the five differences in Table 17 favored the full-time employed over the housewife, but the differences are small. However, the authors reported some significant differences by family life cycle. When preschool children were at home, the differences in evaluation of the marriage favored the mothers who were housewives over those who were employed and enjoyed their work. This finding was true for the husbands as well. When children were all in grade school, evaluation of the marriage was more favorable by those wives (and their husbands) who were employed and enjoyed their work than by the housewives. Later, when only high school children remained in the home, there was little difference between the two categories of wives and their husbands. Other detailed analyses found differences favoring wives who liked their work compared with those who did not when analyses were made within various educational and income categories. When the total sample of full-time employed was compared with the housewives, differences evaporated. Those who liked their work tended to be higher than housewives, those who did not like it were lower. When they were combined, differences became trivial.

The Orden and Bradburn sample was relatively large and random and the analysis more detailed than many, yet it leaves some unresolved questions. Full-time employed, part-time, and housewives differ in a number of characteristics related to marital satisfaction. Full-time employed are older on the average; have fewer children, especially preschool age; and are better educated; yet their husbands earn less on the average and have lower-status occupations. Separate analyses were made within broad income classes and by education of the husband, but nowhere were these variables controlled simultaneously. This procedure is not unusual in research and applies to most of the studies already cited.

However, one problem in this analysis is not encountered elsewhere, that of the halo effect. Although the question was worded to minimize this problem, respondents basically were asked two questions about personal satisfactions: do you like to work and do you have good times with your spouse. A woman who indicated satisfaction on one was somewhat more likely to do so on the other also. Other studies have not faced this problem because the independent variable has been a factual one: Are you employed and, if so, how many hours do you usually work? (The halo problem does not apply to comparisons between totally employed and housewife, and between full-time and part-time employed.)

Birnbaum (1971) compared the marital happiness of married professional women with educated housewives who had graduated "with honors" from a large university. Her findings (p. 154) were that 24 percent of the housewives reported being "not too happy—just average," another 24 percent were "pretty happy," and 52 percent were "very happy." The corresponding percentages for professionals were 0, 32, and 68. If this small sample of gifted women reflects the marital happiness of this segment of the population, then a higher proportion of married women employed in the higher professions are happily married than are comparably gifted, college-educated housewives. Besides the limitations of a small, nonrandom sample, two social characteristics of these women were quite different. Three-fourths of the married professionals had only one or two children compared with three or more for most of the housewives. The other difference is in the occupation of the husbands. Three-fourths of the married professionals were married to professors or scientists compared with 36 percent of the housewives. Sixty-four percent of the housewives were married to business executives or self-employed professionals. Which aspect of these different marriage styles provides the link to marital satisfaction is an open question.

Two studies utilizing non-American samples seem especially relevant. Safilios-Rothschild (1970a), who analyzed data from 896 Greek women, found no difference in marital satisfaction by employment status. However, those employed wives with high work commitment averaged higher marital satisfaction scores than did the nonemployed wives. This means that the employed wives with low work commitment averaged lower on marital satisfaction than did those not employed. Bailyn (1970), studying two hundred British couples in which the wives were university graduates, found that women who favored combining a career with home responsibilities averaged slightly lower on marital adjustment than did those holding traditional attitudes toward women's roles. The employment of the mother was not considered.

Full-Time versus Part-Time Employment

Research on the husband-wife relationship of part-time employed mothers is sparse. Since these women employed only part of the week at any given time number only about one-third of the employed mothers, frequently their numbers are too small for interesting analyses. Too, if one is interested in role conflict or other outcome variables, one might expect that full-time employment would maximize impact on outcomes. Axelson (1963) was one of the few whose studies included analyses of the husband-wife relationship of part-time employed women. He found that the marital satisfaction of the husbands of part-time employed women averaged the same as that of the husbands of housewives and considerably above that of the husbands of full-time employed women. Nye (1963) also analyzed part of his data by part-time, full-time, and housewife categories. He found that the part-time employed mothers averaged higher on satisfaction than did either the full-time employed or the housewives.

The part-time employed seem to enjoy an especially full recreational life (Chapter Nine). They attend more parties, bowl more, and play golf more frequently. In no type of recreation were they significantly lower in participation than the other mothers. They seem to be able to add part-time employment yet have more recreation than other mothers.

Orden and Bradburn (1969) report that their findings suggest that "part-time employment may indeed be the way for a woman to combine the labor market and the home market to achieve optimum adjustment in the marriage relationship both for herself and for her husband. However, only a small proportion of women—just 6 percent of those who are free to make a choice— choose part-time participation in the labor market. This fact may reflect limited opportunities for part-time employment as well as social pressures to put in a 'full day's work.' "

The Orden and Bradburn data add to other findings that part-time employment is related to many outcomes valued by women and their husbands, yet few women voluntarily choose it. Perhaps some of the reasons for preference for full-time employment include much higher incomes, security in employment, and more interesting positions. Only one-fourth of the women seeking employment were looking for part-time positions (U.S. Department of Labor, Women's Bureau, 1968). On the preference for full-time employment, the U.S. Department of Labor, Women's Bureau (1968), indicates, "Thus it is evident that women who work part-time hold, for the most part, the less skilled, less rewarding jobs in our economy. The median income of women who worked at part-time jobs in 1966 was only $827. Even if they worked part time for at least fifty weeks, their median income was only $1,504" (p. 3). The latter figure was only a little more than a third of the average income that year of women employed full time, year around. However, some women prefer part-time employment, despite the lower pay and less attractive positions, yet are unable to find it.

Future Research

The present state of research offers several interesting research challenges. First, while some studies have analyzed the marital adjustment of employed mothers who like or do not like their jobs, no one (to our knowledge) has separated housewives into subcategories on the basis of whether they like the household role or not. Doing so would permit a fourfold analysis of marital satisfactions: employed mothers who like their jobs, employed mothers who do not like their employment, housewives who like housekeeping and child care, and housewives who do not enjoy those household responsibilities.

Second, too little is known of the marital satisfaction of mothers employed part time. Scattered research findings report their marital satisfactions higher than either the full-time employed or the housewives. Yet these findings are hardly sufficiently extensive or systematic to establish this as a firm conclusion. Research focusing specifically on this issue should produce additional insight into the relationship of the marital bond to the economic activity of the wife.

Third, the data show that husbands of employed women earn on the average substantially less than those without employed wives and that employed women on the average are better educated than those not employed; yet no one, to our knowledge, has simultaneously controlled on the husband's income and the wife's education (family income is something quite different). If this were done some additional light might be shed on the relationship of maternal employment to marital success.

Finally, research to date has utilized general samples of families in which husbands have provided most of the income. What are the outcomes in families in which the wife produces an equal or greater amount than the husband? What are the outcomes for the marital satisfaction of the wife and for the husband?

Summary

This chapter asked two broadly related questions: Does the husband-wife relationship differ in families in which the mother is employed and those in which she is not? If the relationship differs, is it attributable to the effects of paid employment? Examination of the research from 1949 to 1973 suggests that it may be necessary to subdivide the first question: Was there a difference in the forties and fifties, during which the employed mother emerged as a major figure? Are the differences still present? If there are differences, are they present in both the middle and working class?

The earliest of these studies, Locke and Mackeprang (1949) failed to find a significant difference in the husband-wife relationship, but most of the studies conducted in the following fifteen years found a small difference favoring wives who were not employed (Gianopulos and Mitchell, 1957; Feld, 1963; Axelson, 1963; Gover, 1963; Powell, 1963; and Nye, 1963). However, Nye found differences in the areas of conflict and living apart but not in marital satisfaction. A variety of measures and many different types of samples were used in these studies; some attempted to hold constant related variables, such as occupation and income of the husband and education of the wife. Although the results of the studies are not uniform, we feel the support for a difference in the marital relationship is stronger than for the alternative of no difference. Having tentatively concluded this to be true, it is important to note that the differences in the husband-wife relationship were quite small. The associations between employment status and marital satisfaction and other measures of the husband-wife relationship were less than 0.20. Thus no more and surely somewhat less than 4 percent of the variance in marital satisfaction and other measures of the marital relationship can be explained by the employment status of the wife.

A subfinding from studies during this period relates to the location of these differences in the social structure. Several of the studies analyzed this relationship within different socioeconomic strata: Feld, by education of the wife; Gover, occupation of the husband; Blood, income of the husband; Nye, occupation of the husband and education; and Feldman and Feldman, poverty-level status. All except Blood located the differences primarily in the lower socioeconomic classes, with almost no differences in the middle class. This finding is consistent with the differences in remarriage found in the Hoffman and Nye samples. Hoffman found, in her largely blue-collar sample, a larger proportion of remarriages (after divorce) among employed mothers than among the housewives. Nye's sample, primarily middle-class, disclosed no significant differences in remarriages between employed mothers and housewives. Blood found the opposite, with considerable differences favoring housewives in the upper income category and employed wives at lower levels. Thus, the research evidence is not entirely consistent but provides predominant support for the thesis that differences favoring the housewife occur mostly in the lower social classes.

The second part of the first question is: Do the differences that existed between the marriages of housewives and of full-time employed wives still persist? We might anticipate that they would not since American society has become accustomed to mothers' holding paid employment. In several categories such women are now in the majority, including the large one of married women with children of school age but none of preschool age. Even among mothers of preschool children, almost one in three is employed. The normative proscriptions against mothers in employment have largely disappeared. Also, more restaurants, cleaning establishments, pre-processed foods, and child-care alternatives are available. Thus, although the conflicts between household and employee roles have not disappeared, many adaptive arrangements and modifications of attitudes may have reduced the stresses associated with role conflict.

Recent research, especially that of Orden and Bradburn (1969), suggests that a change may, indeed, have occurred. In their study, the marriage scores for the husbands were almost identical for those married to housewives and to fully-employed wives; the housewives scored a little higher on happiness but also a little higher on tensions. Their Marital Adjustment Balance Scores were almost identical. This is a single study but the sample was randomly selected and quite large.

The second general question is whether the differences in husband-wife relationship result from employment itself. No one has conducted before-and-after studies in which the marital relationship was assessed before employment, then reassessed afterward. If the two groups of couples were equivalent in other respects, inferences from cross-sectional studies could be made with respect to the effects of employment. Research has shown several differences between the two categories of families (Chapter One). Fully employed wives are older, have fewer children—particularly preschool children—and have more education. Their husbands are older, earn less than average, and are found disproportionately in some occupations. Families of working mothers tend to be concentrated in urban areas. Many of these differences are also related to marital happiness. Older women average somewhat lower in marital happiness; couples with higher education and high income average higher in marital happiness.

Some studies attempted to control these related variables. Blood made his analyses separately with high- and low-income families, as did Gover. Feld held education and family incomes constant. Nye held constant the education of the wife, occupation of the husband, family size, presence of preschool children, and previous marital status. Orden and Bradburn made separate analyses in three family income categories, education of husband and wife, and three stages of the family life cycle. These attempts add to the credibility of the findings, but they are not completely adequate. No study held all the related variables constant simultaneously.

Most of the research findings are consistent with the generalization that in the 1950s and probably early 1960s, the full-time employment of mothers contributed, if only slightly, to more conflict and tensions and less marital happiness. By the late 1960s and

1970s this effect seems to have disappeared in the middle classes. However, the latest study of lower-class families (Feldman and Feldman, 1973) provides substantial evidence for more conflict and less marital satisfaction in lower-class couples in which the mother is employed. Their findings are consistent with virtually all earlier research.

We could sum up the research of almost three decades by concluding that the early studies, in general, showed slightly more marital problems among couples in which the mother was employed; but even in those studies, the difference in tensions and satisfactions occurred mostly at the lower-class levels. Recent studies suggest that the small, sometimes nonsignificant, differences in middle-class families found in earlier studies no longer exist; if the wife enjoys her work, the marital satisfactions of this subgroup of wives may average higher than for housewives in general. However, in lower-class families, research supports the conclusion of continuing differences, favoring couples in which the wife is not employed.

For those wishing to employ these research findings as a basis for making personal decisions concerning their own employment or that of their wives, a caution is in order. Although the average marital adjustment of populations of employed and not-employed wives does not differ substantially, employment of the mother may have a major effect or effects, positive or negative, on any one husband-wife relationship. The consequences are a little more likely to be positive if the number of children at home is small, the job she takes is one she enjoys, the husband's attitude is positive, and the husband and wife have advanced education.

9

Effects on Mother

F. Ivan Nye

Since the employed mother has two clusters of duties, household and employee, which traditionally have been considered full-time occupations, considerable concern has been evinced about her health and well-being. The question is not solely one of the amount of time and energy required since there are special conflicts in which the woman has simultaneous responsibilities in her home and at her place of employment. Further, some studies have suggested that a different set of behaviors, competitive and rational in the office and cooperative and nurturant in the home, are required.

Some repetition cannot be avoided in this chapter because the mother's feelings concerning her child-care role are a part of the effects on the child (Chapter Six), yet one's roles, one's level of competence in them, and one's feelings about them are an integral part of the self. The same is true of the nature of the husband-wife relationship (Chapter Eight). One other problem in assessing effects on the mother is that this issue has attracted less research attention than have effects on the child or the husband-wife relationship. Few studies have directly examined the effects of maternal employment on health, emotions, and self-concept. Thus, whatever research can be reported often was done for other purposes, and the research indicators of the concepts are varied and sometimes not fully appropriate to the questions. Such data as seem appropriate are ex-

Work on this chapter was supported in part by Project #2008 of the Agricultural Research Center, Washington State University.

tracted from these studies, and those studies designed specifically to
assess effects on the mother are reported more completely.

Physical Health

A major study addressed the question of the physical health
of employed mothers (Feld, 1963), with data from a national probability sample of 2,460 adult women. Details of the sample and
findings are given in greater detail in Nye and Hoffman (1963a).
Feld (1963, p. 344) reports:

> *The working mothers clearly report fewer physical
> symptoms than mothers who do not work: only 7 percent
> of the workers report any physical ill health symptoms,
> while 25 percent of the housewives report some of these
> symptoms—pains and ailments in different parts of their
> bodies and not feeling healthy enough to carry out things
> they would like to do. The differences on the physical
> anxiety index are smaller: 36 percent of the workers and
> 44 percent of the housewives report these symptoms.*

About the same proportion of the employed and housewife
respondents reported major illnesses in the past, but housewives were
more likely (18 percent) than employed mothers (11 percent) to
list more than one illness.

Hauenstein and Harburg (1973) studied the effects of
housework and paid employment on the blood pressure of women.
They chose diastolic blood pressure as the indicator because they
reported it to be the best predictor of coronary heart disease for subjects under age sixty. Their research addressed both whether blood
pressure differs between employed wives and housewives, and
whether feelings of dissatisfaction and incompetence in household
and employee roles relate to high blood pressure. They found no
significant differences between employed and nonemployed wives.
Employed wives averaged higher blood pressure, but the differences
were trivial and statistically nonsignificant. When the ages of housewives and working wives were standardized, the average blood pressure became almost identical for the two categories. There was a
similar correspondence in the proportion with hypertensive levels of

blood pressure: 9 percent of the housewives and 11 percent of the working wives.

Feelings about housework and performance of household tasks were found to be related to blood pressure. Those who responded affirmatively to the item "housework is often a strain" and were "often bothered by the feeling I am not doing as good housework as I should be doing" averaged higher blood pressure, while those who felt they were doing well had lower levels. However, attitudes toward paid employment had much less relationship to blood pressure. Surprisingly, those who responded affirmatively to the item "want to quit working (and spend more time at home as a housewife)" averaged lower blood pressure. Thus, strain and feelings of inadequacy in the household roles are related to high blood pressure, but similar strain with respect to the employee role is related to low blood pressure. The latter was especially true for older and overweight women. It may be that wives feel there is no escape from household roles, whereas most feel they can leave paid employment.

Insofar as physical health is concerned, employed mothers as a group appear healthier than housewives. The earlier concerns that the demands of home-centered roles and those of a full-time employee would be unduly taxing on women's health are generally ill-founded. This finding should not be applied to all women as individuals. Some jobs and some in combination with some household responsibilities would be taxing for some women. Nor does this finding apply to several decades ago, when more jobs required heavy physical effort. Yet today, and presumably even more in the future as more heavy labor is eliminated, there seems to be no basis for a general concern about the health of employed mothers. Does employment tend to improve their health? An interesting question but one which would require before-and-after research.

Psychological Health

Anxiety and Feelings of Inadequacy. Concern about combining full-time employment with adequate performance in the child-care and housekeeper roles seems to have been extremely widespread among employed mothers. Some mention of this concern has been made by most of the researchers who studied effects on children. A national survey by the U.S. Department of Labor, Women's Bureau (1971, p. 21), found that half of the 6.5 million women who gave up paid employment in 1970 cited the problem of handling home and child-related responsibilities as the reason for leaving employment. One-third of the women who stated they would like a job but were not seeking work gave this conflict as the reason. Birnbaum (1971) reported that about one-sixth of both married professional women and housewives with comparable education mentioned added conflict as an expected outcome of combining a career with household roles.

The Feld study (1963, pp. 342-343) and a later one by White (1972) addressed the issues more directly. Feld found a larger proportion of employed mothers felt inadequate as parents. While Feld found the relationship existed widely, it was concentrated primarily among high school and college graduates rather than among the least educated in her sample.

In another early study, Kligler (1954) found employed mothers exhibiting marked anxiety and guilt about their roles as mothers. Full-time employed women were happier in their work than housewives but, at the same time, were likely to feel guilty about inadequate performance of household roles.

Kaley (1971, p. 304) found a major difference in orientation between different professional groups. Over a third of married women caseworkers and their supervisors believed conflict was inevitable between employee and housewife roles compared with only 7 percent of married women teachers.

However, employed mothers are not the only ones to have problems with anxiety and guilt. Birnbaum (1971, pp. 189–190) reported from her study of talented college graduates that the full-time housewives were more anxious and overconcerned about their children than were a comparable group of talented women who combined a professional career with motherhood.

The report of earlier researchers of anxiety and guilt feelings on the part of employed mothers led White (1972) to ask whether these anxiety feelings about child-care and socialization roles were different from those of housewives who leave their children to engage in community activities or recreation. His study of 1,092 mothers in a small Washington city disclosed that anxiety was more prevalent among women who left their children with mother substitutes to go to work than among mothers who left them to engage in other activity (Table 18). Maternal anxiety is by no means

Table 18.

ANXIETY LEVELS OF EMPLOYED AND NONEMPLOYED MOTHERS
BY REASON FOR ABSENCE FROM HOME, PERCENT

Level of Anxiety	Employed Mothers for Work Activities	Nonemployed Mothers for Nonwork Activities
High	31.5	15.7
Medium	49.2	54.0
Low	19.4	30.3
Number	124	396

Source: Adapted from White (1972, p. 67).

limited to employed mothers, yet such mothers experience it disproportionately. Mothers who are anxious when leaving children to go to work are more likely, also, to be anxious when leaving them for other activities, but the work situation is more strongly anxiety-producing.

Anxiety is closely related to the evaluation of the mother substitute. Almost all (88 percent) of the mothers with low anxiety levels reported a "good" evaluation of the substitute compared with only 45 percent of the high-anxiety mothers. Lower anxiety scores were found for higher-income families, perhaps because they were able to secure better child-care services. Apparently the beliefs of the mother's parents are relevant also since mothers with traditionalistic parents were more likely to feel anxiety in leaving their children. However, the ideology of the husband was not closely related to anxiety in the wife. In general, the White research indicates that the problem of day care is still anxiety-producing for most employed mothers.

Self-Concept. Employed mothers have a more positive image of themselves than do housewives (Feld, 1963). Eighty percent of the former compared with 65 percent of the latter mentioned self-characteristics that were positive and only 7 percent of the employed compared with 17 percent of the housewives made negative statements. Hacker (1971) found, in a national survey, that both employed wives and housewives attributed a number of favorable characteristics to employed married women; they were viewed as well educated, well informed, ambitious. Only a minority associated them with being "loving mothers" or "good wives." Like Feld, Hacker found desirable personal attributes associated with employment but also role difficulties, with respect to both children and husband. Thus, those employed vary in the direction of self-confidence and a positive self-image, but, in the child-care role, most studies report that the employed see themselves as less adequate than do the full-time housewives.

Mental Illness. Considerable concern has been expressed over the effects of paid employment on the mental health of wives and mothers. Some observers in the psychoanalytic tradition have viewed the activities, values, and relationships of the marketplace as unsuitable for women, either in an absolute sense or because they were the opposite of the attributes needed for maternal and spousal roles. Thus, aggressiveness, rationality, and ruthlessness were seen as functional for the marketplace but dysfunctional in the child-care and therapeutic roles women enact in the home. Sociological perspective anticipated stresses caused by role conflict, both from needing to be at home and at the office simultaneously and from the time and effort required by a combination of provider and household roles.

Two studies bear on this issue. Feld, as part of the research reported above, investigated two indicators of psychosomatic illness: hard heart-beating and shortness of breath. She found these more characteristic of housewives than of employed mothers. Sharp (1963) employed a list of ten psychosomatic symptoms, which in order of increasing affirmative responses were:

> *Have you ever consulted a psychiatrist in the past five years?*
> *Have you ever been troubled with cold sweats?*
> *Do your hands tremble enough to bother you?*
> *Have you ever been bothered by shortness of breath when you were not exercising or working hard?*
> *Are you ever bothered by nightmares?*

Have you ever been bothered by your heart beating
hard?
Have you ever been bothered by pressures or pains
in the head?
Are you ever bothered by nervousness?
Do you have trouble in getting or staying asleep?
Have you ever had spells of dizziness?

A score devised from these symptoms ranged from those who experienced none to those who experienced all. Data were analyzed from 1,982 mothers in three small Washington cities. The investigators had expected to find more symptoms among the employed mothers because of role conflict. However the data did not show the expected differences. Differences that were found were trivial, and symptoms tended to be less frequent among the employed mothers. Although employed mothers reported more anxiety than did housewives, they did not report more of the physical symptoms which anxiety usually produces.

Sharp (1960) reviewed a sample of records in three Washington state hospitals for relationships between employment and mental illness and found one rather large difference. Of the women employed before being hospitalized, almost half (47 percent) were diagnosed to be neurotic rather than psychotic, but only 7 percent of the housewives were. No evidence was found that would suggest that employment is a precipitating factor in mental illness.

Gove and Tudor (1973) have shown that more women than men are treated for mental illness, a difference the authors attribute to differences in male-female sex roles. However, they do not provide a comparison between employed wives and housewives, so the data are not fully appropriate to the present issue.

Even though the data are inadequate, there is no support for the thesis that the mental health of employed mothers is worse than that of housewives. In fact, slight differences favored the employed women.

Recreation

The image of the employed mother as a harried person suggests less time available for recreation. An unstated premise appears to be that recreation is marginal activity which can and is likely to be sacrificed in favor of the requirements of the job and duties of child care, child socialization, and housekeeping. To some extent, therefore, the data on the recreational life of employed mothers test this premise in addition to their usefulness in assessing the costs of employment to mothers.

Research does not support this view of recreation as a marginal interest and activity (Nye, 1958). Some activity, especially that which requires large blocks of day-time hours, such as golf, TV viewing, card-playing, telephoning friends and visiting in the neighborhood, is reduced considerably. Some of these activities may be designed to use surplus time as much as being intrinsically attractive. Entertaining is lessened, also. In addition to requiring considerable time, it requires advance planning and commitments which may be difficult for the employed woman and her family.

In contrast, neither family recreation (if one excludes TV viewing) nor commercial recreation, except golf, were appreciably affected by employment of the wife, suggesting that recreation has a higher priority for women than had been suspected, a value which has since been validated by the tremendous expansion of recreation industries. Mothers seem to have retained those recreational patterns that were meaningful to them, such as joint activity with their families and kin, and such commercial recreation as was of sufficient value to buy, such as dancing, movies, and active physical sports. (Dancing and movies are usually classified as family-participation activities as well as commercial activities.) Those recreational activities which employed mothers participate in less are designed to occupy unused time but also may contain elements of interest and pleasure. We do not know how much, if at all, employed mothers miss these activities.

Community Participation

Employed mothers, particularly those with young children at home, participate less in the leadership of voluntary community organizations. It is not clear that this lessened participation is a cost to employed women, either in rewarding activities foregone or anxiety and guilt feelings incurred because of nonparticipation.

However, a woman's life is different in considerable ways depending on whether appreciable portions of it are invested in community work. This may be sufficient reason for a brief analysis of the relationship between paid employment and voluntary community participation.

The data available are from 1,993 mothers of children in the first through the tenth grades (Sharp, 1963) and also from a "postparental" sample of mothers who had either a son or a daughter married within the year. Contrary to common-sense expectations, younger employed mothers (those with children of school age) belonged to as many organizations as mothers who were not employed. One-fifth of each group indicated no organizational membership, whereas 9 percent of the nonemployed and 7 percent of the employed listed four or more memberships.

The same pattern was found for attendance at organizational meetings. About one-third of the nonemployed and full-time employed said they attended no organizational meetings regularly. Almost the same proportion, 13 and 11 percent, of the nonemployed and full-time employed, respectively, indicated regular attendance at meetings of three or more organizations.

Leadership in community organizations, however, was related to employment status. Less than two-fifths of the employed mothers held an office or a committee chairmanship in an organization; whereas a majority of both nonemployed and part-time employed indicated at least one leadership position. The contrast is even greater for those holding two or more such positions: 13 percent of the nonemployed compared with 4 percent of the full-time employed. The part-time employed mothers appeared to play a more prominent part in organizational leadership than either of the other two groups.

Some causal inference appears warranted from these data. Leadership positions require considerably more time than membership or attendance. Since the three employment categories were matched by sociological variables and since, on the whole, employed mothers should be at least as energetic as the others, it seems safe to conclude that employment does affect leadership roles in community organizations. A mediating sociological mechanism may be a redefinition of the community role of the mother who is a provider. Mothers employed full time define their own community responsibilities as involving fewer leadership roles, a redefinition with which the community concurs. The corollary of such redefinition is the placement of added community responsibility on the nonemployed mother or the professionalization of roles currently filled by volunteers.

Data were also available from 265 mothers whose children were adults or nearly so. The role in the community of these older mothers was possibly less affected by employment since their roles as supervisor, disciplinarian of children, and (probably) housekeeper demanded considerably less time. The role of provider would seem to conflict less with their community role. Consistent with this hypothesis, the employment status of older women was found to be unrelated to membership in organizations or to leadership positions. Although employment reduced the occupancy of leadership positions by mothers with school-age children, during the empty-nest period employment did not reduce leadership by mothers. In looking at specific organizations, differences in organizational participation for these older mothers were found only in those peculiarly related to working hours and occupational activity. Earlier, it was noted that mothers of school-age children were less likely to lead community organizations than those who were not employed. This general difference disappeared after children left home. Apparently, employed mothers whose children were grown could manage the duties of community leadership along with the housekeeper role. Therefore, stage in the family life cycle is an important contingent condition which mediates the relationship between employment and role in the community.

Attitudes Toward Child Care

Chapter Six reviewed the research on effects on children. The concern here is with the effects of children and the responsibilities of child care on mothers.

Birnbaum (1971) reports a major qualitative difference in the problems of child-rearing. Married professional women have problems mainly with the overt behavior of their children and in the conflicts between the child-care and employee roles. She quotes (pp. 189–190) some of the married professional women as follows:

"The hours when one can be free of responsibility become too few to replenish one's own inner resources." "Their irrationality, demandingness, need for attention, and *interruptingness.*" "Always being tied down—can't do anything without planning ahead." "Restraints and restrictions on pursuing one's personal interests at times." Housewives view children differently. The worst things about having children to them are mutual disappointments and a sense of failure; worrying about growth and development; trying to raise children according to standards and ideals; and worrying about their shortcomings. In other words, these women are preoccupied with their achievements as "good mothers." They set or have acquired high standards and often compare themselves to how well they imagine other mothers might do under similar circumstances (p. 190). However, this talented group of married professionals expressed more confidence in their competence in child care than did employed mothers in previous studies.

The Nye research did not ask for a self-rating of competence in the child-care role, but did ask mothers ten questions about their feelings, their interactions with their children, and their feelings about children. Employed mothers were less likely to say that their children made them nervous. Nye interpreted this finding as due both to less time spent in interaction with children and, possibly more important, to preoccupation with work for a large part of the day, which may prevent overconcentration on the problems of the children.

A quasi-scale was also constructed to measure attitudes toward children. The total scores favored the employed mothers slightly; 46 percent of employed mothers fell into the most positive group compared with 42 and 45 percent of the housewives and part-time employed, respectively. Such differences are statistically nonsignificant. However, by utilizing family size as a test variable, a relationship emerged. In small families of one to three children, employed mothers were more positively oriented to the child-care role, but they are not so oriented when they have four or more children. In large families, differences favored the housewife over the employed mother but were not statistically significant. We can suppose that caring for four or more children and holding a full-time paid position frequently created stressful conflicts.

Another test variable, age of children, revealed unexpected relationships. Employed mothers with preadolescent children compared more favorably with housewives than did those with high school-aged children. The implication was that the child-care and socialization roles were more demanding of maternal time and energy in adolescence than during the preadolescent years.

In a related study of 104 employed mothers and a matched sample of 104 housewives who had children aged three to five, a similar but not identical list of items measured attitudes toward children (Nye, Perry, and Ogles, 1963). The differences on ten of twelve items favored the employed mothers, but only two of the differences were large enough to be statistically significant: number of reasons listed for wanting a large family and number of things found enjoyable about one's child. The authors concluded that more employed than nonemployed mothers had positive feelings about their parental activities and about their children. This finding appears to be true of mothers of preschool as well as of school-age children. Since family size was not controlled, however, the employed mothers' more positive attitudes may in part have been a function of having smaller families.

Global Assessments

The specific analyses reported to this point stop short of a general assessment of the impact of employment on the mother's life. In an effort to contribute to a more general assessment, mothers in the Washington study were asked their degree of satisfaction or dissatisfaction with seven broad areas of their lives: family income, house and furniture, recreation, children, husband, community as a place to live, and their daily work. The same questions were asked of mothers in the "post-parental" stage of the family.

Satisfaction with Work. Little in the literature suggests that women enjoy the combination of household and employee roles, and a good deal suggests that they find the combination frustrating and tiring. However, data indicate that those who are employed full time are better satisfied with their daily work than are the housewives and those employed part time. The part-time workers share the interests of outside work and interpersonal relationships but earn less and are less likely to hold professional or supervisory positions. Given higher costs which full-time employed mothers incur in conflicts between household and employee roles and given their much longer working week, they still are more satisfied with their daily work than are those who restrict their responsibilities to housekeeper and child-care roles. Apparently the rewards, economic, psychological and social, are worth the extra effort for most employed mothers.

Satisfaction with Community. The moderate attenuation of community participation of fully employed mothers indicated above might be expected to constitute a deprivation. However, data from Sharp (1963) do not support that perception. Sixty-two percent of the full-time employed mothers were well or completely satisfied with their communities compared with 52 percent of the housewives. The most satisfied, however, were those employed part time. Those who had the most time available for community activity (the non-employed) were, as a group, the most dissatisfied with their communities, which suggests that a low level of satisfaction or a high level of frustration or both are involved in unpaid community work.

No significant differences were found among employment categories with respect to satisfaction with family income, house and furniture, or recreational life. The sample differences favored the employed mother on the first two and the nonemployed mother on the last. Although employed mothers said they worked for added income, they were no better satisfied with their income or standard of living than were nonemployed mothers.

Satisfaction index. Some of these satisfaction items favored the employed mother while others failed to disclose a significant relationship to employment status. To obtain a more general measure of satisfaction, the seven items were combined into a single index (Nye and Hoffman, 1963a). The association between employment and satisfaction total scores was significant, in general favoring the employed, particularly the part-time employed. Among the house-wives was a particularly large proportion of women who were generally dissatisfied with their lives. If the part-time employed were removed from the analysis, the relationship was still significant.

Both part-time and full-time employed mothers were some-what better satisfied than were those not employed. However, employment may be associated with satisfaction under some conditions and not others; it may be reversed under some. Therefore, a number of test variables were introduced into the analysis.

Employed mothers were found generally better satisfied whether the family was large or not, and the presence or absence of preschool children failed to have an appreciable effect as a test variable. Contrary to popular belief, the employed mothers of preschool children verbalized more satisfaction with their daily lives than did their nonemployed equivalents.

Employed mothers with college education showed a considerably smaller proportion in the dissatisfied and a larger proportion in the highly satisfied categories. In contrast, employed mothers with only high school educations were concentrated in the intermediate-satisfaction category and were underrepresented in both the lowest and highest categories.

Satisfactions in Postparental Period. The preceding discussion involved employed mothers in the active period of child-rearing —that is, with minor children at home. In the same study, data were gathered also from a so-called postparental group of 265 mothers who had at least one child who had been married within the last two years. Most were between forty-five and fifty-five years of age.

Much previous literature suggests that women whose responsibilities as mothers were declining require other significant roles from which to obtain social status and a sense of personal worth. The data on postparental mothers, however, were not consistent with this belief. The nonemployed were found to be significantly better satisfied with their recreation and family income. Nonsignificant differences in satisfaction with the relationship to husband, house and furniture, daily work, and children favored the nonemployed mother at the postparental stage.

Since these findings were unexpected, only ad hoc interpretations were offered. The most obvious difference between samples was age. The postparental mothers on the average were eleven years older than the active-stage mothers, which may have been important both psychologically and socially. The reduced energy output of more advanced years may have made the time and energy demands of the job more difficult to meet. Socially, the quest for upward mobility may have run its course, so that the money added did not contribute to distant goals. However, two other differences connected with this older sample may have been important in explaining their lack of satisfaction with employment. The older women had less education and thus less preparation for higher-level positions. These differences were reflected in the positions reported: 40 percent were employed in crafts, operative, service, and household work, contrasted with about 20 percent in these low-status positions among the younger employed mothers. Thus, the older women were typically working in less skilled jobs involving more tiring physical labor for lower pay.

The findings concerning this age period are congruent with those of a small study by Gass (1959). Among eighty-five middle-aged, upper-middle-class women, she found that many were highly satisfied with having considerable time available for leisure and enjoyed the passive role of a full-time housewife with few duties and considerable help: "I enjoy my leisure time but waste a lot of it. However, I enjoy wasting it." Gass states that both the positive aspects of possessing leisure time and the "desire for passivity and their fear of competition and failure" help to keep this group out of employment and relatively satisfied with housewife roles.

National data also show lower involvement of women in the labor force in later middle age, suggesting that employment may be in some ways less profitable. In 1968, there were 6.147 million women forty-five to fifty-five years old employed but only 3.936 million between fifty-five and sixty-four (U.S. Department of Labor, Women's Bureau, 1969, p. 17). Despite the lower participation of women in the labor force after age fifty-five, the proportion working in this category is currently increasing more rapidly than any group. Perhaps the most accurate observation is that there is still a smaller proportion of women aged fifty-five to sixty-four employed than women aged forty-five to fifty-four employed, but the decline is less than previously.

Two general findings can be drawn from the large Washington study of life satisfactions: in the active child-rearing years employed mothers were better satisfied with their lives than were housewives, and during the postparental period, the relationship reversed, with housewives better satisfied than employed mothers.

Birnbaum (1971) studied three groups of talented women: housewives, married women holding professional positions, and single women in professional occupations. Her general conclusion was that "by the middle adult years, the most pressing and poignant problems exist not for the successful career-committed woman, however statistically deviant she may be, but rather for the gifted homemaker who is now faced with a kind of premature retirement as her major life role functions diminish" (p. 1). Most of the married professional women projected a positive image of themselves (Table 19). The Birnbaum research is important, yet the reader is reminded to keep two limitations in mind: the samples are small, and they are drawn from an elite group. The study stimulates a desire for broad-based research with samples of noncollege women; one cannot anticipate whether such research would reveal findings similar to Birnbaum's.

Four studies of the general well being of employed mothers and housewives have been presented. Three of these, the Feld, Birnbaum, and Nye studies of women in the active child-rearing years are in general agreement that where differences in well-being exist, they favor the employed mother over the housewife. However, the Nye study of an older postparental group of mothers, rather heavily weighted toward wives of blue-collar men, found differences favoring the nonemployed. Of these studies, the Birnbaum research with gifted women probably provided the most clear-cut differences favorable to employed women. In the Nye study of women in the active child-rearing years, the largest differences favoring employed mothers was found in the subsample with some college education. There is some support, then, for the idea that the higher the education level of the wife, the more likely that differences in the feelings of well-being will favor employed women.

Summary

The physical health of employed mothers appears to be better than that of housewives. It would be premature to assume a causal linkage, however, since this difference may well be due to selective recruitment of healthier mothers into employment or a tendency of those whose health is poor to leave employment. Still, the difference favoring the employed suggests that the dual set of role responsibilities is not typically damaging to the health of the mother.

Data concerning anxiety, guilt, and self-concept are complex.

Table 19.

Self-Esteem and General Well Being of Talented Women

Variable	Housewife (29)	Married Professional (25) Percent	Single Professional (27)	Significance
Composite self-esteem				
Poor to average	31	4	15	P < .005
Average to good	55	42	31	
Good to very good	14	54	54	
Self-rating on social skills				
Poor to average	66	29	38	P < .02
Good or very good	34	71	62	
Self-rating on child-care skills				
Poor to average	38	18	52	
Good	51	50	29	P < .08
Very good	10	32	19	
General mental-emotional health				
Poor to average	39	12	12	P < .03
Good to very good	61	88	88	
Feelings of uncertainty about self				
Hardly ever	34	64	58	P < .07
Fairly often	66	36	42	
What is missing in life				
Nothing much	27	32	18	
Challenge and creative involvement	42	4	0	
Interpersonal closeness	4	4	18	
More time to do what-ever wanted	27	59	64	P < .001
Marital happiness				
Not too happy—just average	24	0		
Pretty happy	24	32		
Very happy	52	68		P < .03
How does marriage change a woman's life? (responses indicating restrictive, burdensome, demanding)				
None	11	43	27	
Some	37	38	64	
All	52	19	6	P < .004

Source: Constructed from Birnbaum (1971, Tables 4 and 5).

Many early studies and one even as late as 1972 (White) found widespread guilt and anxiety about combining child-care and housekeeper roles with those of provider. Ordinarily, one would expect such anxieties to be accompanied by psychosomatic symptoms of sleeplessness, nervousness, and the like, but no study revealed such consequences of maternal employment. In fact, the Feld study (1963) revealed the opposite; employed mothers were more likely to be free of such symptoms, suggesting that, even then, anxiety and guilt feelings were not severe. Birnbaum (1971) also reported good mental-emotional health for a larger proportion of professionally employed wives than equally able full-time housewives. Perhaps any adverse effects of anxiety and guilt were mitigated by the beneficial effects of the added income and security for children and husband as well as the woman herself. Little research relates this phenomenon to mental illness.

Although many studies reported concern and self-doubt about the child-care role, employed mothers were more likely to enjoy their activities and relationships with children. The change of scene offered by employment appears, for most mothers, to be related to enjoying roles relating to children. However, Nye found this finding limited to families of three or fewer children; with four or more children, housewives were more likely than employed wives to enjoy their maternal roles. Birnbaum also stresses that full-time housewives were more likely to be completely occupied with their children and to have excessive expectations for the children and for themselves as mothers. Although the differences were not necessarily great, for more mothers than not combining provider and child-care roles was associated with enjoying child-care activities and relationships with children.

Studies of self-concept (Feld, 1963; Birnbaum, 1971; Hacker, 1971) revealed more positive and few negative feelings of employed mothers about themselves. The doubts often expressed concerning ability to simultaneously cope with household and employee roles were not typically reflected in doubts of self-worth, perhaps because mothers have not typically internalized a duty to join in the economic support of the family; such contributions are viewed as above and beyond what one is expected to do. Perhaps for this reason, employed mothers project an image of ability and confidence.

Participation in the leadership of voluntary community organizations and in selected recreational activities was less for employed women. While employed mothers belong to as many organizations and are as likely to attend meetings, they take fewer positions of responsibility (until after children leave home, then employed and not employed mothers are equal). It is not clear whether this lesser participation constitutes deprivation. A higher proportion of the employed women evaluated their communities as a satisfactory place to live.

The reduction in recreational participation among employed mothers occurred in TV viewing, day-time neighborhood visiting, formal entertaining, and golf. There were no significant differences in spouse- or family-oriented recreation. No information is at hand concerning whether employed mothers feel the reduction in these activities to be a cost; they may be considered time-fillers for some, if not most, women.

Finally, one attempt to comprehend the general effects of employment on mothers involved research on satisfaction or dissatisfaction with seven major aspects of life. Differences were not great, but they favored young employed mothers compared with housewives, and older housewives over employed mothers. Surprisingly, the items on which younger employed women scored appreciably higher than housewives were in some of the nonmaterial areas: satisfaction with relationships with children, with daily work, and with the community as a place to live.

10

Concluding Remarks

Lois Wladis Hoffman, F. Ivan Nye

The contemporary scene can be viewed as one in which a fundamental change is taking place in the economic activities of women, with corresponding transformation in other roles in the family. But in one sense women's economic activities are not new since in every society they have made economic contributions, either primary in the sense of producing or gathering agricultural products and manufacturing items for trade or secondary in the sense of processing food and fiber for family consumption and wear. As Rossi (1964) and Ridley (1972) and others have pointed out, for women to not be major economic producers is the nontypical situation, rather than the reverse.

Nor, in industrial societies, is it new for women faced with real deprivation to be in the labor force. Thus, in the early years of the Industrial Revolution, women and children in the lower socioeconomic classes were in the factories, as were widows and wives of incapacitated men. What is new is the ever-increasing flow into paid employment of wives of middle-class and blue-collar men who are above the level of absolute economic need.

In paid employment, women contribute to the economic support of their families as they did in the past by directly producing items for family consumption or trade. A difference now is that most employment requires the wife to leave home for most or all of the day, during the working days of the week. While her housekeeping and child-care duties have lessened, they have not ceased; and the decline of the extended family has meant that no other adults at home can assume household responsibilities.

The shift of production from the home to the factory has resulted in increases in efficiency in manufacturing the goods formerly produced at home, to the extent that little is to be gained by the mother's staying home to engage in these activities. Thus, home economic production is generally inefficient, and, as a consequence, housework has declined in prestige and in economic contribution.

The move from home to office and factory production has resulted in certain stresses for women and, probably to a lesser degree, for their families. There are often time conflicts when the employee role requires the woman to be away from home while the care of children or other family and household responsibilities demand her presence in the home. In general, full-time employment, added to child-care and socialization and housekeeper responsibilities, has often resulted in too much work for the mother. Thus American society and, to a lesser extent, other industrial societies have been going through a transitional period in which most mothers, at least after all their children have entered school, have had too little to do at home; but if they take full-time employment, they have too much to do. Aside from the pressures of time and added responsibilities, a further source of strain on the working woman has been the prevailing negative or ambivalent attitude toward maternal employment, which, though it has diminished, has not disappeared and is shared by many of the working mothers themselves (Chapter One).

For all these reasons most research, like most social concern, has looked for negative effects on the child, the marital relationship, and the mother's health. As the situation changes, however, and the social conditions leading to maternal employment become more compelling, the role of the nonemployed mother is likely to become subject to strain. Some of the data reported in this volume support the hypothesis that for families in certain situations—such as when the children are adolescent, or the mother is highly educated, or the mother is the sole support and economic resources are scarce—maternal employment has a positive effect. For example, in Chapter

Six data indicate that adolescent daughters of working mothers showed higher achievement patterns than did those of nonworking mothers, and elementary school children of full-time working mothers in a lower-class black sample showed better social adjustment on psychological tests and school records than did children of nonworking mothers. In Chapter Eight, the data indicate that while the marital adjustment of employed women in blue-collar groups is low, employment status does not differentiate on this variable for white-collar families; and among highly educated women, employment may increase marital satisfaction. Chapter Nine indicates that employed women seem to have better physical and mental health, although the causal sequence here is not clear.

Other studies have found maternal employment associated with lower achievement of children, as has sometimes been the case with sons; more marital difficulties, as in the blue-collar class; and more anxiety about child-care and household roles. Thus, both employment and nonemployment have strains and compensations. A number of the studies reported in this book found part-time employment an unusually successful adaptation to the conflict between the difficulties of being a full-time housewife and the strain of combining this role with full-time employment. These mothers seem to be physically and psychologically healthy, positive toward their maternal roles, and active in recreational and community activities (Chapter Nine). Their children compare favorably to the other two groups with respect to self-esteem, social adjustment, and attitudes toward their parents (Chapter Six); scattered findings suggest that their marital satisfaction is the highest of the three groups (Chapter Eight). This adaptation to the changing distribution of economic activity inside and outside the home has disadvantages at the present time, however. First, appropriate part-time jobs are often difficult to find, although the explanation for this scarcity sometimes seems to be bureaucratic encumbrance rather than the intrinsic aspects of the job. Second, not only the total pay but the rate of pay is often less. Third, various employee benefits, including job security, are typically not extended to part-time workers. Apart from the apparent advantages of part-time employment for mothers, the division of full-time jobs into part-time or the shortening of the work week itself may be necessary changes if the number of women seeking employment increases or if the economy does not expand rapidly enough to create new jobs, both of which are likely to occur.

In Chapters One and Two, the social and psychological factors that led to the increased employment of mothers were analyzed. These included the push away from full-time homemaking because technological, marketing, and medical advances have streamlined household tasks, making employment more feasible and making it seem like a more valuable contribution to the family. Control over fertility has also been an important enabling and motivating factor. Furthermore, maternal employment has become more socially acceptable and fathers have been more willing to help with child-care and household tasks (Chapter Seven). All these social trends are likely to increase. In fact, as pointed out in Chapter Four, the birth rate in the United States has declined dramatically since 1965, traditional sex roles are losing force, women are seeking more college and graduate education, and, consistent with all this, women are becoming more career oriented. However, the social conditions described in Chapter One also include more job opportunities for women because of the expanding economy and the population distribution. The country was going through a period of rapid economic growth. In addition, the increased birth rate in the forties and fifties created more jobs in the conventionally feminine occupations: women workers born in the low-fertility years of the thirties were relatively scarce, while children to teach, nurse, and supply with other commercial services and goods were plentiful. These conditions, which then led to increased job opportunities, no longer prevail; in fact, the current situation is reversed. Here is a dilemma. Women's desire for employment will increase while the availability of jobs may decrease. Even the conditions that create job scarcity—economic recession and decreased birth rates—increase the motivation for employment. In Chapter Three it was pointed out that economic recession increases women's desire for jobs, particularly among whites; in Chapters Two and Four, the increased desire for jobs that results from small family size was discussed. The happy coincidence of a push from the home and a pull from the job market may be over.

However, the job market may change more than diminish.

The expansion of subsidized health services, increased need to care for the elderly, and the growing demand for commercial services may increase the possible jobs in this sphere. Another dimension is being added also as women move into jobs and professions long considered the domain of men—law, medicine, university teaching, the skilled labor trades, and executive positions in all businesses. However, the future does not contain the unusual situation of the recent past, of a small labor force in a rapidly expanding economy. The labor force has been swelled by the maturation of the babies born in the late 1940s and 1950s. Jobs may again be scarce and women taking employment are quite likely to face stiff competition from other women and from men.

If an oversupply of workers develops, it will add to demands for a shorter work week which, by reducing the working day for men, will enable them to more fully share child-care and housekeeper roles at home. A shorter week and a greater sharing of household roles by men will reduce the long hours typically worked by full-time employed mothers and enable more of them to make a commitment to a career.

In any case, the social conditions that existed during the period when most of the research reported in this book was conducted are changing in significant ways. These changes may affect the impact of maternal employment on the family. We have pointed out that the effect of maternal employment depends on the surrounding situation; the effects observed under one condition cannot be generalized to a different condition. For example, we have suggested that some of the strain of maternal employment on the family may stem from the present tendency for the mother to continue to handle the major share of the household and child-care tasks, but if this pattern alters and husbands of working women assume these responsibilities equally with their wives, the stress for the mother and some of the effects noted in Chapters Eight and Nine, such as the marital strain observed in the blue-collar class and the anxieties of the working mother about her domestic roles, might be lessened. On the other hand, as noted in Chapter Six, lack of negative effects on the school-age child might be a result of the conscious effort by working mothers to compensate for their absence by such efforts as deliberately setting aside times for interaction with the child. With the increased acceptance of maternal employment, this pattern might be less common. In a sense, the concern over possible adverse effects of maternal employment on the child may have been overdone, but it may also have led working mothers to make particular efforts which have succeeded in averting these effects. Whether the effects of maternal employment on the child would be equally benign in a situation where maternal employment was not under critical scrutiny in unknown.

In short, the studies reported in this volume were carried out under social conditions that might change. As in all research, whether in the chemistry laboratory or the natural setting, a changed situation can lead to different effects; this is a limitation of all empirical data, whether in the physical or the social sciences.

There is need for a great deal more research. There are no satisfactory studies on the differential outcomes for children of the various substitute child-care arrangements (Chapter Five). Almost nothing is known about the effects of maternal employment on infants (Chapter Six). Frequent reference has been made to the part-time employed mother and to the generally favorable personal and interpersonal outcomes found in such arrangements, but research on this development usually has been a by-product of research on full-time employment. Since most employed mothers work part of the week or part of the year, or both, this phenomenon seems to deserve more than incidental attention from researchers. Particularly important is the observation made repeatedly throughout this volume: most of the existing research has involved white families with two parents present. Research on minority families and families with one parent is urgently needed.

Longitudinal studies are needed to sort out the many questions of causal sequence left unanswered, in order to help differentiate selective factors from effects. In addition, the effect of maternal employment on the child, the marriage, and the mother should be studied at various stages in the family cycle, for the effects at one stage may look different at another.

In addition to these general research directions, specific issues uncovered by empirical results need further exploration. For example, data suggest that maternal employment, particularly in the middle class, has a different effect on boys than on girls, but the dynamics of that effect are not at all clear. Or, as another example, the work-commitment and job-market behavior of black and white women seems to differ, but a full explanation for these patterns is still lacking. Again, the employment-marital adjustment relationship is not the same for women at different ages or for all social classes, and this too needs further investigation.

Finally, the newly emerging patterns need to be researched. As maternal employment becomes the norm, it will be interesting to consider more carefully the nonemployed mother. What are her motivations, her interaction patterns with the other members of her family and her community, her psychological state at various family stages? What will the effects be of massive female employment on the programs that now rely heavily on volunteer womanpower? Another parcel of research will be required to describe and analyze family adaptation to equal careers for women. So far, the employment of the mother has been seen as supplemental to that of the husband. In an increasing number of families, it will become equal to that of the husband, and, in some cases, the mother will be the principal provider, with the father becoming a househusband or employed father supplementing the earnings of his wife.

One aim of this book has been to describe the present state of knowledge on the effects of maternal employment on the family. An equally important goal is to stimulate further research. The questions still unanswered and the new ones that are arising seem to indicate that behavioral scientists should be readying their theoretical and conceptual tools for the challenges presented.

References

ABBOTT, E. *Women in Industry*. New York: Appleton-Century Crofts, 1910.

ADDISS, L. K. "Job-Related Expenses of the Working Mother." *Children*, 1963, *10*(6), 219–223.

ALDOUS, J. "Wives' Employment Status and Lower-Class Men as Husband-Fathers: Support for the Moynihan Thesis." *Journal of Marriage and the Family*, 1969, *31*, 469–476.

ALMQUIST, E. M., and ANGRIST, S. S. "Role Model Influences on College Women's Career Aspirations." *Merrill-Palmer Quarterly*, 1971, *17*(3), 263–279.

American Council on Education. *National Norms for Entering College Freshmen—Fall 1966*. Research report 2(1). Washington, D.C.: 1967.

American Council on Education. *The American Freshman: National Norms for Fall 1972*. Research report 7(1). Washington, D.C.: 1972.

ANGRIST, S., and LAVE, J. R. "Issues Surrounding Day Care." *The Family Coordinator*, 1973, *22*(4), 457–464.

ASTIN, H. S. *The Woman Doctorate in America*. New York. Russell Sage Foundation, 1969.

ATKINSON, J. W. (Ed.) *Motives in Fantasy, Action and Society*. New York: Van Nostrand, 1958.

AXELSON, L. "The Marital Adjustment and Marital Role Definitions of Husbands of Working and Nonworking Wives." *Marriage and Family Living*, May 1963.

233

AXELSON, L. "The Working Wife: Difference in Perception Among Negro and White Males." *Journal of Marriage and the Family,* 1970, *32*(6), 457–464.

BABCHUK, N. "Primary Friends and Kin, A Study of the Associations of Middle Class Couples." *Social Forces,* 1965, *43,* 483–493.   .

BAHR, S. J. *A Methodological Study of Conjugal Power: A Replication and Extension of Blood and Wolfe.* Unpublished doctoral dissertation. Washington State University, 1972.

BAHR, S. J., BOWERMAN, C. E., and GECAS, V. "Adolescent Perceptions of Conjugal Power." *Social Forces,* 1974, *52,* 357–367.

BAILYN, L. "Notes on the Role of Choice in the Psychology of Women." *Daedalus,* 1964, *93,* 700–710.

BAILYN, L. "Career and Family Orientations of Husbands and Wives in Relation to Marital Happiness." *Human Relations,* Apr. 1970.

BANDUCCI, R. "The Effect of Mother's Employment on the Achievement, Aspirations, and Expectations of the Child." *Personnel and Guidance Journal,* 1967, *46,* 263–267.

BARUCH, G. K. "Maternal Influences upon College Women's Attitudes Toward Women and Work." *Developmental Psychology,* 1972a, *6*(1), 32–37.

BARUCH, G. K. *Maternal Role Pattern as Related to Self-Esteem and Parental Identification in College Women.* Paper presented at meeting of the Eastern Psychological Association, Boston, Apr. 1972b.

BARUCH, R. *The Achievement Motive in Women: A Study of the Implications for Career Development.* Unpublished doctoral dissertation. Harvard University, 1966.

BAUMRIND, D., and BLACK, A. E. "Socialization Practices Associated with Dimensions of Competence in Preschool Boys and Girls." *Child Development,* 1967, *38,* 291–327.

BECKER, W. C. "Consequences of Different Kinds of Parental Discipline." In M. L. Hoffman and L. W. Hoffman (Eds.), *Review of Child Development Research.* Vol. 1. New York: Russell Sage Foundation, 1964.

BELOW, H. I. *Life Styles and Roles of Women as Perceived by High-School Girls.* Unpublished doctoral dissertation. Indiana University, 1969.

BETTELHEIM, B. *The Children of the Dream.* London: Macmillan, 1969.

BIRNBAUM, J. A. *Life Patterns, Personality Style and Self-Esteem in Gifted Family Oriented and Career Committed Women.* Unpublished doctoral dissertation. University of Michigan, 1971.

BLAKE, J. "Demographic Science and the Redirection of Population Policy." In M. C. Sheps and J. C. Ridley (Eds.), *Public Health and Population Change*. Pittsburgh: University of Pittsburgh Press, 1965.

BLAKE, J. "Population Policy for America: Is the Government Being Misled?" *Science*, 1969, *164*, 522–529.

BLAKE, J. "Reproductive Motivation and Population Policy." *BioScience*, 1971, *21*(5), 215–220.

BLAUNER, R. *Alienation and Freedom: The Factory Worker and His Industry*. Chicago: University of Chicago Press, 1964.

BLOOD, R. O., JR. "The Husband-Wife Relationship." In F. I. Nye and L. W. Hoffman (Eds.), *The Employed Mother in America*. Chicago: Rand McNally, 1963.

BLOOD, R. O., JR. *Love Match and Arranged Marriage*. New York: Free Press, 1967.

BLOOD, R. O., JR., and HAMBLIN, R. L. "The Effect of the Wife's Employment on the Family Power Structure." *Social Forces*, 1958, *36*, 347–352.

BLOOD, R. O., JR., and WOLFE, D. M. *Husbands and Wives*. New York: Free Press, 1960.

BLUMER, H. *Symbolic Interactionism: Perspective and Method*. Englewood Cliffs, N.J.: Prentice-Hall, 1969.

BOTT, E. *Family and Social Network*. London: Tavistock, 1957.

BOURNE, P. G. "What Day Care Ought To Be." *The New Republic*, 1972, pp. 18–23.

BOWEN, W. G., and FINEGAN, T. A. *The Economics of Labor Force Participation*. Princeton, N.J.: Princeton University Press, 1969.

BOWERMAN, C. E. "Adjustment in Marriage: Over-All and in Specific Areas." *Sociology and Social Research*, 1957, *41*.

BOWLBY, J. A. "Some Pathological Processes Engendered by Early Mother-Child Separation." In M. J. E. Senn (Ed.), *Infancy and Childhood*. New York: Josiah Macy, Jr. Foundation, 1953.

BOWLBY, J. A. "The Nature of the Child's Tie to His Mother." *International Journal of Psycho-Analysis*, 1958, *39*, 350–373.

BOWLBY, J. A. *Attachment*. New York: Basic Books, 1969.

BRONFENBRENNER, U. "Some Familial Antecedents of Responsibility and Leadership in Adolescents." In L. Petrullo and B. M. Bass (Eds.), *Leadership and Interpersonal Behavior*. New York: Holt, Rinehart, and Winston, 1961.

BRONFENBRENNER, U. *Two Worlds of Childhood: U.S. and USSR*. New York: Russell Sage, 1970.

BRONFENBRENNER, U. *Is Early Intervention Effective?* Paper presented at biennial meeting of the Society for Research in Child Development, Philadelphia, Mar. 1973.

BRONFENBRENNER, U., and OTHERS. *Day Care U.S.A.: A Statement of Principles.* Washington, D.C.: Office of Child Development, 1970.

BROVERMAN, I. K., VOGEL, S. R., BROVERMAN, D. M., CLARKSON, F. E., and ROSENKRANTZ, P. S. "Sex-Role Stereotypes: A Current Appraisal." *Journal of Social Issues,* 1972, *28*(2), 59–78.

BROWN, S. W. *A Comparative Study of Maternal Employment and Nonemployment.* Unpublished doctoral dissertation. University Microfilms 70–8610. Mississippi State University, 1970.

BUMPASS, L., AND WESTOFF, C. *The Later Years of Childbearing.* Princeton, N.J.: Princeton University Press, 1970.

BURCHINAL, L. G. "Personality Characteristics of Children." In F. I. Nye and L. W. Hoffman (Eds.), *The Employed Mother in America.* Chicago: Rand McNally, 1963.

BURCHINAL, L. G., AND LOVELL, L. *Relation of Employment Status of Mothers to Children's Anxiety, Parental Personality and PARI Scores.* Unpublished manuscript 1425. Ames: Agricultural Experiment Station, Iowa State University, 1959.

BURGESS, E. W., AND WALLIN, P. *Engagement and Marriage.* Philadelphia: Lippincott, 1953.

BURIC, O., AND ZECEVIC, A. "Family Authority, Marital Satisfaction and the Social Network in Yugoslavia." *Journal of Marriage and the Family,* 1967, *29,* 325–336.

CAIN, G. G. *Married Women in the Labor Force.* Chicago: University of Chicago Press, 1966.

CALDWELL, B. M. "The Effects of Infant Care." In M. L. Hoffman and L. W. Hoffman (Eds.), *Review of Child Development Research.* Vol. 1. New York: Russell Sage Foundation, 1964.

CALDWELL, B. M., WRIGHT, C. M., HONIG, A. S., AND TANNENBAUM, J. "Infant Day Care and Attachment." *American Journal of Orthopsychiatry,* 1970, *40* (3), 397–412.

CARLSON, J. "The Recreational Role." Unpublished paper. Moscow, Idaho: Department of Sociology, University of Idaho, 1973.

CARTWRIGHT, D. "Influence, Leadership, and Control." In J. G. March (Ed.), *Handbook of Organizations.* Chicago: Rand McNally, 1965.

CARTWRIGHT, L. K. "Conscious Factors Entering into Decisions of of Women to Study Medicine." *Journal of Social Issues,* 1972, *28*(2), 201–215.

CAUMAN, J. "Family Day Care and Group Day Care: Two Essential Aspects of a Basic Child Welfare Service." *Child Welfare,* 1961, *40,* 20–23.

Center for Applied Behavior Analysis. *An Experiment to Facilitate National Day Care Policy Decisions.* Lawrence, Kan., 1962.

CENTERS, R., RAVEN, B. H., AND RODRIGUES, A. "Conjugal Power Structure: A Re-examination." *American Sociological Review,* 1971, *36,* 264–278.

CHAMBLISS, W. J. "The Selection of Friends." *Social Forces,* 1965, 370–380.

CHAPMAN, J. E., AND LAZAR, J. B. *A Review of the Present Status and Future Needs in Day Care Research.* Paper prepared for the Interagency Panel on Early Childhood Research and Development, 1971.

Child Welfare League of America. *Standards for Day Care Service.* New York, 1969.

CHILMAN, C. S. "Probable Social and Psychological Consequences of an American Population Policy Aimed at the Two-Child Family." In E. Milner (Ed.), *The Impact of Fertility Limitation on Women's Life, Career and Personality.* New York: New York Academy of Sciences, 1970.

CHO, L. J., GRABILL, W. H., BOGUE, D. J., and OTHERS. *Differential Current Fertility in the United States.* Chicago: Community and Family Study Center, 1970.

CLASS, N. E. *Licensing of Child Care Facilities by State Welfare Department.* Washington, D.C.: Social and Rehabilitation Service, Children's Bureau, Department of Health, Education, and Welfare, 1968.

CLAUSEN, J. A. "Family Structure, Socialization and Personality." In L. W. Hoffman and M. L. Hoffman (Eds.), *Review of Child Development Research.* Vol. 2. New York: Russell Sage Foundation, 1966.

CLAUSEN, J. A., and CLAUSEN, S. R. "The Effects of Family Size on Parents and Children." In J. Fawcett (Ed.), *Psychological Perspectives on Fertility.* New York: Basic Books, 1973.

COLLINS, A. H. "Some Efforts to Improve Private Family Day Care." *Children,* 1966, *13.*

COLLINS, A. H. *The Home-Centered Woman as a Potential Protective*

Service Resource. Paper presented at the National Conference on Social Welfare, Authors Forum, Dallas, May 1971.

COLLINS, A. H. "Natural Delivery Systems: Accessible Sources of Power for Mental Health." *American Journal of Orthopsychiatry,* 1973, *43,* 46–52.

COLLINS, A. H., EMLEN, A. C., and WATSON, E. L. "The Day Care Neighbor Service: An Interventive Experiment." *Community Mental Health Journal,* 1969, *5,* 219–224.

COLLINS, A. H., and WATSON, E. L. *The Day Care Neighbor Service: A Handbook for the Organization and Operation of a New Approach to Family Day Care.* Portland, Ore.: Tri-County Community Council, 1969a.

COLLINS, A. H., and WATSON, E. L. "Exploring the Neighborhood Family Day Care System." *Social Casework,* 1969b, *50,* 527–533.

COLLVER, O. A. "Women's Work Participation and Fertility in Metropolitan Areas." *Demography,* 1968, *5*(1), 55–60.

COLLVER, O. A., and LANGLOIS, E. "The Female Labor Force in Metropolitan Areas: An International Comparison." *Economic Development and Cultural Change,* 1962, *10,* 367–385.

CONSTANTINOPLE, A. "Masculinity-Femininity: An Exception to a Famous Dictum?" *Psychological Bulletin,* 1973, *80,* 389–407.

CONYERS, J. E. "Employers' Attitudes Toward Working Mothers." In F. I. Nye and L. W. Hoffman (Eds.), *The Employed Mother in America.* Chicago: Rand McNally, 1963.

COSTANTINI, E., and CRAIK, K. H. "Women as Politicians: The Social Background, Personality, and Political Careers of Female Party Leaders." *Journal of Social Issues,* 1972, *28*(2), 217–236.

COSTIN, L. B. *The Training of Personnel for the Licensing of Family Homes in Child Welfare.* Urbana, Ill.: University of Illinois, 1965.

COSTIN, L. B. *Child Welfare: Policies and Practice.* New York: McGraw-Hill, 1972.

CROSS, K. P. *Beyond the Open Door.* San Francisco: Jossey-Bass, 1971.

CYRUS, D. "Problems of the Modern Homemaker-Mother." In J. Landis and M. Landis (Eds.), *Readings in Marriage and the Family.* Englewood Cliffs, N.J.: Prentice-Hall, 1952.

DAHL, R. A. "The Concept of Power." *Behavioral Science,* 1957, *2,* 201–218.

DAVIS, K. "Population Policy: Will Current Programs Succeed?" *Science,* 1967, *158,* 730–739.

Day Care and Child Development Reports. 1971, 1974.

Day Care Policy Studies Group. *Final Report. Part I: Alternative Federal Day Care Strategies for the 1970s, Summary Report.* Minneapolis: Institute for Interdisciplinary Studies, 1972.

DELORIA, D. J. *A Design for a National Day Care Cost-Effectiveness Experiment.* Ypsilanti, Mich.: High/Scope Educational Research Foundation, 1972.

DENNIS, W., and NAJARIAN, P. "Infant Development Under Environmental Handicap." *Psychological Monographs,* 1957, *71* (Whole No. 436).

DITTMAN, L. L. (Ed.) *Early Child Care: The New Perspectives.* Chicago: Aldine-Atherton, 1968.

DIZARD, J. *Social Change in the Family.* Chicago: Community and Family Study Center, University of Chicago, 1968.

DOKECKI, P. R., and OTHERS. *The Training of Family Day Care Workers: A Feasibility Study and Initial Pilot Efforts.* Vol. 4. Nashville: Darcee Papers and Reports, 1971.

DONOGHUE, B. A. *Utility of the Marlowe-Crowne Social Desirability Scale in an Interviewing Situation.* Unpublished master's thesis. University of Portland, 1973.

DOUVAN, E. "Employment and the Adolescent." In F. I. Nye and L. W. Hoffman (Eds.), *The Employed Mother in America.* Chicago: Rand McNally, 1963.

DREW, J. B. "Training Child Care Aides." *Children Today,* 1973.

DUNCAN, O. D., SCHUMAN, H., and DUNCAN, B. *Social Change in Metropolitan Detroit.* Ann Arbor: Population Studies Center, University of Michigan, 1972.

DUVAL, E. B. *Conceptions of Mother Roles by Five and Six Year Old Children of Working and Non-Working Mothers.* Unpublished doctoral dissertation. Florida State University, 1955.

EDWARDS, E. "Family Day Care in a Community Action Programme." *Children,* 1968, *15,* 55–58.

EMERSON, P. E., and SCHAFFER, H. R. "The Development of Social Attachments in Infancy." *Monographs of the Society for Research in Child Development,* 1964, *29* (3, Whole No. 94).

EMLEN, A. C. *Neighborhood Family Day Care as a Child-Rearing Environment.* Paper presented at annual meeting of the National Association for the Education of Young Children, Boston, Nov. 1970a.

EMLEN, A. C. "Realistic Planning for the Day Care Consumer." In *Social Work Practice, 1970.* New York: Columbia University Press, 1970b.

EMLEN, A. C. "Family Day Care Research: A Summary and Critical Review." In *Family Day Care West: A Working Conference.* Pasadena, Calif.: Pacific Oaks College, 1972.

EMLEN, A. C. "Slogans, Slots and Slander: The Myth of Day Care Need." *American Journal of Orthopsychiatry,* 1973, *43,* 23–36.

EMLEN, A. C. "Day Care for Whom?" In A. Schoor (Ed.), *Children and Decent People.* New York: Basic Books, 1974.

EMLEN, A. C., DONOGHUE, B. A., and CLARKSON, Q. D. *The Stability of of the Family Day Care Arrangements: A Longitudinal Study.* Corvallis, Ore.: DCE Books, 1974.

EMLEN, A. C., DONOGHUE, B. A., and LAFORGE, R. *Child Care by Kith: A A Study of the Family Day Care Relationship of Working Mothers and Neighborhood Caregivers.* Corvallis, Ore.: DCE Books, 1971.

EMLEN, A. C., and WATSON, E. L. *Matchmaking in Neighborhood Day Care: A Descriptive Study of the Day Care Neighbor Service.* Corvallis, Ore.: DCE Books, 1971.

EPSTEIN, C. F. *Woman's Place: Options and Limits in Professional Careers.* Berkeley: University of California Press, 1970.

EPSTEIN, C. F. "Law Partners and Marital Partners." *Human Relations,* 1971, *24,* 549–564.

EPSTEIN, C. F. *The Woman Lawyer.* Chicago: University of Chicago Press, in press.

EYDE, L. D. *Work Values and Background Factors as Predictors of Women's Desire to Work.* Bureau of Business Research Monograph 108. Columbus: College of Commerce and Administration, Ohio State University, 1962.

EYDE, L. D. "Work Motivation of Women College Graduates: Five-Year Follow-Up." *Journal of Counseling Psychology,* 1968, *15*(2), 199–202.

FALLER, L. A. *Bantu Bureaucracy.* Chicago: University of Chicago Press, 1965.

FARLEY, J. "Maternal Employment and Child Behavior." *Cornell Journal of Social Relations,* 1968, *3,* 58–70.

FARLEY, J. "Graduate Women: Career Aspirations and Desired Family Size." *American Psychologist,* 1970, *25*(12), 1099–1100.

FEATHERSTONE, J. "Kentucky Fried Chicken: The Day Care Problem." *The New Republic,* Sept. 1970.

FEIN, G. G., and CLARKE-STEWART, A. *Day Care in Context.* New York: Wiley, 1973.

FELD, S. "Feelings of Adjustment." In F. I. Nye and L. W. Hoffman

(Eds.), *The Employed Mother in America*. Chicago: Rand McNally, 1963.

FELDMAN, H. *Development of the Husband-Wife Relationship*. Research report to the National Institute of Mental Health. Ithaca, N.Y.: Department of Human Development and Family Studies, Cornell University, 1965.

FELDMAN, H., and FELDMAN, M. *The Relationship Between the Family and Occupational Functioning in a Sample of Rural Women*. Ithaca, N.Y.: Department of Human Development and Family Studies, Cornell University, 1973.

FIDELL, L. S. "Empirical Verification of Sex Discrimination in Hiring Practices in Psychology." *American Psychologist*, 1970, *25*(12), 1094–1098.

FINKELMAN, J. J. *Maternal Employment, Family Relationships, and Parental Role Perception*. Unpublished doctoral dissertation. Yeshiva University, Israel, 1966.

FISHER, M. S. "Marriage and Work for College Women." *Vassar Alumnae Magazine*, 1939, *24*, 7–10.

FITCHER, J. H. *Graduates of Predominately Negro Colleges: Class of 1964*. Publication 1571. Washington, D.C.: Government Printing Office, 1969.

FITZSIMMONS, S. J., and ROWE, M. P. *A Study in Child Care 1970–71*. Vol. 1. *Findings*. Cambridge, Mass.: Abt Associates, 1971.

FOGARTY, M. P., RAPOPORT, R., and RAPOPORT, R. N. *Career, Sex and Family*. London: Allen and Unwin, 1971.

FOLEY, F. A. "Family Day Care for Children." *Children*, 1966, *13*, 141–144.

FORTNEY, J. A. *Achievement as an Alternate Source of Emotional Gratification to Childbearing*. Paper presented at meeting of the Population Association of America, Toronto, Apr. 1972.

FRANKEL, E. "Characteristics of Working and Non-Working Mothers Among Intellectually Gifted High and Low Achievers." *Personnel and Guidance Journal*, 1964, *42*, 776–780.

FREEDMAN, R., WHELPTON, P. K., and CAMPBELL, A. A. *Family Planning, Sterility, and Population Growth*. New York: McGraw-Hill, 1959.

FREEMAN, L. C. *Elementary Applied Statistics: For Students in Behavioral Science*. New York: Wiley, 1965.

FUCHS, R. "Different Meanings of Employment for Women." *Human Relations*, 1971, *24*, 495–499.

GALAMBOS, E. C. *Income Tax Deductions for Family Day Care Homes*.

Southeastern Day Care Bulletin 1. Atlanta: Southeastern Day Care Project, Southern Regional Education Board, 1971.

Gallup Opinion Index. *Report No. 91.* Princeton, N.J.: Jan. 1973.

GARBER, J. *Problem Areas in the Establishment of Day Care Centers.* SWRRI Publication 5. Chestnut Hill, Mass.: Boston College, 1972a.

GARBER, J. *Proprietary Day Care.* SWRRI Publication 13. Chestnut Hill, Mass.: Boston College, 1972b.

GARLAND, T. N. "The Better Half? The Male in the Dual Profession Family." In C. Safilios-Rothschild (Ed.), *Toward a Sociology of Women.* Lexington, Mass.: Xerox College Publishing, 1972.

GARVIN, C. and OTHERS. *Decision Making in the WIN Program: First Year Progress Report.* Ann Arbor: University of Michigan School of Social Work, 1970.

GASS, G. Z. "Counseling Implications of Woman's Changing Role." *Personnel and Guidance,* Mar. 1959.

GENDELL, M. *The Influence of Family Building Activity on Woman's Rate of Economic Activity.* Paper presented at the United Nations' World Population Conference, Belgrade, 1965.

GIANOPULOS, A., and MITCHELL, H. E. "Marital Disagreement in Working Wives: Marriages as a Function of Husband's Attitude Toward Wife's Employment." *Marriage and Family Living,* Nov. 1957.

GINZBERG, E. *Educated American Women: Life Styles and Self-Portraits.* New York: Columbia University Press, 1971.

GLUECK, S., and GLUECK, E. "Working Mothers and Delinquency." *Mental Hygiene,* 1957, *41,* 327–352.

GOLD, M. *A Social-Psychology of Delinquent Boys.* Ann Arbor, Mich.: Institute for Social Research, 1961.

GOLDBERG, P. *Misogyny and the College Girl.* Paper presented at meeting of the Eastern Psychological Association, Boston, Apr. 1967.

GORDON, B. "Foster Family Day Care Services." *Child Welfare,* 1959, *38,* 18–21.

GOVE, W. R., and TUDOR, J. F. "Adult Sex Roles and Mental Illness." *American Journal of Sociology,* Jan. 1973.

GOVER, D. O. "Socio-Economic Differential in the Relationship Between Marital Adjustment and Wife's Employment Status." *Marriage and Family Living,* Nov. 1963.

GRAHAM, P. A. "Women in Academe." *Science,* 1970 *169*(3952), 1284–1290.

GRAY, S. W. *Parental Environment of Very Young Children.* Paper presented at annual conference of the National Association for the Education of Young Children, Boston, Nov. 1970.

GRIFFEN, A. *How to Start and Operate a Day Care Home.* Chicago: Regnery, 1973.

GROTBERG, E. H. (Ed.) *Critical Issues in Research Related to Disadvantaged Children.* Princeton, N.J.: Educational Testing Service, 1969.

GROTBERG, E. H. (Ed.) *Day Care: Resources for Decisions.* Washington, D.C.: Office of Economic Opportunity, 1971.

GROTBERG, E. H., SEARCY, W., and SOWDER, B. *Toward Interagency Coordination: An Overview of Federal and Development Activities Relating to Early Childhood, Second Annual Report.* Washington, D.C.: George Washington University, 1972.

HACKER, H. M. "The Feminine Protest of the Working Wife." *Indian Journal of Social Work,* Jan. 1971, *31.*

HALL, F. T., and SCHROEDER, M. P. "Time Spent on Household Tasks." *Journal of Home Economics,* 1970, *62*(1).

HALLER, M., and ROSENMAYER, L. "The Pluridimensionality of Work Commitment." *Human Relations,* 1971, *24, 501*–*518.*

HAMAMSY, L. "The Role of Women in a Changing Navaho Society." *American Anthropologist,* 1957, *59, 101*–*111.*

HARBESON, G. *Choice and Challenge for the American Women.* Cambridge, Mass.: Schenkman, 1967.

HARLOW, H., and HARLOW, M. H. "Learning to Love." *American Scientist,* 1966, *54*(3), *244*–*272.*

HARTLEY, R. E. "Children's Concepts of Male and Female Roles." *Merrill-Palmer Quarterly,* 1960, *6, 83*–*91.*

HARTLEY, R. E. "What Aspects of Child Behavior Should Be Studied in Relation to Maternal Employment?" In A. E. Siegel (Eds.), *Research Issues Related to the Effects of Maternal Employment on Children.* University Park, Pa.: Social Science Research Center, 1961.

HAUENSTEIN, L. S., and HARBURG, E. *Housework Stress and Blood Pressure Among Married Black and White Women.* Unpublished paper. Ann Arbor: Program for Urban Health Research, Department of Psychology, University of Michigan, 1973.

HAWKINS, D. F., AND OTHERS. *Industry Related Day Care: The KLH Child Development Center, Part I.* Cambridge: Massachusetts Institute of Technology, n.d.

HAYGHE, H. "Labor Force Activity of Married Women." *Monthly Labor Review,* Apr. 1973.

HEER, D. M. "Dominance and the Working Wife." In F. I. Nye and L. W. Hoffman (Eds.), *The Employed Mother in America.* Chicago: Rand McNally, 1963a.

HEER, D. M. The Measurement and Bases of Family Power: An Overview." *Marriage and Family Living,* 1963b, *25,* 133–139.

HEINICKE, C. M., and WESTHEIMER, I. *Brief Separations.* New York: International Universities Press, 1965.

HEINICKE, C. M., FRIEDMAN, D., PRESCOTT, E., PUNCEL, C., AND SALE, J. S. "The Organization of Day Care: Considerations Relating to the Mental Health of Child and Family." *American Journal of Orthopsychiatry,* 1973, *43,* 8–22.

HEINICKE, C. M., STRASSMAN, L. H., HAVER, K., STRATHEY, E., RAMSEY-KLEE, D., and SPINGATH, T. *Relationship Opportunities in Day Care: Changes in Child and Parent Functioning.* Los Angeles: University of California, 1973.

HELLMUTH, J. (Ed.) *Disadvantaged Child.* Vol. 3: *Compensatory Education: A National Debate.* New York: Brunner/Mazel, 1970.

HENNIG, M. M. "Family Dynamics for Developing Positive Achievement Motivation in Women: The Successful Woman Executive." *Annals of the New York Academy of Sciences,* 1973, *208,* 76–81.

HENSHEL, A. *Anti-Feminist Bias in Traditional Measurements of Masculinity-Femininity.* Paper presented at meeting of the National Council on Family Relations, Estes Park, Colo., Aug. 1971.

HERZOG, E. *Children of Working Mothers.* Washington, D.C.: Children's Bureau, 1960.

HESS, H. "Ethology and Developmental Psychology." In P. Mussen, (Ed.), *Carmichael's Manual of Child Psychology.* New York: Wiley, 1970.

HESS, R. D., and OTHERS. "Parent-Training Programs and Community Involvement in Day Care." In E. H. Grotberg (Ed.), *Day Care: Resources for Decisions.* Washington, D.C.: Office of Economic Opportunity, 1969.

HIRSHI, T., and SELVIN, H. C. *Delinquency Research: An Appraisal of Analytic Methods.* New York: Free Press, 1967.

HOFFMAN, D. B., and OTHERS. *Parent Participation in Preschool Day Care.* Atlanta: Southeastern Educational Laboratory, 1971.

HOFFMAN, L. W. "The Father's Role in the Family and the Child's Peer Group Adjustment." *Merrill-Palmer Quarterly,* 1961, *7*(2), 97–105.

HOFFMAN, L. W. "The Decision to Work." In F. I. Nye and L. W. Hoffman (Eds.), *The Employed Mother in America.* Chicago: Rand McNally, 1963a.

HOFFMAN, L. W. "Effects on Children: Summary and Discussion." In F. I. Nye and L. W. Hoffman (Eds.), *The Employed Mother in America.* Chicago: Rand McNally, 1963b.

HOFFMAN, L. W. "Mother's Enjoyment of Work and Effects on the Child." In F. I. Nye and L. W. Hoffman (Eds.), *The Employed Mother in America.* Chicago: Rand McNally, 1963c.

HOFFMAN, L. W. "Parental Power Relations and the Division of Household Tasks." In F. I. Nye and L. W. Hoffman (Eds.), *The Employed Mother in America.* Chicago: Rand McNally, 1963d.

HOFFMAN, L. W. "Early Childhood Experiences and Women's Achievement Motives." *Journal of Social Issues,* 1972a, *28*(2), 129–155.

HOFFMAN, L. W. "A Psychological Perspective on the Value of Children to Parents: Concepts and Measures." In J. T. Fawcett (Ed.), *The Satisfactions and Costs of Children: Theories, Concepts, Methods.* Honolulu: East-West Center, 1972b.

HOFFMAN, L. W. "The Professional Woman as Mother." In R. B. Kundsin (Ed.), *A Conference on Successful Women in the Sciences.* New York: New York Academy of Sciences, 1973.

HOFFMAN, L. W. "Fear of Success in Males and Females." *Journal of Consulting and Clinical Psychology,* 1974, *42,* 353–358.

HOFFMAN, L. W., and HOFFMAN, M. L. "The Value of Children to Parents." In J. T. Fawcett (Ed.), *Psychological Perspectives on Population.* New York: Basic Books, 1973.

HOFFMAN, L. W., and LIPPITT, R. "The Measurement of Family Life Variables." In P. Mussen (Ed.), *Handbook of Research Methods in Child Development.* New York: Wiley, 1960.

HOFFMAN, L. W., and WYATT, F. "Social Change and Motivations for Having Larger Families: Some Theoretical Considerations." *Merrill-Palmer Quarterly,* 1960, *6,* 235–244.

HOLMSTROM, L. L. *The Two-Career Family.* Cambridge, Mass.: Schenkman, 1972.

HORNER, M. S. "Femininity and Successful Achievement: A Basic Inconsistency." In J. M. Bardwick, E. Douvan, M. S. Horner, and D. Gutman (Eds.), *Feminine Personality and Conflict.* Monterey, Calif.: Brooks/Cole, 1972a.

HORNER, M. S. "Toward an Understanding of Achievement-Related Conflicts in Women." *The Journal of Social Issues,* 1972b, *28* (2), 157–175.

HORNER, M. S., and WALSH, M. R. *Causes and Consequences of the Existence of Psychological Barriers to Self-Actualization.* Paper presented at the New York Academy of Science Conference, New York, May 1972.

HUNT, J. M. *Intelligence and Experience.* New York: Ronald Press, 1961.

HUNTINGTON, D. C., PROVENCE, S., and PARKER, R. K. (Eds.) *Day Care: Serving Infants.* Washington, D.C.: Office of Child Development, 1971.

"Illinois Bell Day Care Referral Made Permanent Because of Savings and Improved Company Relations." *Day Care and Child Development Reports,* 1971, *1.*

Internal Revenue Service. *Your Federal Income Tax, 1972 Edition.* Washington, D.C.: Government Printing Office, 1972.

JACOBSON, W. D. *Power and Interpersonal Relations.* Belmont, Calif.: Wadsworth, 1972.

JENCKS, C. *Inequality: A Reassessment of the Effect of Family and Schooling in America.* New York: Basic Books, 1972.

JOHNS, J. R., and GOULD, R. S. *Day Care Survey 1970.* Bladenburg, Md.: Westinghouse Learning Corporation, Westat Research, 1971.

JOHNSON, C. L. *Leadership Patterns in Working and Non-Working Mother Middle Class Families.* Unpublished doctoral dissertation. University Microfilms 69–11. University of Kansas, 1969.

JONES, J. B., LUNDSTEEN, S. W., and MICHAEL, W. B. "The Relationship of the Professional Employment Status of Mothers to Reading Achievement of Sixth Grade Children." *California Journal of Education Research,* 1967, *43*(2), 102–108.

KAGAN, J. "Continuity of Cognitive Development During the First Year." *Merrill-Palmer Quarterly,* 1969, *15,* 101–119.

KALEY, M. M. "Attitudes Toward the Dual Role of the Married Professional Woman." *American Psychologist,* Mar. 1971.

KANDEL, D. B., and LESSER, G. S. "Marital Decision-Making in American and Danish Urban Families: A Research Note." *Journal of Marriage and the Family,* 1972, *34,* 134–138.

KAPPEL, B. E., and LAMBERT, R. D. *Self Worth Among the Children of Working Mothers.* Unpublished manuscript. Waterloo, Ontario: University of Waterloo, 1972.

KEIDEL, K. C. "Maternal Employment and Ninth Grade Achievement in Bismarck, North Dakota." *Family Coordinator,* 1970, *19,* 95–97.

KELLER, S. *The Urban Neighborhood: A Sociological Perspective.* New York: Random House, 1968.

KEYSERLING, M. D. *Windows on Day Care.* New York: National Council of Jewish Women, 1972.

KHARCHEV, A., and GOLOD, S. "The Two Roles of Russian Working Women in an Urban Area." In A. Michel (Ed.), *Family Issues of Employed Women in Europe and America.* Leiden, E. J. Brill, 1971.

KIEVIT, M. B. *Review and Synthesis of Research on Women in the World of Work.* Columbus: ERIC Clearinghouse for Vocational and Technical Education, Center for Vocational and Technical Education, Ohio State University, 1972.

KIM, S. *Determinants of Labor Force Participation of Married Women 30–44 Years of Age.* Unpublished doctoral dissertation. Ohio State University, 1972.

KING, K., MC INTYRE, J., and AXELSON, L. J. "Adolescents' Views of Maternal Employment as a Threat to the Marital Relationship." *Journal of Marriage and the Family,* 1968, *30*(4), 633–637.

KIRKPATRICK, C. "Inconsistency in Marriage Roles and Marriage Conflict." In J. Landis and M. Landis (Eds.), *Readings in Marriage and the Family.* Englewood Cliffs, N.J.: Prentice-Hall, 1952.

KLEIMAN, C. "Industry Steps Up Its Day Care Output." *Day Care and Early Education,* Sept. 1973, *1*, 27–30.

KLIGLER, D. *The Effects of Employment of Married Women on Husband and Wife Roles: A Study in Culture Change.* Unpublished doctoral dissertation. Yale University, 1954.

KOHN-RAZ, R. "Mental and Motor Development of Kibbutz, Institutionalized, and Home-Reared Infants in Israel." *Child Development,* 1968, *39*, 489–504.

KOMAROVSKY, M. "Cultural Contradictions and Sex Roles: The Masculine Case." *American Journal of Sociology,* 1973, *78*(4), 873–885.

KORNFELD, M. "Home-Safe: A New Approach in Day Care for the Young Child." *American Journal of Orthopsychiatry,* 1974, *44* (2), 238–239.

KRIESBERG, L. *Mothers in Poverty: A Study of Fatherless Families.* Chicago: Aldine, 1970.

KURTH, S. B. "Friendships and Friendly Relationships." In G. J. McCall (Ed.), *Social Relationships.* Chicago: Aldine, 1970.

LAFOLLETTE, C. T. *A Study of the Problems of 652 Gainfully Employed*

Married Homemakers. New York: Teachers College, Columbia University, 1934.

LAJEWSKI, H. C. *Child Care Arrangements of Full-Time Working Mothers.* Washington, D.C.: Children's Bureau, 1959.

LAMOUSE, A. "Family Roles of Women: A German Example." *Journal of Marriage and the Family,* 1969, *31,* 145–152.

LATRIDIS, D. *Child Care in an Urban World.* Report 1: *Social Policy Perspectives and Dilemmas.* Chestnut Hill, Mass.: Boston College, 1972.

LEBERGOTT, S. "Population Change and the Supply of Labor." In *Demographic and Economic Change in Developed Countries.* Princeton, N.J.: Princeton University Press, 1960.

LEHMAN, E. W. "Toward a Macrosociology of Power." *American Sociological Review,* 1969, *34,* 453–464.

LESLIE, G. R. *The Family in Social Context.* New York: Oxford University Press, 1973.

LEVENSTEIN, P. "Cognitive Growth in Preschoolers Through Verbal Interaction with Mothers." *American Journal of Orthopsychiatry,* 1970, *40*(3), 426–432.

LEVENSTEIN, P. *Verbal Interaction Project: Aiding Cognitive Growth in Disadvantaged Preschoolers Through the Mother-Child Home Program July 1, 1967–August 31, 1970.* Washington, D.C.: Office of Child Development, Children's Bureau, Department of Health, Education, and Welfare, 1971.

LEVINE, A. G. *Marital and Occupational Plans of Women in Professional Schools: Law, Medicine, Nursing, Teaching.* Unpublished doctoral dissertation. Yale University, 1968.

LEVINE, J. A. "Whither Day Care . . . And the Foundation Dollar?" *Foundation News,* 1974.

LEWIS, M., and GOLDBERG, S. "Perceptual-Cognitive Development in Infancy: A Generalized Expectancy Model as a Function of the Mother-Infant Interaction." *Merrill-Palmer Quarterly,* 1969, *15,* 81–100.

LIPMAN-BLUMEN, J. "How Ideology Shapes Women's Lives." *Scientific American,* 1972, *226*(1), 34–42.

LITWAK, E. "Extended Kin Relations in an Industrial Society." In E. Shanas and C. F. Streib (Eds.), *Social Structure and the Family Generational Relations.* Englewood Cliffs, N.J.: Prentice Hall, 1965.

LOCKE, H. J., and MACKEPRANG, M. "Marital Adjustment of the Employed Wife." *American Journal of Sociology,* May 1949.

LOPATA, H. Z. *Occupation: Housewife*. New York: Oxford University Press, 1971.

LOW, S., and SPINDLER, P. B. *Child Care Arrangements of Working Mothers in the United States*. Publication 461. Washington, D.C.: Children's Bureau, 1968.

LOZOFF, M. M. *Changing Life Styles and Role Perceptions of Men and Women Students*. Paper presented at conference sponsored by Radcliffe Institute, Radcliffe College, Cambridge, Mass., Apr. 1972.

LUNDBERG, F., and FARNHAM, M. *Modern Women, the Lost Sex*. New York: Harper and Row, 1947.

LUNNEBORG, P. W. *Stereotypic Aspect in Masculinity-Femininity Measurement*. Paper presented at meeting of the American Psychological Association, San Francisco, Sept. 1968.

LUPRI, E. "Contemporary Authority Patterns in the West German Family: A Study in Cross-National Validation." *Journal of Marriage and the Family*, 1967, *31*, 134–144.

MAAS, H. S. "Childrens' Environments and Child Welfare." *Child Welfare*, 1971, *59*, 131–142.

MC CLELLAND, D. C., ATKINSON, J. W., CLARK, R. A., and LOWELL, E. L. *The Achievement Motive*. New York: Appleton-Century Crofts, 1953.

MACCOBY, E. E. "Children and Working Mothers." *Children*, 1958, *5*(3), 83–89.

MACCOBY, E. E. "Sex Differences in Intellectual Functioning." In E. E. Maccoby (Ed.), *The Development of Sex Differences*. Stanford, Calif.: Stanford University Press, 1966.

MC CORD, J., MC CORD, W., and THURBER, E. "Effects of Maternal Employment on Lower-Class Boys." *Journal of Abnormal and Social Psychology*, 1963, *67*, 177–182.

MC CORD, W., and MC CORD, J. *Origins of Crime*. New York: Columbia University Press, 1959.

MASLOW, A. II., RAND, H., and NEWMAN, S. "Some Parallels Between Sexual and Dominance Behavior of Infra-Human Primates and the Fantasies of Patients in Psychotherapy." *Journal of Nervous and Mental Disease*, 1960, *131*, 202–212.

MATHEWS, S. M. "The Development of Children's Attitudes Concerning Mothers' Out-of-Home Employment." *Journal of Educational Sociology*, 1933, *6*, 259–271.

MEADE, M. "The Politics of Day Care." *Commonweal*, 1971, *94*.

MEIER, H. C. "Mother-Centeredness and College Youths' Attitudes

Toward Social Equality for Women: Some Empirical Findings."
Journal of Marriage and the Family, 1972, *34*, 115–121.

MICHEL, A. "Comparative Data Concerning the Interaction in French
and American Families." *Journal of Marriage and the Family*,
1967, *29*, 337–344.

MICHEL, A. "Interaction and Goal Attainment in Parisian Working
Wives' Families." In A. Michel (Ed.), *Family Issues of
Employed Women in Europe and America*. Leiden: E. J.
Brill, 1971.

MIDDLETON, R., AND PUTNEY, S. "Dominance in Decisions in the Family:
Race and Class Differences." *American Journal of Sociology*,
1960, *65*, 605–609.

MOGEY, J. "Family and Community in Urban-Industrial Societies."
In H. T. Christenson (Ed.), *Handbook of Marriage and the
Family*. Chicago: Rand McNally, 1964.

MONDALE, W. *American Families: Trends and Pressures, 1973*. Senate
Subcommittee Hearings on Children and Youth. Washington:
Government Printing Office, 1974.

MOORE, T. "Children of Working Mothers." In S. Yudkin and H.
Holme (Eds.), *Working Mothers and Their Children*. London:
Michael Joseph, 1963.

MORGAN, J. N., DAVID, M., COHEN, W., AND BRAZER, H. *Income and
Welfare in the United States*. New York: McGraw-Hill, 1962.

MOSS, H. A. "Sex, Age and State as Determinants of Mother-Infant
Interaction." *Merrill-Palmer Quarterly*, 1967, *13*, 19–36.

National Manpower Council. *Womanpower*. New York: Columbia
University Press, 1957.

NELSON, D. D. "A Study of School Achievement Among Adolescent
Children with Working and Nonworking Mothers." *Journal
of Educational Research*, 1969, *62*, 456–457.

NELSON, D. D. "A Study of Personality Adjustment Among Adolescent
Children with Working and Nonworking Mothers." *Journal
of Education Research*, 1971, *64*, 1328–1330.

NOLAN, F. L. "Effects on Rural Children." In F. I. Nye and L. W.
Hoffman (Eds.), *The Employed Mother in America*. Chicago:
Rand McNally, 1963a.

NOLAN, F. L. "Rural Employment and Husbands and Wives." In F.
I. Nye and L. W. Hoffman (Eds.), *The Employed Mother in
America*. Chicago: Rand McNally, 1963b.

NYE, F. I. *Family Relationships and Delinquent Behavior*. New York:
Wiley, 1958.

NYE, F. I. "The Adjustment of Adolescent Children." In F. I. Nye and L. W. Hoffman (Eds.), *The Employed Mother in America.* Chicago: Rand McNally, 1963.

NYE, F. I. *The Delineation of Substantive Family Roles.* Paper presented at annual meeting of the National Council on Family Relations, Chicago, Oct. 1970.

NYE, F. I. GECAS, V., AND DILLMAN, D. A. *Sexism: An Examination of the Oppression Hypothesis and Implications for Institutional Change.* Unpublished manuscript. Pullman, Wash., 1973.

NYE, F. I., and HOFFMAN, L. W. (Eds.) *The Employed Mother in America.* Chicago: Rand McNally, 1963a.

NYE, F. I., and HOFFMAN, L. W. "The Socio-Cultural Setting." In F. I. Nye and L. W. Hoffman (Eds.), *The Employed Mother in America.* Chicago: Rand McNally, 1963b.

NYE, F. I., AND MAC DOUGAL, E. "The Dependent Variable in Marital Research." *The Pacific Sociological Review,* Fall 1959.

NYE, F. I., PERRY, J. B., JR., AND OGLES, R. H. "Anxiety and Anti-Social Behavior in Preschool Children." In F. I. Nye and L. W. Hoffman (Eds.), *The Employed Mother in America.* Chicago: Rand McNally, 1963.

OBERG, K. "Kinship Organization of the Banyankole." *Africa,* 1938, *11,* 129–159.

OLSON, D. H., AND RABUNSKY, C. "Validity of Four Measures of Family Power." *Journal of Marriage and the Family,* 1972, *34,* 224–234.

OPPENHEIMER, V. K. *The Female Labor Force in the United States: Demographic and Economic Factors Governing Its Growth and Changing Composition.* Population Monograph Series 5. Berkeley: University of California, 1970.

OPPENHEIMER, V. K. "Demographic Influence on Female Employment and the Status of Women." *American Journal of Sociology,* Jan. 1973, *78.*

OPPONG, C. "Conjugal Power and Resources: An Urban African Example." *Journal of Marriage and the Family,* 1970, *32,* 676–680.

ORDEN, S. R., and BRADBURN, N. M. "Dimensions of Marital Happiness." *American Journal of Sociology,* May 1968.

ORDEN, S. R., AND BRADBURN, N. M. "Working Wives and Marital Happiness." *American Journal of Sociology,* Jan. 1969.

ORTH, M. "The American Child Care Disgrace." *Ms.,* May 1973.

PARKER, R. K., and DITTMAN, L. L. (Eds.) *Day Care: Staff Training.* Washington, D.C.: Office of Child Development, 1971.

PARKER, R. K., and KNITZER, J. "Day Care and Preschool Services: Trends in the 1960's and Issues for the 1970's." In *Government Research on the Problems of Children and Youth*. Washington, D.C.: Government Printing Office, 1971.

PARNES, H. S., SHEA, J. R., RODERICK, R. D., ZELLER, F. A., KOHEN, A. I., and ASSOCIATES. *Years for Decision: A Longitudinal Study of the Educational and Labor Market Experience of Young Women*. Vol. 1. Manpower Research Monograph 24. Washington, D.C.: Government Printing Office, 1971.

PARNES, H. S., SHEA, J. R., SPITZ, R. S., ZELLER, F. A., and ASSOCIATES. *Dual Careers: A Longitudinal Study of Labor Market Experience of Women*. Vol. 1. Manpower Research Monograph 21. Washington, D.C.: Government Printing Office, 1970.

PERRUCCI, C. C. "Minority Status and the Pursuit of Professional Careers: Women in Science and Engineering." *Social Forces*, 1970, *49*, 245–258.

PERRY, J. B. "The Mother Substitutes of Employed Mothers: An Exploratory Inquiry." *Marriage and Family Living*, 1961, *23*, 362–367.

PERRY, J. B. "Mother Substitutes." In F. I. Nye and L. W. Hoffman (Eds.), *The Employed Mother in America*. Chicago: Rand McNally, 1963.

PETERSON, E. T. *The Impact of Maternal Employment on the Mother-Daughter Relationship and on the Daughter's Role-Orientation*. Unpublished doctoral dissertation. University of Michigan, 1958.

PIOTROWSKI, J. "The Employment of Married Women and the Changing Sex Roles in Poland." In A. Michel (Ed.), *Family Issues of Employed Women in Europe and America*. Leiden: E. J. Brill, 1971.

PITTMAN, A. "A Realistic Plan for the Day Care Consumer." In *Social Work Practice, 1970*. New York: Columbia University, 1970.

POHLMAN, E. H. *Psychology of Birth Planning*. Cambridge, Mass.: Schenkman, 1969.

POLOMA, M. M. "Role Conflict and the Married Professional Woman." In C. Safilios-Rothschild (Ed.), *Toward a Sociology of Women*. Lexington, Mass.: Xerox College Publishing, 1972.

POLOMA, M. M., and GARLAND, T. N. *The Myth of the Egalitarian Family*. Paper presented at meeting of the American Sociological Association, Washington, D.C., 1970.

POWELL, K. S. "Family Variables." In F. I. Nye and L. W. Hoffman

(Eds)¦, *The Employed Mother in America.* Chicago: Rand McNally, 1963a.

POWELL, K. S. "Personalities of Children and Child-Rearing Attitudes of Mothers." In F. I. Nye and L. W. Hoffman (Eds.), *The Employed Mother in America.* Chicago: Rand McNally, 1963b.

PRESCOTT, E. *Children in Group Day Care: The Effect of a Dual Child-Rearing Environment.* Los Angeles: Welfare Planning Council, 1964.

PRESCOTT, E. *The Large Day Care Center as a Child-Rearing Environment.* Pasadena, Calif.: Pacific Oaks College, 1970.

PRESCOTT, E. "Group and Family Day Care: A Comparative Assessment." In *Family Day Care West: A Working Conference.* Pasadena, Calif.: Pacific Oaks College, 1972.

PRESCOTT, E. *A Comparison of Three Types of Day Care and Nursery School-Home Care.* Paper presented at biennial meeting of the Society for Research in Child Development. Philadelphia, Mar.–Apr. 1973a.

PRESCOTT, E. *Who Thrives in Group Day Care?* Part 2: *Assessment of Childrearing Environments: An Ecological Approach.* Pasadena, Calif.: Pacific Oaks College, 1973b.

PRESCOTT, E. *Is Day Care as Good as a Good Home?* Paper presented at annual meeting of the American Orthopsychiatric Association, San Francisco, Apr. 1974.

PRESCOTT, E., and JONES, E. *Group Day Care as a Child-Rearing Environment.* Pasadena, Calif.: Pacific Oaks College, 1967.

PRESCOTT, E., and JONES, E. *An Institutional Analysis of Day Care.* Pasadena, Calif.: Pacific Oaks College, 1970a.

PRESCOTT, E., and JONES, E. *Group Day Care as a Panacea.* Pasadena, Calif.: Pacific Oaks College, 1970b.

PRESCOTT, E., and JONES, E. "Day Care for Children—Assets and Liabilities." *Children,* 1971, *18,* 54–58.

PROPPER, A. M. "The Relationship of Maternal Employment to Adolescent Roles, Activities, and Parental Relationships." *Journal of Marriage and the Family,* 1972, *34,* 417–421.

RABKIN, L. Y., and RABKIN, K. "Children of the Kibbutz." *Psychology Today,* 1969, *3*(4), 40.

RADINSKY, E. K. "Follow-Up Study on Family Day Care Service." *Child Welfare,* 1964, *43,* 305–308.

RAINWATER, L. *And the Poor Get Children.* Chicago: Quadrangle, 1960.

RAINWATER, L. *Family Design, Family Size and Contraception*. Chicago: Aldine, 1965.

RANA, A. *Is Part-Time Child Care Surrogate Parenting?* Paper presented at Annual Meeting of the American Orthopsychiatric Association, San Francisco, Apr. 1974.

RAPOPORT, R., and RAPOPORT., R. "The Dual-Career Family: A Variant Pattern and Social Change." In C. Safilios-Rothschild (Ed.), *Toward a Sociology of Women*. Lexington, Mass.: Xerox College Publishing, 1972.

REES, A. N., and PALMER, F. H. "Factors Related to Change in Mental Test Performance." *Developmental Psychology Monograph*, 1970, *3*(2, Pt. 2).

Report in Preschool Education. Washington, D.C.: Capitol Publications, 1972.

RHEINGOLD, H. "The Modification of Social Responsiveness in Institutional Babies." *Monographs of the Society for Research in Child Development*, 1956, *21* (2, Serial No. 63).

RHEINGOLD, H., and BAYLEY, N. "The Later Effects of an Experimental Modification of Mothering." *Child Development*, 1959, *30*, 363–372.

RHEINGOLD, H., GEWIRTZ, J. L., and ROSS, H. W. "Social Conditioning of Vocalizations in the Infant." *Journal of Comparative Physiological Psychology*, 1959, *52*, 68–73.

RIDLEY, J. C. "The Changing Position of American Women: Education, Labor Force Participation, and Fertility." In *The Family in Transition*. Fogarty International Proceedings 3. Washington, D.C.: Government Printing Office, 1969.

RIDLEY, J. C. *Fertility, Family Planning, and the Status of Women in the United States*. Unpublished manuscript. Washington, D.C.: Georgetown University, 1972.

RIEBER, M., and WOMACH, M. "The Intelligence of Preschool Children as Related to Ethnic and Demographic Variables." *Exceptional Children*, 1967, *34*, 609–614.

RIEGE, M. G. "Parental Affection and Juvenile Delinquency in Girls." *The British Journal of Criminology*, 1972, *12*, 55–73.

RIESMAN, D., GLAZER, N., and DENNY, R. *The Lonely Crowd*. Garden City, N.Y.: Doubleday, 1953.

ROBINSON, J. B. "Historical Changes in How People Spend Their Time." In A. Michel (Ed.), *Family Issues of Employed Women in Europe and America*. Leiden: E. J. Brill, 1971.

ROBY, P. "Structural and Internalized Barriers to Women in Higher

Education." In C. Safilios-Rothschild (Ed.), *Toward a Sociology of Women.* Lexington, Mass.: Xerox College Publishing, 1972.

ROBY, P. (Ed.) *Child Care—Who Cares.* New York: Basic Books, 1973.

RODMAN, H. "Marital Power and the Theory of Resource in Cultural Context." *Journal of Comparative Family Studies,* 1972, *3,* 50–69.

ROETHLISBERGER, F. J., and DICKSON, W. J. *Business Research Studies.* Cambridge, Mass.: Division of Research, Harvard Business School, 1939.

ROSENFELD, C., and PERRELLA, V. C. "Study in Mobility." *Monthly Labor Review,* 1965, *88*(9), 1077–1082.

ROSSI, A. S. "Women in Science: Why So Few?" *Science,* 1965, *148* (3674), 1196–1202.

ROWE, M. P. *Economics of Child Care.* Testimony for the Senate Finance Committee. Cambridge: Abt Associates, 1971.

ROWE, M. P., and HUSBY, R. D. "Economics of Child Care: Costs, Needs, and Issues." In P. Roby (Ed.), *Child Care—Who Cares.* New York: Basic Books, 1973.

ROWE, R. R., and OTHERS. *Child Care in Massachusetts: The Public Responsibility.* Cambridge: Massachusetts Early Education Project, 1972.

ROY, P. "Adolescent Roles: Rural-Urban Differentials." In F. I. Nye and L. W. Hoffman (Eds.), *The Employed Mother in America.* Chicago: Rand McNally, 1963.

RUDERMAN, F. A. *Child Care and Working Mothers: A Study of Arrangements Made for Daytime Care of Children.* New York: Child Welfare League of America, 1968.

RUOPP, R. R. *A Study in Child Care 1970–71.* Vol. IIB: *Systems Case Studies.* Cambridge: Abt Associates, 1971.

RUOPP, R. R., O'FARRELL, B., WARNER, D., ROWE, M., and FREEDMAN, R. *A Day Care Guide for Administrators, Teachers, and Parents.* Cambridge, Mass.: MIT Press, 1973.

RUSSELL, B. *Power.* London: George Allen and Unwin, 1938.

RUSSO, N. F. *Sex and Race Differences in Conceptions of the Woman's Role.* Paper read at meeting of the American Psychological Association, Washington, D.C.: Sept. 1971.

RUTMAN, L., and CHOMMIE, P. W. "A Comparison of Families Using Commercial and Subsidized Day Care Services." *Child Welfare,* 1973, *52,* 287–297.

RYDER, N. B., and WESTOFF, C. F. *Reproduction in the United States 1965.* Princeton, N.J.: Princeton University Press, 1971.

SAFILIOS-ROTHSCHILD, C. "A Comparison of Power Structure and Marital Satisfaction in Urban Greek and French Families." *Journal of Marriage and the Family,* 1967, *29,* 345–352.

SAFILIOS-ROTHSCHILD, C. "Family Sociology or Wives' Family Sociology? A Cross-Cultural Examination of Decision-Making." *Journal of Marriage and the Family,* 1969a, *31,* 290–301.

SAFILIOS-ROTHSCHILD, C. "Sociopsychological Factors Affecting Fertility in Urban Greece: A Preliminary Report." *Journal of Marriage and the Family,* 1969b, *31,* 595–606.

SAFILIOS-ROTHSCHILD, C. "The Influence of the Wife's Degree of Work Commitment upon Some Aspects of Family Organization and Dynamics." *Journal of Marriage and the Family,* 1970a, *32,* 681–691.

SAFILIOS-ROTHSCHILD, C. "The Study of Family Power Structure: A Review 1960–1969." *Journal of Marriage and the Family,* 1970b, *32,* 539–552.

SAFILIOS-ROTHSCHILD, C. "Towards the Conceptualization and Measurement of Work Commitment." *Human Relations,* 1971, *24,* 489–493.

SALE, J. S. "Family Day Care: One Alternative in the Delivery of Developmental Service in Early Childhood." *American Journal of Orthopsychiatry,* 1973, *43,* 37–45.

SALE, J. S. *A Self-Help Organization of Family Day Care Mothers as a Means of Quality Control.* Paper presented at annual meeting of the American Orthopsychiatric Association, San Francisco, Apr. 1974.

SALE, J. S., with TORRES, Y. L. *I'm Not Just a Babysitter.* Pasadena, Calif.: Pacific Oaks College, 1971.

SALE, J. S., and OTHERS. *Open the Door . . . See the People.* Pasadena, Calif.: Pacific Oaks College, 1972.

SAUNDERS, M. M., and KEISTER, M. E. *Family Day Care: Some Observations.* Greensboro: North Carolina University, 1972.

SCANZONI, J. H. *Opportunity and the Family.* New York: Free Press, 1970.

SCANZONI, J. H., and MC MURRY, M. "Continuities in the Explanation of Fertility Control." *Journal of Marriage and the Family,* 1972, *34,* 315–322.

SCHAEFER, E. *Education in the Home.* Paper presented at annual conference of the National Association for the Education of Young Children. Boston, 1970.

SCHIENFELD, D. R., and OTHERS. *Parent's Values, Family Networks and Family Development: Working with Disadvantaged Families.* Research report 6.9. Chicago: Institute for Juvenile Research, 1969.

SCHULTZE, C. L., and OTHERS. *Setting National Priorities: The 1973 Budget.* Washington, D.C.: Brookings Institution, 1972.

SHARP, L. J. "Employment Status of Mothers and Some Aspects of Mental Illness." *American Sociological Review,* Oct. 1960.

SHARP, L. J. "Maternal Mental Health." In F. I. Nye and L. W. Hoffman (Eds.), *The Employed Mother in America.* Chicago: Rand McNally, 1963.

SHEA, J. R., SOOKIN, K., and RODERICK, R. D. *Dual Careers: A Longitudinal Study of Labor Market Experience of Women.* Vol. 2. Manpower Research Monograph 21. Washington, D.C.: Government Printing Office, 1973.

SHERIDAN, M. L. "Family Day Care for Children of Migrant Farmworkers." *Children,* 1967, 13–18.

SIEGEL, A. E., and HAAS, M. B. "The Working Mother: A Review of Research." *Child Development,* 1963, *34,* 513–542.

SILVERMAN, W., and HILL, R. "Task Allocation in Marriage in the United States and Belgium." *Journal of Marriage and the Family,* 1967, *29,* 353–359.

SMITH, H. C. *An Investigation of the Attitudes of Adolescent Girls Toward Combining Marriage, Motherhood and a Career.* Unpublished doctoral dissertation. University Microfilms 69–8089. Columbia University, 1969.

SOBOL, M. G. "Commitment to Work." In F. I. Nye and L. W. Hoffman (Eds.), *The Employed Mother in America.* Chicago: Rand McNally, 1963.

SOBOL, M. G. "A Dynamic Analysis of Labor Force Participation of Married Women of Childbearing Age." *The Journal of Human Resources,* 1973, *8*(4), 497–505.

SPAULDING, B. *Family Day Care Project, Third Progress Report.* Fitzroy, Victoria, Australia: Brotherhood of St. Laurence, 1972–1973.

Special Analyses, Budget of the United States Government, Fiscal Year 1972. Washington, D.C.: Government Printing Office, 1972.

Special Analyses of the United States Government, Fiscal Year 1973. Washington, D.C.: Government Printing Office, 1973.

SPIRO, M. E. *Children of the Kibbutz.* New York: Schocken, 1965.

SPITZ, R. A. "Hospitalism: An Inquiry into the Genesis of Psychiatric

Conditions in Early Childhood." *Psychoanalytic Studies of the Child,* 1945, *1,* 53–74.

SPREY, J. "Family Power Structure: A Critical Comment." *Journal of Marriage and the Family,* 1972, *34,* 235–238.

STEINER, G. Y. *The State of Welfare.* Washington, D.C.: Brookings Institution, 1970.

STEINFELS, M. O. *Who's Minding the Children? The History and Politics of Day Care in America.* New York: Simon and Schuster, 1973.

STOLZ, L. M. "Effects of Maternal Employment on Children: Evidence from Research." *Child Development,* 1960, *31,* 749–782.

STRODTBECK, F. L. "Husband-Wife Interaction over Revealed Differences." *American Sociological Review,* 1951, *16,* 468–473.

STYCOS, J. M., and WELLER, R. H. "Female Working Roles and Fertility." *Demography,* 1967, *4*(1), 210–217.

SUSSMAN, M. B. "Needed Research on the Employed Mother." *Marriage and Family Living,* 1961, *23,* 368–373.

SWANSON, R. M. *A Descriptive Study of Attitudes Toward and Utilization of Day Care Among Ramsey County, Minnesota Mothers.* St. Paul: Community Health and Welfare Planning Council, 1971.

SWEET, J. A. "Family Composition and the Labor Force Activity of American Wives." *Demography,* Apr. 1970, *7.*

SZOLAI, A. "The Multinational Comparative Time Budget: A Venture in International Research Cooperation." *American Behavioral Scientist,* 1966, *10,* 1–31.

TANGRI, S. S. *Role-Innovation in Occupational Choice Among College Women.* Unpublished doctoral dissertation. University of Michigan, 1969.

TANGRI, S. S. "Determinants of Occupational Role Innovation Among College Women." *Journal of Social Issues,* 1972a, *28*(2), 177–199.

TANGRI, S. S. "Policies That Affect the Status of Women and Fertility." *Journal Supplement Abstract Service, Catalog of Selected Documents in Psychology,* 1972b, *2,* 107.

THIBAUT, J., and KELLY, H. *The Psychology of Groups.* New York: Wiley, 1959.

THOMAS, G. *A Baseline Evaluation of Child Caring Institutions in Georgia.* Athens: University of Georgia, 1973.

TIZARD, B., COOPERMAN, O., JOSEPH, A., and TIZARD, J. "Environmental Effects on Language Development: A Study of Young Children in Long-Stay Residential Nurseries." *Child Development,* 1972, *43,* 337–358.

TRAVIS, N. E., and OTHERS. *Bulletins of the Southeastern Day Care Project.* Atlanta: Southern Regional Educational Board, 1971.

TROUT, B. E., and BRADBURY, D. E. *Mothers for a Day: The Case of Children in Families Other Than Their Own.* Publication 319. Washington, D.C.: Children's Bureau, 1946.

TURK, J. L., and BELL, N. W. "Measuring Power in Families." *Journal of Marriage and the Family,* 1972, *34*(2).

TURNER, R. H. *Family Interaction.* New York: Wiley, 1970.

UDRY, J. R. "Marital Instability by Race, Sex, Education and Occupation Using 1960 Census Data." *American Journal of Sociology,* 1966, *72.*

University of Michigan, Office of Research Administration. "Household Work 1926–1965." *Research News,* 1973, *22*(12), 6–7.

U.S. Bureau of Labor Statistics. *Special Labor Report No. 13.* Washington, D.C.: Government Printing Office, 1971.

U.S. Bureau of the Census. *Statistical Abstract of the United States.* (61st ed.) Washington, D.C.: Government Printing Office, 1940.

U.S. Bureau of the Census. *Occupational Trends in the United States, 1900–1950.* Working paper 5. Washington, D.C.: Government Printing Office, 1958.

U.S. Bureau of the Census. *Current Population Reports, Series P-23, No. 36.* Washington, D.C.: Department of Commerce, 1971.

U.S. Bureau of the Census. *Statistical Abstract of the United States* (93rd ed.) Washington, D.C.: Government Printing Office, 1972.

U.S. Bureau of the Census. *Employment Status and Work Experience.* Washington, D.C.: Government Printing Office, 1973a.

U.S. Bureau of the Census. *Statistical Abstract of the United States.* (94th ed.) Washington, D.C.: Government Printing Office, 1973b.

U.S. Children's Bureau. *On Rearing Infants and Young Children in Institutions.* Washington, D.C., 1967.

U.S. Department of Labor. *Federal Interagency Day Care Requirements.* Federal Panel on Early Childhood, Office of Economic Opportunity, Department of Health, Education, and Welfare. Washington, D.C., 1968.

U.S. Department of Labor. *Day Care Services: Industry's Involvement.* Bulletin 296. Washington, D.C.: Government Printing Office, 1971.

U.S. Department of Labor. *Federal Funds for Day Care*. Washington, D.C.: Government Printing Office, 1972.

U.S. Department of Labor, Women's Bureau. *College Women Seven Years After Graduation, Resurvey of Women Graduates—Class of 1957*. Bulletin 292. Washington, D.C.: Government Printing Office, 1966.

U.S. Department of Labor, Women's Bureau. *Part-Time Employment of Women*. WB 68–151. Washington, D.C.: Government Printing Office, 1968.

U.S. Department of Labor, Women's Bureau. *Handbook on Women Workers*. Bulletin 294. Washington, D.C.: Government Printing Office, 1969.

U.S. Department of Labor, Women's Bureau. *Background Facts on Women Workers in the United States*. Washington, D.C.: Government Printing Office, 1970.

U.S. Department of Labor, Women's Bureau. *Working Women and Their Family Responsibilities: United States Experience*. 1–40. Washington, D.C., 1971.

U.S. Department of Labor, Women's Bureau. *Facts on Women Workers of Minority Races*. Washington, D.C.: Government Printing Office, 1972a.

U.S. Department of Labor, Women's Bureau. *Who Are the Working Mothers?* Employment Standards Administration Leaflet 37 (Stock 2916–0007). Washington, D.C.: Government Printing Office, 1972b.

U.S. Department of Labor, Women's Bureau. *Day Care Facts*. Washington, D.C.: Government Printing Office, 1973.

U.S. Department of Labor, Women's Bureau. *Women as Workers*. D-65. Washington, D.C.: Government Printing Office, n.d.

U.S. Monthly Vital Statistics Report, Mar. 1974.

U.S. Senate Hearings on S. 1512. *Comprehensive Child Development Act of 1971*. Washington, D.C.: Government Printing Office, 1971.

VERNON, E., and WILLNER, M. *Magnitude and Scope of Family Day Care Problems in New York City*. New York: Medical and Health Research Association of New York City, 1966.

VOGEL, S. R., BROVERMAN, I. K., BROVERMAN, D. M., CLARKSON, F. E., and ROSENKRANTZ, P. S. "Maternal Employment and Perception of Sex Roles Among College Students." *Developmental Psychology*, 1970, *3*, 384–391.

VON MERING, F. H. "Professional and Non-Professional Women as Mothers." *Journal of Social Psychology,* 1955. *42,* 21–34.

WALDMAN, E. "Marital and Family Characteristics of the U.S. Labor Force." *Monthly Labor Review,* May 1970.

WALDMAN, E. "Changes in the Labor Force Activity of Women." In N. Glazer-Malbin and H. Y. Waehrer (Eds.), *Woman in a Man-Made World.* Chicago: Rand McNally, 1972a.

WALDMAN, E. "Marital and Family Characteristics of the U.S. Labor Force." *Monthly Labor Review,* May 1972b, 18–27.

WALDMAN, E., and GOVER, K. R. "Children of Women in the Labor Force." *Monthly Labor Review,* July 1971.

WALDMAN, E., and YOUNG, A. M. "Marital and Family Characteristics of Workers, March 1970." *Monthly Labor Review,* Mar. 1971.

WALKER, K. E. "Homemaking Still Takes Time." *Journal of Home Economics,* 1969, *61*(8), 621–624.

WALKER, K. E. "How Much Help for Working Mothers? The Children's Role." *Human Ecology Forum,* 1970a, *1*(2), 13–15.

WALKER, K. E. *Time-Use Patterns for Household Work Related to Homemakers' Employment.* Paper presented at meeting of the Agricultural Outlook Conference, Washington, D.C., Feb. 1970b.

WALKER, K. E., and WOODS, M. E. *Time Use for Care of Family Members.* Use-of-Time Research Project, working paper 1. Ithaca, N.Y.: Cornell University, 1972.

WALLER, W., and HILL, R. *The Family: A Dynamic Interpretation.* (rev. ed.) New York: Holt, Rinehart, and Winston, 1951.

WARNER, D. W., ROWE, M. P., and BOTKIN, J. *Sliding Fee Schedules: A Simulation Analysis of Child Care Service and Cost Under Welfare Reform.* Cambridge, Mass.: Abt Associates, 1972.

WARNER, D., and RUOPP, R. R. *Publicly Funded Day Care in Maryland: Technical Report.* Cambridge, Mass.: Abt Associates, 1974.

WEIL, M. W. "An Analysis of the Factors Influencing Married Women's Actual or Planned Work Participation." *American Sociological Review,* 1961, *26,* 91–96.

WEISS, E. J. *They Carry the Burden Alone: The Socio-Economic Living Pattern of Oregon Women with Dependents.* Salem: Oregon Bureau of Labor, 1968.

WEISS, R. S., and SAMELSON, N. M. "Social Roles of American Women: Their Contribution to a Sense of Usefulness and Importance." *Marriage and Family Living,* 1958, *20,* 358–366.

WELLER, R. H. "The Employment of Wives, Dominance, and Fertility." *Journal of Marriage and the Family*, 1968, *30*, 437–442.

WELLER, R. H. "The Impact of Employment Upon Fertility." In A. Michel (Ed.), *Family Issues of Employed Women in Europe and America*. Leiden: E. J. Brill, 1971.

WELLS, A. *Day Care: An Annotated Bibliography*. Minneapolis: Institute for Interdisciplinary Studies, 1971.

Westinghouse Learning Corporation and Westat Research, Inc. *Day Care Survey*. Bladenburg, Md.: Westat Research, 1970.

WHELPTON, P. K., CAMPBELL, A. A., and PATTERSON, J. E. *Fertility and Family Planning in the United States*. Princeton, N.J.: Princeton University Press, 1966.

WHITE, L. C. "Maternal Employment and Anxiety over Mother Role." *Louisiana State University Journal of Sociology*, Spring 1972.

WHITE, M. S. "Psychological and Social Barriers to Women in Science." *Science*, 1970, *170*, 413–416.

WHITE, S. H., and OTHERS. *Federal Programs for Young Children: Review and Recommendations*. Vols. 1, 2, 3, 4. Washington, D.C.: Government Printing Office, 1973.

WILLIAMS, T. M. *Infant Care: Abstracts of the Literature*. Washington, D.C.: Consortium on Early Childbearing and Childrearing, 1972.

WILLNER, M. "Day Care: A Reassessment." *Child Welfare*, 1965, *44*, 125–133.

WILLNER, M. "Unsupervised Family Day Care in New York City." *Child Welfare*, 1969, *45*, 342–347.

WILLNER, M. "Family Day Care: An Escape from Poverty." *Social Work*, 1971, *16*, 30–35.

WINTERBOTTOM, M. R. "The Relation of Need for Achievement to Learning Experiences in Independence and Mastery." In J. W. Atkinson (Ed.), *Motives in Fantasy, Action, and Society*. New York: Van Nostrand, 1958.

WISHNOV, B. *Determinants of the Work-Welfare Choice, A Study of AFDC Women*. SWRRI Publication 15. Chestnut Hill, Mass.: Boston College, 1973.

WOLFE, D. M. "Power and Authority in the Family." In D. Cartwright (Ed.), *Studies in Social Power*. Ann Arbor: Institute for Social Research, University of Michigan, 1959.

WOODS, M. B. "The Unsupervised Child of the Working Mother." *Developmental Psychology*, 1972, *6*(1), 14–25.

WORTIS, R. P. "The Acceptance of the Concept of the Maternal Role by

Behavioral Scientists: Its Effects on Women." *American Journal of Orthopsychiatry,* 1971, *41* (5), 733–746.

YARROW, L. J. "Separation from Parents During Early Childhood." In M. L. Hoffman and L. W. Hoffman (Eds.), *Review of Child Development Research.* Vol. 1. New York: Russell Sage Foundation, 1964.

YARROW, M. R., SCOTT, P., DE LEEUW, L., and HEINIG, C. "Childrearing in Families of Working and Non-Working Mothers." *Sociometry,* 1962, *25,* 122–140.

YOUNG, A. M. "Children of Working Mothers." *Monthly Labor Review,* Apr. 1973, 37–40.

YOUNG, D. R., NELSON, R. R., and OTHERS. *Public Policy for Day Care of Young Children.* Lexington, Mass.: Lexington Books, 1973.

YUDKIN, S., and HOLME, A. *Working Mothers and Their Children.* London: Michael Joseph, 1963.

ZAMOFF, R. B., and LYLE, J. R. "Who Needs What Kind of Day Care Center." *Child Welfare,* 1973.

ZARATE, A. O. "Differential Fertility in Monterrey Mexico: Prelude to Transition?" *Milbank Memorial Fund Quarterly,* 1967, *45,* 93–108.

ZISSIS, C. "A Study of the Life Planning of 550 Freshman Women at Purdue University." *Journal of the National Association of Women Deans and Counselors,* 1964, *28,* 153–159.

Index